SAINT OR SATAN?

Alexander John Lowney

B.Sc., M.Phil

29ᵗʰ January 2000

About Authentic Voices

AUTHENTIC VOICES is a new series designed specifically to give a voice in the West to those writers and commentators now emerging from the former Communist Bloc.

For too long we have heard only the opinions of Western journalists and foreign correspondents on the political, intellectual and cultural lives of this massive mixture of nations, races and creeds. And yet we are perhaps not much closer to understanding their feelings, thoughts and attitudes. We continue to be surprised and shocked by the events taking place in the countries of the former Soviet dictatorship and are sometimes too keen to criticize or dismiss them.

AUTHENTIC VOICES aims to give us the understanding and insight which only the Insider's View can provide. In these books, "insiders" will voice their concerns, their opinions, their hopes. And although their use of language and expression may differ considerably from our own, the intention of this series is to keep as closely as possible to the original style, emphasis and use of words.

The titles in this AUTHENTIC VOICES series will be carefully chosen for their relevance to world affairs, or for the kind of unique observations only the insider can provide. These books may seriously challenge accepted views; certainly they will be thought-provoking. We hope that you, the reader, will find them of considerable interest.

Already published in the AUTHENTIC VOICES series:

Conflict in the Caucasus: Georgia, Abkhazia and the Russian shadow
by Svetlana Chervonnaya. Foreword by Eduard Shevardnadze
ISBN 0 906362 30 X

SAINT OR SATAN?

The Life and Times of Russia's New Rasputin, Anatoly Kashpirovsky

by Galina Vinogradova

edited by Anthony Anderson
and translated by Galina Vinogradova
with initial help from Daphne West

GOTHIC IMAGE
PUBLICATIONS

First published 1996 by
Gothic Image Publications
7 High Street, Glastonbury,
Somerset, BA6 9DP

© Galina Vinogradova 1996

Editorial service and setting
in Acorn Monotype Garamond by
Abbey Press Glastonbury

Cover design by Frameworks

Printed and bound in Great Britain by
WBC Book Manufacturers, Bridgend, Mid-Glamorgan

All rights reserved. No part of this publication may be
reproduced or utilized in any form or by any means
without written permission from the Publisher

A catalogue record for this book is available
from the British Library

ISBN 0 90632 31 8

To my husband Alex:
without his support and understanding,
this book would never have been possible.

To Frances, Jamie, Josie and James;
to Tom, Caryne, Joey and Asher;
to the road to Kobuleti,
an unforgettable journey which is not yet over.

Contents

About the Author		x
Acknowledgements		xi
Introduction		xiii
1	The Struggle for Survival	1
2	Hypnosis? No, Suggestion	21
3	The Travelling Hypnotist	41
4	From Vinnitsa to Moscow	65
5	Healing the Nation	99
6	Crisis of Confidence	131
7	In His Own Words	153
8	Politics and the Man	175
Bibliography		201
Index		209
Illustrations		after page 108

The poems and extracts used to head each chapter were regularly used by Dr Kashpirovsky during his healing seances

About the Author

Galina Vinogradova is a Russian from St Petersburg who spent many years working as an Intourist guide and interpreter, travelling all over the former Soviet Union. Now living and working as a freelance writer in the USA, she spent four years researching this book, both in the US and in Russia, during which time she attended many of Dr Anatoly Kashpirovsky's healing sessions and conducted a series of interviews with him.

She believes that the story of the amazing Dr Kashpirovsky offers important insights into the psychology of Russian society in transition.

Acknowledgements

Special thanks to Frances Howard-Gordon, who initiated this venture in an effort to promote more understanding of Russian culture, and for publishing this book. Her faith in me as a writer helped me to live through four years of joy and pain while working on this book.

I am grateful to all those who have contributed to the book: especially to Tony Anderson, who edited the book and made it readable; to my daughter Katya and to my mother, who during this period of time did not receive my full attention but constantly provided me with the latest information from Russia;

To Marina Venskaya for editing the initial Russian version of the book; to Mikhail Zimmerman, who helped to make the first contacts with Anatoly Kashpirovsky possible; to Tamara Pasternak, the devoted friend of Kashpirovsky, for her great interest in the book and for arranging interviews;

To Professor Modest Kabanov, director of the Bekhterev Psychoneurological Research Institute, St Petersburg; Professor Daniel Golubev, New York, and Professor Alexander Golbin, Chicago, who provided me with information on the subject of psychotherapy and the use of hypnosis in the Soviet Union;

To Tatiana Syrchenko, editor-in-chief of *Anomalia*, St Petersburg, for her interviews with Kashpirovsky in Russia at my request; to Alexander Grant, *Novoye Russkoye Slovo*, for providing material and photographs, to Tatiana Bogdanova, *Lyra* programme, Leningrad television; to the late Svetlana Kirilova for contacts with the programme *Fifth Wheel*; to Allan Chumak, journalist and psychic, Moscow, for information about Soviet television during perestroika; to Dr Valery Lunin, member of the Supreme Soviet of Russia, for insight into the political situation in Russia today; to Olga Zatsepina, Moscow University, for helping to contact Mikhail Gorbachev and Sergei Mikhalkov; to Irina Razumnova, USA-Canada Institute, for briefing on the political and economic situation in Russia; to Elena Fedotova for information on the subject; to Dr Leon Tek and Dr Joan Hass for providing expertise and explanations about psychotherapy in America;

To Lee Russell, Boris Neyman and Helen Maxie for doing research and providing excellent information via Lexis-Nexis; to the staff of the Slavic division of New York Public Library; to Jeffrey Schneider for technical support; to Ruth Steinkraus-Cohen and the International Hospitality Committee for providing materials and moral support;

And last but not least, to Anatoly Kashpirovsky, for interviews, photographs and video materials.

Galina Vinogradova
Connecticut, January 1996

Introduction

When I returned to Leningrad in September 1989 from a trip to England, I could not understand what was going on. In the West, I had heated discussions with my friends about the ways in which the Soviet Union should move towards capitalism and democracy; but in the Soviet Union, it seemed the entire country was under some hypnotic spell. People did not want to discuss anything except the healing "seances" of Dr Anatoly Kashpirovsky which were being shown on television.

The taxi driver from the airport warned me: "Don't miss the seance tonight. Kashpirovsky not only heals everything, he can change the colour of grey hair back to normal, scars dissolve and warts disappear."

"But how can you be so sure that it really happens?" I asked him.

"People write him letters or send him telegrams and he reads them before the show," he said. And he proudly showed me his own hand where, he said, there had been a scar until he had watched Kashpirovsky on television. "But scars are nothing compared to what people claim in their testimonials," he went on. "I heard a woman say that she had cancer, and after just watching Kashpirovsky on television, it had gone. She even had a paper from her doctor."

Then he told me the first Kashpirovsky joke I'd heard: "You know, someone complained to Kashpirovsky about having warts on his penis. 'I've been watching your seances,' he wrote to Kashpirovsky, 'but the warts are still there. However, my penis has disappeared. What should I do?'"

Introduction

Of course, the health system in the Soviet Union was in a dreadful state. There were universal shortages and I myself had had some really gloomy encounters with official medicine. Besides, the emerging private hospitals and clinics were beyond the means of the majority of the population. Kashpirovsky's treatment, however, was free and it was so comfortable. Just sit in front of your TV set and after half an hour, all your troubles are over, and after all, he was a qualified psychotherapist. So everyone sat nightly in front of their televisions waiting for a miracle.

I had seen Kashpirovsky once before. In March 1988 he had been on *Vzglyad*. This TV programme was the voice of Gorbachev's perestroika and attracted the most controversial and outspoken personalities. He did not talk much. But what on earth was he doing? What was going on? The other participants were doing the oddest things in response to his simple commands and gestures. Vadim Belozerov, the presenter, allowed his hand to be pierced with needles; he smiled and felt no pain. And this was all done via a TV link: Kashpirovsky uttered a word of command from Kiev and in the studio in Moscow a dozen people fell flat on their backs. The programme was broadcast over the entire Soviet Union.

Like many others I became fascinated by Dr Kashpirovsky, the extraordinary claims his patients made for him, and the power he exerted over the whole nation. I decided to try to track him down.

Our first meeting took place in November 1991 in New York at a Polish club in Green Point. I came to interview him for an article I was planning to write. I never imagined that it would be so easy to see him in person. Remembering the crowds and police cordons whenever he appeared in the Soviet Union, I expected the same here in the USA. But this time there were no crowds, no police, nothing of the kind. I entered a small dressing-room and saw a man in a black leather coat. He did not in the least resemble the larger-than-life figure I had seen on Soviet television. "What do you want?" he asked me, and started talking without waiting for my reply. While he was talking, he looked me over. I felt his penetrating gaze. I don't know why, but my heartbeat went up. "What if he hypnotizes me and I fall into a

Introduction

trance?" I asked myself, remembering the scenes at his television performances when women would sway and roll in their seats, apparently out of control. I was so nervous that I couldn't concentrate on what he was saying. Eventually I calmed down enough to hear him coming to the end of an impassioned defence of his work, and then the interview was over.

At our second meeting, also in a Polish club, this time in New Jersey, Mikhail Zimmerman, his manager, invited me into the dressing room where the Master was preparing himself. When I stepped into the room, Kashpirovsky was trying on a black polo shirt. It was too big. "Shit," he said, instead of "Hello," and continued to pull the shirt off. "How many times do I have to tell him to choose the right size! Idiot!"

I stood in front of him waiting for the right moment to interrupt and greet him. But he paid no attention to me. Then he looked at me sharply and said, "And who are you? Where are you from? Who sent you here? What do you want to know?" I was so astonished that I didn't know what to say.

"Don't you remember? You gave me an interview a couple of days ago and said that I could come."

"There are so many people who want to see me and talk to me," he retorted. "What kind of questions do you have?"

I suddenly felt that I didn't want to ask any questions. "I can see that you're upset and nervous, so I'd better come back later," I said and was ready to leave the room.

"I'm never nervous. What is this performance? Nothing special. I've had audiences of millions of people, and I never felt any fear." And he went on without a pause: "Didn't I tell you how I was invited to go to Moscow to heal Leonid Brezhnev?

"No, you didn't tell me anything," I said, trying to ignore his rudeness and turning my recorder on.

"They called me to ask if I could come and help him. You know he was very ill. So I said that I would go. I remember that we were driving in the car and I started to have doubts: what if I really help him? And if he died? The KGB major said, 'If Brezhnev dies it will be

xv

a great misfortune for the country and the people.' I said, 'You can pick up any of these drunkards who are lining up to buy some beer and put them in his position and the country would be better off.' At that moment we were passing a food market and there were lots of people around. 'If you like, we can stop and ask them.' The major turned red and almost exploded."

At that moment Mikhail Zimmerman entered the room. "It's time to start, Anatoly Mikhailovich. People are becoming impatient."

"Don't tell me what to do! You'd do better to take care of what you're supposed to do. Why did you pick this size? How can I appear before the audience in such a shirt?" His manager tried to say something but Kashpirovsky didn't listen. He started to continue his story.

I said, "Maybe I'll come another time?"

"Maybe there won't be another time," he replied. Suddenly he stopped and said, "I must go now. Come back in two weeks. I'll call you when I'm back in New York after the tour to San Francisco and Los Angeles."

But he never called me. I knew that he was leaving for Russia so I phoned Mikhail Zimmerman. He told me that Kashpirovsky would be performing at Brighton Beach. "But you know," he said, "I will not be his manager anymore. He said that he doesn't want me to work for him. He has found somebody else." Despite this, Zimmerman continues to regard his former boss as a genius and is utterly convinced of his abilities.

The performance, as usual, attracted many Soviet emigrés, desperate to be healed. I eventually attended dozens of his sessions and got used to them, but at this point I was confused by everything. I could clearly see that some people fell into a trance, while others would sit with their eyes open. "Close your eyes! You're distracting me!" Once he looked at me, forgetting that I was supposed to keep my eyes open and record the session. I felt his eyes burning me all over.

At the end people would come up to the stage to shake hands or simply to touch him. I joined the queue. Finally it was my turn. "What if he won't recognize me?" I thought.

"I lost your telephone number," he said. And then without pausing, "I have decided to grant you some interviews."

"But when?" I asked him. "When, er, when—I come back here in the spring."

"But you did not tell me the end of the story about Brezhnev. Did you get to see him?"

"OK," he said, "You can come backstage now." He made a sign to his guards to let me go. But behind the curtain was a crowd of lucky patients. I had to wait while he finished talking to them. Almost all of them were women. Finally, he came up to me and said, "You see, this is neither the place nor the time to talk to you."

"Anatoly Mikhailovich, please help me!" A woman was standing next to us showing her hand to him.

Kashpirovsky immediately became irritated. "Who allowed you to come here? Don't you see that I'm busy right now?" His tone of voice and the expression on his face did not bode well. But surprisingly enough, the woman paid no attention. She continued to wave her hand around until finally he burst out: "You, get out of here!"

"Please, please, help me!" pleaded the woman. "You are my only hope. Nothing can cure my eczema!" She was trying to make him take a look. Finally, she brought her hands very close to his face. "Take your hands away from my face! Why do you do this? If I become angry, your hands will become even worse!"

I was standing there watching the scene, thinking that he didn't behave quite in the way that I'd expected him to. He didn't seem like a healer, he was so rude.

Kashpirovsky immediately understood my reaction and said, "You see, all these people, they never leave me alone. I'm sick and tired of their demands. They think they have the right to stop me anywhere. I have no privacy at all." But sensing that I still had reservations, he said, "I must go. When I come in the spring, we'll meet again. I'll call you."

I knew that he would never call me. I was upset but decided to try again. "Why don't we set up a date now, before you leave?"

But Kashpirovsky was not listening. He was surrounded by his fans, who were asking him the same thing. "I'm not sure when I'll be here," he was telling them. Then, looking at me and seeing that I was still not happy, he said quite unexpectedly, "Tamara Iosifovna, help this woman to contact me. She is a writer."

Tamara Iosifovna was his greatest fan and devoted patient. She followed him everywhere and helped him to manage his sessions. She lives in Philadelphia now. In 1991 she was literally carried into one of his seances in New York. She had a large wound after an operation on her spine to remove a cancerous tumour. Soon her wound healed completely. "My doctor could not believe his eyes." she told me. "When he saw the result of Kashpirovsky's treatment, he said: 'Your Russian doctor must be a very capable man. I would never have believed that such a thing was possible.' He is an oncologist and didn't believe in miracles. But this is what Kashpirovsky is all about."

The following spring I did get the chance to interview him at greater length. I was invited to his house in Long Island, where he was living with his son Seryozha. Kashpirovsky was having a hard time because he was going through a divorce and had other problems at home. He told me about his childhood and his student years at Vinnitsa Medical School, about his desire to travel and how he had started his performances.

I was listening to his story and I tried to ask him about his "supernatural" powers. He would only laugh in reply. But once he became really angry. "Why can't you believe that I'm an ordinary man? I'm the same as other people. Nobody believes me. People want me to admit that I have some supernatural power because somehow in this way it's easier for them to understand my influence."

"But how do you influence people? You say that you don't actually hypnotize them."

"I do not hypnotize anybody. I'm a psychotherapist and psychotherapy is a science. I'm not a miracle worker like those charlatans who say that they have ESP. I have nothing to do with that lot. Try to understand me."

I tried to understand but I felt lost. "Have you heard of Emerson and his technique?" I asked and immediately regretted it.

Introduction

"I'm not interested in any of them. They can't teach me anything. I've learnt everything myself through more than seventeen hundred performances. I have met thousands and thousands of people, and now you're telling me about Emerson. I don't want to hear about such people anymore."

So I went away and read books by Pavlov, and by Platonov who taught Kashpirovsky, and by Bekhterev on healing and many others, to try to get to grips with the subject. I interviewed hundreds of people, his supporters and his enemies. He inspired the most extreme adulation on the one hand, and utter hatred and contempt on the other.

I never became friends with Kashpirovsky. I think it's impossible to get close to him. He's a difficult and complex man. He would disappear for months and then one day call me and say something that would make me change all my ideas about him. At one point I was going to write an "authorized" biography; he wanted me to record his exact words, not to change anything. He even accepted my proposal that we should work on the book together, though this proved quite impossible. "All these writers and journalists always distort everything I say," he told me. "But I like the way you seem to understand me and my work."

It was not true. I did not understand at all. But I decided to try.

1

The Struggle for Survival

What if life deceives and baits you,
Never bridle, never grieve!
Bide the dismal day, believe
That a day of joy awaits you.

By the future lives the heart;
And if dreary be the present,
All is fleeting, will depart,
And departed, will be pleasant.

(Alexander Pushkin 1825)

In the spring of 1995 a group of nouveaux-riches Russians went on a little trip from St Petersburg to Moscow along the river. It was the Russian Orthodox Easter and everyone was on holiday. Their cruise ship stopped at the town of Uglich, known in Russian history as the place where Tsarevich Dmitri, the son of Ivan the Terrible, was assassinated.

In town the church was full of worshippers and sightseers. Those who could not enter the church were standing on the steps or milling around. People were in a festive mood. "Christ is risen!" they greeted each other and kissed three times. The newcomers from the cruise ship attracted the attention of some old women with *kulitch*s and *paskha*s (Easter cakes), who had come to have their Easter food blessed by the priest. Suddenly whispers began to spread among them: "Look, there goes the Devil! Satan is here!" The visitors seemed to pay no attention and proceeded to the church. "I say, the Devil is here! Don't let him in!" The voices became louder and others in the crowd joined in. The tourists could now hear them clearly. They stopped in front of the crowd not knowing what to do. "What are they talking about? Who do they mean?" they asked each other. They did not understand what the fuss was all about. The old women were shouting at the top of their lungs pointing at a short man with a Roman haircut and dressed all in black. "He is the Devil! Don't let him in!"

"You fools, you don't know what you are talking about!" the man retorted angrily. Is it not enough that I have helped so many of you? You are an ungrateful lot. Your priests have brainwashed you. I don't want to waste my time here." He turned around sharply and went back to the ship fuming and cursing. That man was Anatoly Kashpirovsky.

Just a few years previously he had been unquestionably the most popular man in the Soviet Union.

* * *

He was born on August 11, 1939, at four o'clock in the morning in a small Ukrainian village called Stavnitsa, Medzhibozh *raion* (district), in the Khmelnitsky *oblast* (region). He is convinced that he can remember himself from the day he was born, from the very moment of his birth. "It seems to me that even then I comprehended in the same way as I do now. I remember being carried to the window and shown to relatives. I wanted to say something to them and I couldn't," Kashpirovsky told me.

Yadviga Nikolayevna, Anatoly's mother, was a practical, farsighted woman. She insisted that her son's birth certificate should indicate as his place of birth not the village of Stavnitsa but the town of Proskurov (renamed Khmelnitsky in 1954), where she was living with her husband. She couldn't reconcile herself to the idea that Anatoly, her son, would be considered a country bumpkin just because she had given birth to him while visiting her mother's village.

This wasn't just a woman's caprice. In Stalin's era, villagers did not have internal passports and could not move to the cities to work or study. Family joy on the birth of a son was clouded because Anatoly's father would soon be going to the war. Indeed, in two months Kashpirovsky senior was sent to fight in Finland, part of Stalin's plan to strengthen the USSR's borders in case of war with Germany. Mikhail Yakovlevich Kashpirovsky, like all Soviet citizens, believed Stalin's propaganda that the Red Army was the strongest army in the world and that war with little Finland would not last long. He comforted his wife, promising to come home soon. Finland, however, did not want to submit to occupation by Soviet forces and war lasted longer than he expected.

Soon he was transferred to the western Ukraine, to the town of Strii, near Lvov, which had been annexed from Poland under the secret pact with Hitler. Stalin hoped that by keeping to the conditions of the pact he could hold off the war with Germany for a bit longer.

Yadviga Nikolayevna, who loved her husband with all her heart, followed him there, her baby son in her arms. "My mother was exceptionally beautiful," reminisced Anatoly. "All her life she remained faithful to my father. She was a true soldier's wife; she followed my father wherever he was posted. For many years she had to endure hunger, hardship and many dangers, but she never complained."

Anatoly always had a special relationship with his mother. To him she was the ideal woman, a devoted wife and mother, the best counsellor in all his affairs. Her difficult nomadic life gave her a tough character and she learned great resourcefulness and self-reliance.

"The peoples of eastern Poland and western Ukraine are happy to join Stalin's Family of Peoples," said the captions in the newspapers. Newsreels showed "liberated people" greeting Russian soldiers. Yadviga Nikolayevna, however, soon learned the truth, that the local community hated the "liberators", and looked upon her as one of them. She felt lonely and anxious because her husband was constantly on training exercises, preparing for the war with Germany. Before fleeing the German advance, the Soviet occupational regime murdered thousands of Ukrainian civilians, mainly members of Lvov's intelligentsia.

"As soon as the war broke out, my father was sent to the front. A true patriot, he was prepared to give his life for his motherland and Stalin. Like other soldiers he joined the Communist Party to demonstrate his loyalty. My mother took me to Stavnitsa to my grandmother's. Nobody had anticipated that the Germans would advance so swiftly into our country, and that by November the whole of the Ukraine would already be occupied. My mother decided to flee. She was terrified that the Nazis would execute the family of a Soviet soldier."

She was lucky to get hold of two carts and horses. They abandoned all their belongings and set off for Russia towards Voronezh, which was still in Soviet hands. There were nine of them: seven adults and two small children, Anatoly and his cousin. Fearing they might run into Germans, they had to travel mainly at night. Several times their carts came under fire. It took them four months to reach Voronezh.

There the army confiscated their horses and without any explanation put them aboard a freight train along with hundreds of other refugees. Soon they found out that they were heading east. They slept on the floor, men, women, children. There was no food nor any essentials. Whenever the train stopped, they tried desperately to get water and something to eat. Finally they arrived. They had reached Kazakhstan, the other end of the country; it seemed to be a sandy, barely inhabited desert. They had no idea what to do. There was no one to take care of them and they were left to fend for themselves. The local people regarded them as an added burden because they themselves did not have enough food. But at last the family managed to get settled in Krasnoarmeisky village, not far from the river Chu.

"To start with," Kashpirovsky remembered, "we had no roof over our heads. The only thing we could do was to buy a yurt and live like Kazakhs. It was very difficult for us. Most of all we suffered because of the climate. Nights were extremely cold. To keep warm we slept on the floor because the flue from the stove passed underneath it. But during the daytime it was impossible to survive because of the heat. The sand got so unbearably hot that it burned my feet through my shoes. From morning till night we were kept busy foraging for food because, like other evacuees, we were left without any means of subsistence.

"Now, many years later," said Kashpirovsky, "life in evacuation does not seem to have been so bad. I recall the smell of my mother's pancakes, which I like to the present day; my first dog, Aryks; the Dzhigiti, tribal horsemen who could perform extraordinary tricks and who seemed to be heroes out of a fairy tale. I tend to romanticize everything from those days. But it is difficult to imagine now what our mothers had to go through to survive and bring their children up during the war."

He was eventually put into a nursery school. "I liked it there, because we played war. Even at two or three years old, I did know that Hitler was the worst possible thing in the world and I had to fight him. I particularly liked the game when my favourite nanny took part in it as a nurse. I was happy to be wounded so she would carry me off the battlefield. Perhaps it was at this time that my interest in women was first aroused. But most of all, of course, I loved my mother. If she went out somewhere, I would sit for hours and wait for her.

"We lived three long years in Kazakhstan. All this time we didn't know what was happening to father. Mother tried to locate him, wrote to the military enlistment office, but never received an answer. We thought we would never see him again. But one day mother came to the nursery school and called me. I saw a man standing behind her. He looked like a giant in a long greatcoat. My mother pushed me gently forward, saying: 'This is your father!'"

Then Kashpirovsky senior was ordered back to the Ukraine and obtained permission to move his family with him. Arriving at the town of Rovno in the Sumy district, again they had no place to live. By October 1944 the Ukraine was completely liberated from the Germans, but the war had left terrible scars. More than a quarter of the Ukrainian population was homeless, since more than seven hundred towns and villages had been destroyed. The family wandered from place to place. Only after his mother had got a job at a military depot did they get a flat—a small room, and a corridor which did not have a roof. They settled there with their relatives who returned with them from Kazakhstan. Nine people shared one small room, but they were happy to be together and back in the Ukraine.

Soon they were separated yet again. Father had to return to his unit, to fight the Germans. He sent his wife and son to stay with his mother. She lived in the village of Markovtsy in the Khmelnitsky region. But their life there was no easier than before. "At night we used candles because there was no electricity. We could not get coal or wood for heating. To warm the house and to cook we burned straw in the stove. But I liked it there. I used to sit by a small window, watching the snowflakes swirl. I imagined how huge wolves or bandits from fairy tales would appear and I would fight with them to defend my mother. After mother had read me *White Fang* by Jack London I became obsessed with dogs. I desperately wanted to have my own White Fang."

There was a lot of snow that winter. The only way to travel was by sledge. Uncle Peter worked as a coachman in the *kolkhoz* (collective farm). Anatoly, who adored horses, loved to be taken for a ride. "I would settle in the sledge, on straw bedding covered with a sheepskin coat, ready to be driven anywhere. I felt no cold nor other discomfort. I still have vivid images of the ruts left by the horses, the flashing of hooves.

"At last the war ended. The Soviet Union celebrated. People were so happy; they hoped victory would end their sufferings. Mother rushed back to Stavnitsa; she was sure her husband and brother would return soon. Time went by but no word came from them. Although the war was over, people continued to receive the 'killed in battle' notices and many soldiers were missing in action. Many of mother's acquaintances had been either killed or wounded. She was desperate. To find her husband she wrote letters everywhere but with no success.

"Then one day my uncle returned home. The happiness and joy of his return soon gave way to concern, because he brought a woman with him. My family did not know how to react to this. They had gone through so much together with his wife, who had no inkling of the new arrangement. But this did not bother me at all. Faina Mikhailovna was young and beautiful. I fell in love with her instantly. When, after work, my mother, sisters and Faina would spin yarn and sing, I would run into another room, and throw myself on a bed and listen with a trembling heart. They sang sad, melodic Ukrainian songs that overwhelmed me with strange feelings of pain and happiness. They all sang well, but I thought that Aunt Faina sang best of all. I was in love."

Then the long-awaited event! Father returned home from the war. "We ran to the *voenkomat* (military commissariat) where he was waiting for us. My mother almost lost her reason. She was crying and laughing at the same time. She could not believe her eyes. He had participated in all the major battles and had not been wounded once. 'Misha, maybe you are charmed?' she asked him, laughing through the tears. He had left for the war as a sergeant and returned as a major. He showed me his medals and I was so happy—my father was a real hero!"

It turned out that father was to be posted to Belorussia, so it meant they had to pack again. But there, too, they had to move from place to place. They rented two rooms in the house of a German who had other officers as tenants. There was unrest and the army was sent to suppress the "bandits". These bandits were in fact those who opposed Soviet rule, and they were attacking officers and soldiers. Once, when the Kashpirovskys were visiting their landlord, someone fired through the open window. Uncle pushed Anatoly under the table, and the others just got down on the floor. Father and the other officers rushed outside, but by that time there was no trace of the attackers.

"I was always proud that my father was an officer and deputy commander of the regiment. What made me feel particularly superior among my friends was father's American truck, a Studebaker, which had been assigned to him. When I was lucky, he would take me along for a ride." Sometimes they would go to Minsk, the capital of Belorussia, almost completely destroyed by the Fascists. There they saw German prisoners of war who walked with their heads bowed. People pointed and shouted at them. Once he went with his father to a prisoner-of-war camp which surprised him with its neatness and cleanliness.

At Minsk railway station, packed with people who had been waiting for trains for days, Anatoly witnessed an incident that deeply impressed him. "An officer came into the centre of the hall and right there, in front of everyone, began to urinate. When people rebuked him for this, he got his Nagant revolver out and began shooting, and not just into the air, but indiscriminately. My feelings were hurt. I could not handle the idea that this was a Soviet officer, not a Fascist."

In Zhirovitsy, a small Belorussian town, Anatoly went to school for the first time. The school occupied a single-storey building.

Teaching was in Belorussian, which Anatoly had difficulty understanding. "The teacher spoke at length about something or other and I just sat there, looking out of the window and waiting for her to say, 'You, boy, go home!' For me, starting school meant the loss of all my freedom."

After the war not only schools were in short supply, but there weren't enough teachers, not to mention textbooks or exercise books. The classes were overcrowded and children of various ages were put in the same class. But schooling was free, available to everybody. In all republics, towns and villages in the Soviet Union, education was carried out according to the programme developed by the ministry of education in Moscow. So throughout the country, on any given day, everyone would study exactly the same thing.

Right from nursery school Anatoly and his peers were taught that Stalin was the wisest and kindliest man on Earth and that they were the most fortunate children in the world to live in the Soviet Union. The first word that he learned to read and write was *Stalin*.

Anatoly Kashpirovsky grew up with an inquisitive mind. He was interested in many things and, because of his travels, was much better informed than his peers. But school lessons were agonizingly tedious to him. He continued to attend school praying each day for release. Suddenly his sufferings stopped.

"Tomorrow we are going home to the Ukraine," his father announced. "Pack your things!" Anatoly's father had been demobbed. He could have stayed in the army longer, but mother insisted that he resign his commission. She didn't approve of his drinking bouts with his superior officers. After demobilization he received no special privileges, nor was he even given a military pension.

In the Ukraine they had no place to stay but with their relatives. They knew there was no food there, so Mikhail Yakovlevich sold his shotgun and other things brought from Germany, his trophies, to buy some sacks of grain.

In Medzhibozh he got a job in the roads department. "My father worked very hard and gained the respect of his colleagues. Although he never occupied a high position, he behaved as if he were a high Party functionary of the *Obkom* (regional party committee), a powerful organization which controlled everything in the region. He had an analytical mind and could formulate his thoughts impressively on paper. A letter from him to an organization received instant attention," said Kashpirovsky, and I could feel that he was really proud of his father.

Anatoly started the second class in a Russian school and it turned out he had learned nothing in Belorussia. He found studies difficult and school boring. All his dreams were directed to the fortress built in the Middle Ages to protect the town from frequent Tatar attacks, which was located not far from the school. The fortress was an enormous place, with round towers and drawbridges, a legacy of the Lithuanian knights. In this ancient mysterious structure, Anatoly and his friends liked most of all to play at Cossack brigands and run amok in all the underground passages.

Joining a new school meant that he had to prove himself to a new lot of children. In order to win prestige among the children at the Russian school, Anatoly decided to jump from a second-floor window at the school. This was very high up, but he managed it and won the acclaim of his peers, although his father was summoned to the headmaster.

Life began to improve for the family. At last they could build a house of their own and bought a cow too. Anatoly was moved to a Ukrainian school. He took a liking to this school at once. The teachers there treated children with warmth, even respect. Isaac Gervets, the mathematics teacher, surprised him by addressing thirteen-year-olds formally as adults. Although Anatoly was given the lowest mark nine times for his algebra, he really liked the mathematics teacher and didn't want to look a complete fool in this teacher's eyes. So he sacrificed his summer holidays by staying at home and taking private lessons. The additional lessons helped him to become one of the best mathematicians in the school.

But Anatoly's favourite subject was physical education. From an early age he had been attracted by strong people, like the heroes of Jack London. "As a child, I used to fight all day long and my pride was terribly hurt whenever I got beaten." But PE lessons, two hours a week, were clearly not enough to enable him to realize his dream of becoming strong. He was only eleven years old when he began additional training. The school was about four kilometres away, so he had to get up early to have time to do his exercises.

"Once, on the way to school, I saw a group of classmates trying to lift weights in the yard of the military commissariat. Without a moment's thought I approached them and tried to lift one myself. To my horror, I failed. The boys started sneering at me. I knew that I could not survive this disgrace. I swore to myself that I would do anything in the world to become the strongest in school." So the same day he found some scrap iron on which he hung metal gearwheels from a combine harvester, and with these homemade weights he began to pump his muscles. But still it was not enough, and he dreamed of the barbell that he had seen in the yard.

One evening he got his chance. "There was no one in the yard. The barbell looked so tempting that I simply could not leave it there. I had to steal it! Nothing could stop me, neither the weight of two *pud*s, thirty-six kilos, which was almost equal to mine, nor the distance of four kilometres to my house. I tore my chest muscles, but I got it home. I trained with it all the time and later took it with me to Vinnitsa." At the school sports competitions he demonstrated his new strength: he could lift two weights and, balancing them on his fingers, could push them up five times. Now he really was the strongest boy in the school! A local football team wanted him to play with them, but then he smashed his left kneecap and could hardly walk. Yadviga Nikolayevna could not bear to see him hobbling around. But when she saw that the injured leg had become thinner than the other one, she took him to a doctor. Their local doctors, however, could not do much for him. So she was advised by her relations to see a babushka who was reputed to be a miracle-worker.

Officially, of course, the Soviet Union was the country of atheism, but people never stopped believing in the supernatural, in amazing cures and other miracles. In the Ukraine, places like the Kiev-Pechersky cathedral, churches, and monasteries enjoyed great popularity because of the powerful sacred relics and miraculous ikons that were kept there. People believed that they could make the blind see and cripples walk.

It has always been a Russian tradition to turn to sorcery for help. People, especially in rural areas, took potions and herbs accompanied by charms and incantations, often words from prayers, psalms and ecclesiastical writings. Officially such treatment was banned. So they charmed illnesses away in secret settings, as a rule *tete-à-tete* with the patient. It was possible to get to see folk healers only with the help of friends and acquaintances whom healers trusted. Anatoly, however, had been brought up at school to be an atheist and a rationalist and he never believed in miracles or cures. Yadviga Nikolayevna had some trouble in persuading her son to visit a sorceress.

"The babushka looked to be about a hundred years old. The skin on her hands was so transparent that her veins and bones showed through. I could hardly keep myself from laughing when, with a serious look, she began to pass her hands over me and whispered something or other. The healing session ended with promises that all would be well. But nothing happened and I understood that I would have to take care of it myself. When the plaster cast was removed, I began squatting exercises that were very painful. I tried to ignore the pain and continued training. Later I even put a weight on my shoulders. Gradually I increased the weight to ten kilos, then twenty, forty and so on. That is how the 'miracle' happened and my leg no longer bothered me."

For the Kashpirovsky family, Stalin's death was a great tragedy. In spite of all the burdens and deprivations, and although every family had had someone arrested, shot or exiled, Mikhail Yakovlevich taught his son that Stalin was a real hero, that he had won the war against Hitler. If his father came across some obvious injustice, then, like everyone else, he looked for others to blame, for unknown enemies, spies or slovenly bureaucrats from the leader's entourage.

Although his father was a staunch communist, Anatoly did not become an activist in the Pioneer or Komsomol organization (Young Communists); he was not among the sincerely dedicated or active members. He found their meetings boring and the gymnasium gave him far greater pleasure. The school administration approved his sporting progress as it contributed to the school's credit.

When Nikita Khrushchev started his period of reforms, people initially greeted many of them with enthusiasm. Kashpirovsky remembers being desperately unhappy that, because of his studies, he was not allowed to go to the Virgin Lands—Khrushchev's campaign to raise crops from virgin grasslands in Kazakhstan—nor to take part in the Komsomol building projects in Siberia and the Far East, which Khrushchev had instigated. "But it turned out that nothing was done for the volunteers: there was no housing, no food, no medical service."

Even though Khrushchev wanted to feed the nation, his programmes for improving the country's agriculture led to yet greater difficulties with the food supply. An obsession with increasing the consumption of meat and dairy products drove the controversial agricultural programme. After his visit to America, he was convinced that the Soviet Union could overtake the United States in its production of milk, meat and butter. Slogans exhorted people to participate in the competition with America. "Soon everyone will be able to buy milk at a state dairy store," he assured the peasants, who did not want to give their cattle away to *kolkhoz*es and *sovkhoz*es (state-owned collective farms). "No need to worry. The State will take care of you!"

But the Kashpirovskys, like other people, did not share his enthusiasm. They did not want to give away their cow, which had helped them to survive through the first postwar years. Besides, the stores remained empty.

Anatoly finished school and like all lads of the postwar era, dreamed of becoming a pilot. But Yadviga Nikolayevna had her own ideas. Not far from their house lived a doctor. Whenever she met him, she held her breath with admiration because he looked so sedate and important. Yadviga Nikolayevna kept on telling her son, "You must become a surgeon, just like Dr Krut."

Neither of his parents had had a chance to complete their secondary education, but they helped their son not only to finish secondary school but also to get a higher education and become a doctor. However, even in her wildest dreams Kashpirovsky's mother could not have imagined that her son would be compared to Jesus Christ, and that pilgrims would come to him from all over the country. Although Anatoly didn't want to go into medicine, he gave in to his mother's insistence and went off with a friend to Vinnitsa to take his entrance examinations for the medical institute.

In order to be accepted at the Vinnitsa Medical Institute, as competition could be very great, parents had to hire tutors for extra lessons. These teachers were in fact often professors who were paid extra money by the parents to guarantee their children's place at the institute, a covert form of bribery. But of course Yadviga Nikolayevna did nothing of the kind because she didn't know the ways of the city and would never have considered such a thing. So Anatoly had to face the challenge on his own. He didn't want to be a loser nor to disappoint his mother, so he had to use his wits. Examinations in physics and chemistry had to be taken, as well as essays in Russian and Ukrainian. He coped easily with the humanities, but anticipated difficulties with the science.

"The morning of the physics exam was beautiful and the sun was shining brightly. I woke up feeling triumphant. I knew that I had to be bold, to take a risk and then I would be successful. The examiner actually gave me my chance. When he asked if anyone would answer questions without preparation, I decided to risk it. 'I will,' I said and drew a card with questions. I realized immediately that I knew something about the second question, but nothing about the others. I looked straight into the eyes of the examiner and said: 'I'll start with the second question.' This, of course, was normally an impossible thing to get away with. But amazingly, he accepted. Then he asked me to solve the problem set in the third question. I said that I had had no time to think about it in detail. So he asked me what my first step would be. I named it. He said that I was correct and gave me an excellent mark."

It only remained for Anatoly to get a good grade in chemistry, a subject he knew absolutely nothing about. But at that examination he repeated exactly the same trick. He volunteered to answer first and overwhelmed the examiner with his self-confidence. He got a total score of eighteen out of a possible twenty; he had passed. This came as a complete surprise to everyone, not least to himself. Kashpirovsky said that this kind of behaviour always brought him success. He learned to take risks.

Anatoly now had to live apart from his family. Of course, life in Vinnitsa, a regional centre, seemed to be exciting and more interesting than in his own village. After all, Vinnitsa was a large town with a population of about four hundred thousand. After the war the town had developed into a large industrial and cultural centre. "The ruins of the monasteries impressed me, of course, but most of all I liked the museum of Nikolai Pirogov. He was a Russian surgeon, and lived in Vinnitsa in the last century. Not far from his house is a small mausoleum with the mummified body of Pirogov. The doctor himself prepared the embalming fluids, and its composition still remains a secret. I believe that Pirogov's body is better preserved than Lenin's, although it was mummified over a hundred years ago."

Thus Anatoly started his independent life. Vinnitsa Medical Institute had a reputation as a good school and he found it both challenging and stimulating: "I was not the best, although everything depended, of course, on the subject. Blood, surgery, medicine, were not my cup of tea. I was interested in man as a whole being. I loved philosophy and got excellent grades for that, but anatomy became a real problem. In the second year I nearly left the institute because of it."

There were no grounds for complaining about tuition at the institute, but the living conditions were unspeakably awful. As an out-of-town student, Anatoly had the right to stay in a hostel, but it did not have sufficient rooms for all the students. So he had to rent a corner in a little room, not much bigger than a coffin, paying for it with a large proportion of his modest student grant. "I shared the room with a sixth-year student from the medical institute. As always, I got up early in the morning to do my exercises, and it irritated me that he liked to stay in bed half the day and to come home late at night."

April 12, 1961, the day Yury Gagarin was launched into space, was a day of national celebration. "I shall never forget that day," said Kashpirovsky. "I was at the institute when the news came. Everyone was overcome with such joy that students ran out into the streets congratulating each other most sincerely, shouting and crying with rapture. I was so excited! I knew that we were the first in space and soon space would be ours. I desperately wanted to go into space myself one day." He dreamed of becoming an astronaut and worked hard on self-improvement.

At the institute he had the reputation of being an ascetic: he didn't drink, smoke nor allow himself anything excessive. Striving for self-perfection, he imposed a system of restrictions on himself and stuck rigidly to it. It became difficult to maintain when he got a room in the hostel, sharing a dormitory with twelve beds. His neighbours would return just before daybreak, brew tea and chat loudly. Sometimes they brought girls with them. But Anatoly had no time for such diversions. He spent all his spare time on training and sport.

"In 1956, when I had just arrived in Vinnitsa, I saw the man of my dreams on a trolleybus. I was envious of his muscular physique. Most young men of my age would sooner follow a good-looking girl, but I followed this man to the Lokomotiv stadium. The man I followed, Vasili Ivanovich Bob, turned out to be the trainer there. Without wasting any time, I approached a hundred-kilo barbell and lifted it. No one expected this from a novice. I think I was able to do this only through the force of my pride. I lacked technique. But within the year I could compete as a middleweight and would lift a hundred and fifty kilos. I became friends with Piotr Korol, the future Olympic champion. This connection proved very important later on. Then I won the Vinnitsa championship and became the middleweight champion of the Ukraine."

The team consisted of eight athletes from light to heavyweight. "They were strong and young and they solved their conflicts with their fists. I, as their captain, had to intervene." Once, when they arrived in Odessa for a competition, Kashpirovsky was told that their heavyweight was missing. "He was supposed to stay in his room and drink water to gain eight kilos for the next day's competition in the superheavyweight category. But he disappeared and no one knew where to find him. I was furious, because we had a real chance to win the team competition but without him our chances were nil. At last we found him. He was having a good time with his girl, and even managed to lose two more kilos. So, what can one do with such an idiot? Of course, the team got even with him. I'm sure he will remember it for the rest of his days. I beat him up and I made him drink a bucketful of water in one go. He went from eighty-two to ninety kilos, so he was able to take part in the competition."

There were often fights and conflicts on the train on the way to a competition when the lads were excited and nervous, anticipating the coming event. "There was a young lightweight in our team, a Jew. Although he was young, he had become a Master of Sport. In our compartment, besides me and that boy, was a woman and a heavyweight. This heavyweight was really full of himself. And he started to make fun of the lightweight, making rude remarks about his race. I told him to stop, but he paid no attention. Then I said: 'Listen, stop showing off in front of this woman. If you won't stop now, I'll give you a box on the ear!' He was over a hundred kilos and much bigger than I, but when I was enraged it did not matter. He said: 'You and whose army!' I leapt onto my feet and hit him with a bottle. He hardly had time to cover his face with his hands. The rest of the way he was no trouble. He understood that I was ready for anything.

In the summer students were sent to the *kolkhoz* to work in the fields as work experience. "We were harvesting corn, the 'queen of the fields' as it was called in the press. Perhaps with all this corn, Khrushchev wanted to solve all the food-supply problems at one go. But the Party functionaries went to absurd lengths to satisfy Nikita Sergeyevich's desires. It was planted everywhere, even in the polar regions. After Khrushchev's visit, the seedlings would be dug up and transported to the next place he was to visit," said Kashpirovsky.

During one of his stints as a student worker, he went to a dance for the first time in his life—at the age of twenty-three. "I looked around and noticed a girl standing alone. I felt sorry for her. She was so ugly and lonely that I invited her to dance. Surprisingly enough she rejected me. Perhaps she understood that I felt pity for her. I decided never to go there again." He went to dances only if he was asked to protect someone or stand up for the honour of a girl, since he had a reputation as a fighter. Everyone knew about his strength and fearlessness, but it did not make him happy. He felt lonely. He still hadn't made any friends at the institute, and he hadn't kept in contact with his former classmates, who now considered him a city type. In spite of a tendency to fall in love, which revealed itself early on in his life, he always behaved in a restrained way with girls. He was shy. A particular incident in his childhood had a lasting affect on his attitude to women.

One summer's day he was helping his mother on the farm, as usual. He was walking along the road with the cow, and their black-and-white dog, Rosa, was running alongside. When he turned round he noticed a string of carts following him, and a girl, who looked to be older than him, about thirteen or fourteen, was running in front of the carts. Deep in thought, he didn't notice that the girl had caught up with him. She ran past without taking any notice of him. Not really knowing why, he suddenly shouted after her to ask her to walk with him. But she didn't stop. The string of carts overtook him and he saw that the girl had stopped and was waving at him. He became worried. Suppose she took up his suggestion? But he decided he couldn't back out of it and ran up to her. She asked in a businesslike way: "What will you give me for it? Have you got any money?" He hadn't any.

"Then I remembered that I had some pancakes which my mother had given me for lunch. She nodded her head and I followed her into the oat field. She headed in the direction of a small clearing, settled down there and tore off her dress. At this point I really did take fright. I realized that I ought to do something, but I didn't know quite what. Without undressing, I climbed on top of her. Then I suddenly felt as if someone were watching us. I looked around and saw that my Rosa was sitting there looking at us. Her eyes were so full of reproach that I instantly jumped up and ran off as fast as I could."

After this incident, and especially because of the shame he felt in front of his mother, he decided to have nothing to do with girls until he got married. And he kept the promise he made to himself.

Anatoly started his final sixth year and as before lived in the hostel. At this point a rumour started that an unusually beautiful girl, a gypsy, had appeared on the scene and was occupying the room on the next floor. They met by chance in the corridor, she smiled at him, and that was enough. Soon after their meeting he knocked on her door and when she appeared he blurted out: "I'm going to marry you!" and ran away.

At the time she was just finishing her first year, and both needed to prepare for their examinations. Anatoly suggested that they should go off into the forest to do some work and to sunbathe. Hardly had they managed to spread a blanket out on a clearing when some uninvited guests paid them a visit. "There were six lads, carrying real clubs. I realized that there would be a fight, and I didn't even have a stick. They came closer and I still did not know what to do. Then I saw the bottles of soft drinks that we brought with us. I banged them together, sprang at one of the lads and pushed a splinter of glass to his throat: 'There are six of you,' I said to him, 'but I'll take two of you with me to the next world and you'll be one of them!' Taking advantage of his confusion, I seized the club from him. 'Come on then! Who's going to join me in the next world?' I shouted, but the bandits, who didn't expect such a turn of events, showed a sensible preference for retreat." His behaviour brought the desired results: in the eyes of his girlfriend he was a knight in shining armour.

"Some time later we married. She continued her studies, but my salary at the hospital was not enough to live on. In winter we had nothing to buy fuel. So as not to freeze I had to steal coal from the factory. But all the same we were happy to begin with, she loved me very much. In the mornings, before lectures, she would rush to the market to get milk for me. But we lived together only for a short time, no more than eighteen months or so. There were many reasons for the divorce, but the main one was that she could not have children."

Kashpirovsky had graduated at the age of twenty-three in 1962. He was not a specialist; he just had a diploma from the medical faculty, a rather lowly qualification, with little prestige attached to it. At this time a system of allocation operated in the country: on graduation from an educational institution, the student himself was not free to choose the clinic where he wanted to work. He was sent off into the back of beyond, to the most primitive sort of hospitals. Only when they had worked three years on allocation could "young specialists", as they were known then in official documents, move to some other place. Most graduates preferred not to go to a village, as life seemed impossible there. To stay in a city, students resorted to various cunning schemes, including fictitious marriages, and some managed to stay using personal connections through the back door.

As Kashpirovsky was a sportsman and a member of the Ukrainian weightlifting team, he had a real chance of staying on in Vinnitsa. Sporting achievements were valued much more highly than professional ones. However, another record-holding athlete, a hammer-thrower, took his place, and Kashpirovsky was sent to a railway hospital in the tiny town of Zhmerenka, about forty kilometres from Vinnitsa.

"The Zhmerenka hospital administration did not know what to do with me and I was appointed as a physical training therapist. My salary was low, sixty-three roubles a month, half of which went on the flat. I worked as a doctor for football players, for whom, as a weightlifter, I had little respect. Besides, my duties irritated me. I hated studying tests, cardiograms, and most of all I hated having to fill in patients' record cards." Conflict with the team's trainer was not slow in coming, and finally Kashpirovsky used *blat* (connections for personal gain) to get a transfer to the psychiatric hospital in Vinnitsa in April 1963. Psychiatry was a popular speciality because doctors could receive additional pay, forty-two days leave per year, and other benefits.

In the Soviet Union, as Paul Calloway wrote in *Russian and Western Psychiatry*, the most outdated and abuse-ridden area of health protection was the system of psychiatric services. It continued to operate primarily on the outdated principles on which it was originally based in the 1950s. This was Pavlovian conditioned-reflex psychology, a black-and-white approach to the diagnosis of mental illness, heavy reliance on psychotropic drugs, very little practice of individual or group counselling, and an emphasis on work as the best form of treatment and therapy. In Soviet psychiatry, as in all of Soviet medicine, the social dimension was given great weight in all diagnoses and treatments. The average Soviet citizen avoided seeking psychiatric help, convinced it was better to suffer than have one's life ruined, an almost certain outcome of Soviet psychiatric clinics and services.

"At first I wasn't much interested in psychiatry, nor had I been trained as a psychiatrist. But after I'd read *Notes of a Psychiatrist* by L. Bogdanovich, I started to feel a calling for this work." Vinnitsa hospital was a big one, with two thousand beds. Conditions were terribly shabby and cramped with eighty to ninety patients in each ward. "To start with, I worked in the neurosis department, treating people with depression. Then I was transferred to the women's geriatric department. I had my fill of looking at the dying. I don't know why, but people die mostly at night. So, when I worked a night shift, I often had to sit with an old lady, watching her dying, her body hardening. The smell of death—I'll never forget it. Yet in a strange way I was happy: it gave me the opportunity to ponder at length about life and death. Later I came to the understanding that many effects of old age could be reversed. My treatment has produced many such examples.

"So my mother's dream came true, her son became a doctor, but like other Soviet doctors I continued to live in extreme poverty. My situation was particularly hard because I did not have the *propiska* (internal passport) that would allow me permanent residency. My semi-legal status in Vinnitsa made me move from flat to flat. Sometimes I slept in an attic, going to bed in a coat. I would get up frozen to the marrow, covered with frost. Afterwards, I had to go to work in the hospital. In the evenings, during my first three years of working as a doctor, I used to work as a loader at the railway station to earn some extra money. But my life of poverty seemed to me quite normal. I had never lived in comfortable conditions, never even thought about it. I felt that I was young, strong, and full of expectations for the future."

2

Hypnosis? No, Suggestion

*My uncle—high ideals inspire him;
but when, past joking, he fell sick,
he really forced one to admire him—
and never played a shrewder trick.*

*Let others learn from his example!
But God, how deadly dull to sample
sickroom attendance night and day
and never stir a foot away!*

*And the sly baseness, fit to throttle,
of entertaining the half-dead:
one smoothes the pillows down in bed,
and glumly serves the medicine bottle,
and sighs, and asks oneself all through:
When will the devil come for you?*

*(Chapter one of Eugene Onegin,
Alexander Pushkin)*

*I*n 1964 Anatoly Kashpirovsky was offered the opportunity to go to Kharkov on an advanced training course to study psychotherapy. "I was not interested in psychotherapy then; besides, we had to listen to lectures on Marxism-Leninism and attend military training," he said "but I was happy to go there, because I had no place to live. Four months in Kharkov would give me a breathing spell in my unsettled existence."

Kharkov was the only city in the Soviet Union other than Moscow and Leningrad where such courses were offered. The city's population was about two thirds Ukrainian and one third ethnic Russian. Like almost everywhere in the Ukraine, the teaching was done in Russian. "Our course was organized by the Institute for Professional Enhancement," recalls Kashpirovsky. "Our lecturers were famous Soviet psychotherapists: Platonov, Velvovsky, Doubrovsky and other professors from Kharkov University or Medical Institute. My course was organized by Konstantin Platonov, the father of Soviet psychotherapy, a devoted follower of Bekhterev and Pavlov, who believed that hypnosis was central to psychotherapy. He continued to teach despite the various political ups and downs. He was absolutely convinced that verbal input alone could influence and cure his patients, hence his monograph *The Word as Physiological and Therapeutic Factor*. He taught us how to induce hypnosis and I remember becoming terribly impatient during the demonstrations, desperate to have a go myself."

Kharkov University had an established tradition of study in psychology. In the first few decades after the imposition of Soviet rule in the Ukraine, this course was subjected to rigid Party control and the ideas of materialism were imposed upon the science. General psychology began to disappear even as an area of research. The Kharkov psychologists had worked with a purely physical, reflexological, theory of the mind. This was a mechanistic concept of human behaviour determined solely by physiology and environment. So the development of psychology was hampered by its links to dialectical materialism and utilitarian considerations of social policy. However, at the time of Khrushchev's "Thaw", while Kashpirovsky was studying at Kharkov, attitudes were beginning to change.

Most importantly, Kashpirovsky was introduced to the works of Freud, still difficult to obtain in the Soviet Union, and banned for many years; his theory of psychoanalysis did not fit into the framework of Soviet scientific thought. "It appeared that I was not the only one who was looking for his books, but I pulled some strings and read everything I could get my hands on. Freud was a breath of fresh air in the stagnant atmosphere of Soviet scientific dogma. His references to literary images and symbols, his descriptions of the subconscious, were immediately recognizable to me. They resonated with my own experiences. Freud struck me with the depth of his penetration into the inner self. I could never have imagined such frank discussions between a patient and a doctor. Soviet people would never have revealed their inner thoughts in this way. I envied Freud's brilliance and was angry that I had not been able to read him earlier in my student years. My life could have been quite different. However, despite my excitement, it was virtually impossible to put these new ideas into practice. The powers that be would simply not countenance them."

One of his teachers, Dr Doubrovsky, had returned from seventeen years in a labour camp. Local administrators were reluctant to employ ex-prisoners, who were generally still looked upon with great suspicion. He was, in fact, very lucky after this to have gained his job as a consultant at the university, though he never received the recognition he deserved. He had achieved some remarkable results using techniques of rapid hypnosis in various treatments, particularly with stuttering. But he suffered much criticism from colleagues in his own department. Even though Platonov and others were progressive for the time and were trying to break away from the old mechanistic modes of thought, Doubrovsky's methods were regarded with scepticism. Kashpirovsky, however, was deeply impressed.

Doubrovsky was one of many thousands of prisoners liberated from Stalin's labour camps at this time. The return of so many victims of Stalin's terror, among them men like Alexander Solzhenitsyn, seemed at first to open up and signal a real change in Soviet society. However, Khrushchev's "Thaw", the prototype of Gorbachev's "glasnost", was erratic and inconsistent. Very soon popular writers and artists found themselves victimized again. When the novel *Doctor Zhivago* was published abroad and earned Pasternak a Nobel Prize, the Soviet government reacted with fury. The book was banned and the author was forced to decline the honour.

Kashpirovsky's personal problems preoccupied him so much that he hardly registered the shifting tides of social and political reform. "News of Khrushchev's retirement I took rather calmly. Although he made a lot of promises to grant cultural freedom, economic flexibility and social justice, none of them were fulfilled." In fact, life in Kharkov was very hard. "A group of young doctors from all over the Ukraine were housed four or six to a room in new dormitories built for the Medical Institute. Food was scarce. This was the time when, thanks to Khrushchev's agricultural reforms, even bread disappeared. The builders of the dormitories 'forgot' to build the road to the bus stop. Every day I had to walk three kilometres through a swamp to get there. We were cut off from the world and, in our free time, had nothing to do but drink and fight. Imagine how I felt! In order to keep myself fit and not get involved in the fights, I used to spend my time at the gym at the Kharkov tractor factory. There I met Igor Rybak, an Olympic champion and local celebrity who helped me later on.

"When I left Kharkov and returned to Vinnitsa, I was eager to test myself, to see if I could use hypnosis and actually put patients into trance. I worked in the department of neurosis. My patients were young women with all sorts of depressions, fears and phobias. I decided to try hypnosis on them and started with a group of stutterers in my department. I did exactly as I had seen Dr Doubrovsky do. I told them to line up against the wall and gave them a little talk on speech and how it works. I tried to convince them that there was nothing inherently wrong with them. Many could speak perfectly well when not under stress. I started with some tests to check their suggestibility. I told them they would feel themselves falling backwards, and I could see that they started to do so. Then I said something was pulling them forwards, and they would start to fall forwards. I told them I was certain they would stop stuttering, and they did. As you see, the method is very simple. There is nothing mysterious about it."

The following day the chief surgeon asked to see Kashpirovsky. "What did you do yesterday?" he asked. The doctor looked serious, but he had laughter in his eyes. "What have you done to your patients? Now it's the doctors who are all stuttering in amazement!" Kashpirovsky realized he had permission to continue his experiments. Little by little, the news spread all round the hospital. He never lacked willing guinea-pigs. Women patients, particularly, got hooked on his treatment, followed him everywhere and waited to waylay him at every corner. They wrote him love letters and threatened suicide when he did not reply. His life in the department of neurosis became impossible—everyone was much too neurotic—and he asked for a transfer.

"This is how I came to work on ward 22, a ward for the criminally insane. I worked with murderers and rapists and other deeply disturbed people. Their treatment depended upon psychotropic drugs and I couldn't practise my hypnosis on them." However, he did continue his sessions of hypnosis after-hours, although the administration did not provide him with a room to work in. He conducted his sessions in the corridors, arguing with the cleaners who tried to shoo away his patients.

One noticeable effect of Khrushchev's Thaw was that all kinds of investigation into phenomena previously dismissed as "bourgeois" was now possible: telepathy, faith-healing, psychokinesis, auras around plants and animals, astrology, levitation, dowsing, acupuncture, witchcraft and hypnotism. All these began to be studied and popularized and lectured about all over the country.

"I remember attending the lectures of so-called 'hypnotists' who began to spring up like mushrooms after heavy rain and travel all round the country. The lectures were organized by local philharmonic societies, which also organized concerts and different kinds of entertainment. These performers gathered crowds of people and claimed they could read thoughts telepathically like Messing, make instant calculations or do psychological tricks," recalled Kashpirovsky. "I have never been a believer in all this nonsense about paranormal phenomena. I think most of these ESPers should be examined thoroughly at a mental hospital. I saw a film about Ninel Kulagina, the famous psychic who said she could move objects without touching them, with her mind alone. She became a sensation. But I think she was just a fraud. I myself have never felt the need to use anything that goes beyond psychotherapy. Its influence is so powerful and multifaceted."

In 1967 he was married for the second time. Valentina was only seventeen and still studying. He loved her very much, but their marriage was never an easy one, though it was to last for twenty-five years. Their early life together always suffered from problems with money. A doctor's wage was barely enough to make ends meet. "I got about a hundred to a hundred and twenty roubles a month. Because of the acute shortage of housing, I had been on the waiting list for a room for years. I could not buy a cooperative flat; this was beyond my means and my social position was not good enough to expect a flat as a perk or benefit. I lacked influential friends who could help me to bypass the long waiting period. So the only way was to rent a flat and pay half my salary for it. When the children were born, a daughter, Lena, and a son, Seryozha, I had to turn to our parents for help. At first we moved into my parents' home. Then we lived with her parents. Life seemed unbearable, but now I think it was a kind of real happiness: all of them were alive and tried to do everything to help us. But soon it was we who had to help our parents. My father was ill for a long time and died on the very day that Lena started school and Seryozha was born; my father-in-law died when Lena finished school, so that she attended the graduation ball with a black mourning ribbon in her plait.

"Life in Vinnitsa was difficult and many of the social problems now associated with the post-glasnost era were prevalent then. For example, hooliganism was awful. Women were afraid to walk the streets without a man to protect them. The newspapers never wrote about this, but everyone knew the situation. Bandits threatened people everywhere, and the militia could do nothing about it. Once, when I finished my shift at the hospital at nine o'clock in the evening and was about to go home, a doctor asked me to accompany her because she was afraid to go home alone.

"So that evening we walked along the lane through the park. The benches on both sides of the alley were full of young lads, smoking, drinking, playing cards. Suddenly, one of them loudly insulted my companion. She lowered her head and I could see tears on her cheeks. I stopped and told her not to move, then sharply turned towards the loudmouth. Everyone stopped laughing and watched me with interest. They were sure I would never spot the one who had insulted her. But I spotted him immediately. I bent over him and whispered into his ear. After that I joined my companion and we started off. No one stopped us or said anything. I was sure of success, never doubted myself. I merely said to him, 'You speak too loudly,' and nothing else. But he did not expect it, so I got him off his guard and won the day."

But such small trials of strength and will did little to assuage his sense of frustration and his restlessness, and his work with mentally sick criminals was making his life miserable. He wanted to test his worth on a wider stage, to travel, to see more of the great world beyond his provincial town. Always eager for something different, already excited by the lectures in hypnosis that he had attended in Kharkov, he went one evening to see a performance by Gennady Smertin, a stage hypnotist from Odessa. What he saw made him think he could do just as well. He too could explain the fundamentals of hypnosis and even show the odd trick. "I thought it would give me the chance to express myself. I knew I could do much better. Besides, I did not like the way Gennady Smertin performed—too much noise and very little confidence in himself. Neither did I like the way he looked. His hat was too big, his huge boots with spurs were too noticeable and distracted the public's attention. But I got friendly with him and it was Smertin who advised me to go to the local *Znanie* (knowledge society)."

The Znanie had a network of centres all over the country with the headquarters in Moscow, aimed at popularizing academic knowledge of all kinds and spreading this knowledge throughout the country through lectures. Hypnosis was only one of many topics.

At the Znanie in Vinnitsa, Kashpirovsky was told that according to instructions from Moscow, public demonstrations of hypnosis were banned unless as part of a lecture on hypnosis and suggestion and that a special, officially approved documentary film should be shown before the lecture. In the film Vladimir Rozhnov, a leading Russian psychiatrist, director of the All-Union Psychotherapy Centre in Moscow, explained the essence of hypnosis and its usage in medical practice. Rozhnov insisted on prohibiting the use of hypnosis without special training. He cited other countries like Great Britain where, he claimed, the use of hypnosis on stage had been banned. His position was supported by other scientists, such as W. A. Karle, who wrote:

> Because hypnosis is a powerful process, it has the potential for achieving important beneficial effects when properly used. Equally, however, simply because it is powerful, it is also dangerous in the wrong hands.

Control over its use did not in fact exist in Britain, where anyone could advertise himself as a hypnotherapist and treat patients without any recognized medical or psychological training or qualifications. Certainly the abuse of hypnosis in stage demonstrations was limited by the Hypnotism Act of 1952 which restricted such performances to clubs, but in other countries such demonstrations were outlawed altogether.

Rozhnov later became a fierce critic of Kashpirovsky, who himself had little time for the professor's strictures. "It seems to me that Rozhnov simply wanted to be famous as the only scientist who knew everything about hypnosis, to create his own cult. He could not reconcile himself to the idea that other doctors could do hypnosis better than he. He did everything to limit our use of hypnosis." All these restrictive instructions had been thought up in Moscow and, as usual, were quite ridiculous. It simply hadn't occurred to the bureaucrats that there were no projectors to show Rozhnov's film in remote provincial towns.

"I never showed any films or paid much attention to their rules and regulations. I organized my lectures the way I wanted," said Kashpirovsky. "Later I learned how to get round the official ban. The posters to announce the coming lecture would have 'HYPNOSIS' in capital letters at the top, and in small letters at the bottom 'No, suggestion,' and suggestion could be talked about without any restrictions or filmed instructions."

So Kashpirovsky started out on his lecture tours. "I presented a script of my lecture on the history of hypnosis, where I talked about Braid, Mesmer and Coué, the early fathers of hypnotism, trying hard to make it interesting. In my text I had to include information on the remarkable achievements of the founders of Russian psychotherapy and their materialistic approach to the problems of hypnosis and suggestion; otherwise it would not have been allowed by the censor. When the censor passed it, I was licensed as a lecturer for Znanie. I shall never forget my very first lecture, given on June 17, 1970, in the small town of Yampol, not far from Vinnitsa. My first audience were peasants who came to the local club straight after a long working day in the fields. My lecture was called 'Hypnosis and Suggestion' and I was going to tell them about the Russian psychotherapists Sechenov and Pavlov. But they would not listen, so to quieten them down, I started reading an extract from Kuprin's story *Moonlit Night*.

"It is a short story written in 1893. Kuprin was evidently interested in the subconscious and in hypnotism. The story is basically a conversation between the author and his companion, Gamov. They were walking from a dacha in the countryside to Moscow. They had met before many times, but this time they had to walk home during a moonlit night:

> Suddenly Gamov asked a question: "Are you afraid of anything?" He looked like a man who had suffered a great tragedy.
> "Most of all," he said, "I fear moonlit nights. Cold light, which is neither white nor blue, dead. Dead, lonely, moon deprived of life and air. Myriads of silver dots ... and the Earth as a dot, a grain of sand flying through the eternal darkness ... Everything is covert when lit by the Moon's false light. I can feel that I am being watched by a pair of invisible eyes. They look at me from the sides and from behind. Worst of all is that they look at me from behind, and I have a strong urge to look back. My heart pounds so hard that it can be heard by the 'invisible' being who can also hear how my hair is standing on end."
> "I believe that a man has two wills," said Gamov. "One will is conscious. By this will I control my actions and I am aware of it in me every minute of my life. The second one is subconscious. In some cases the subconscious controls the person without him being aware of it, sometimes even against his will. A person cannot understand it, he is not aware of its existence. When you walk, you move your legs, swing your arms. But you do not think about your arms and legs because you are engrossed in our conversation. Who is making them move if it is not the second will, the subconscious? And what about hypnotism, when one subject submits himself to the commands of another against his will?"
> "I'm afraid of this mysterious part of man," continued Gamov. "I believe that if this second will exists, it means there is a physical organ related to it, which can be affected by disease. But a man does not know anything about his second will and does not know that he is sick. And this is the worst of all. Lunatics, madmen, criminals with obsessive disorders, epileptics—they all suffer from the same disease, the disorder of their second will. I'm afraid of myself, of you, of anything ..."

"I liked the story very much and hoped it would help to create an atmosphere conducive to hypnosis. Alas, the villagers were bored and could not relate to the essence of the conversation between the characters. My listeners stirred only when I was reading the description of a murder. I could see interest rising in their eyes when I was reading about blood, and the horrible details about the death of a beautiful young woman:

> "Do you know that a killer is always attracted to the place of a murder?" asked Gamov. "What would you say if your companion, whom you know as a quiet person, who does not like to talk much, with whom you just used to walk side by side, would make a confession that he had committed a murder two years ago, right here at this very spot?" Gamov pointed out a place in front of him. "That he killed the woman he loved most of all?"

"When I continued, I knew my audience was ripe. They felt the same fear which was described in the story. Since that time I have learnt that if you want to make people believe in you, that you are capable of doing the impossible, you must show blood, pain and suffering. All this makes people very receptive to what you do. That is why I decided later on to show surgical operations on national television. I knew they were more convincing than a million words."

But here, at his first lecture, after he had just finished reading the story, somebody yelled out: "What about some tricks? Show us something interesting or we'll go home!" The audience supported him, nodding their heads in approval. "I've got a better idea," replied Kashpirovsky. "Come on up. Anyone who's not afraid, come up on stage." He started repeating "Sleep, sleep" in a monotone, as recommended by Rozhnov, but people did not obey his commands. It appeared more difficult than he had imagined. The villagers were much more difficult to deal with than his patients. To his patients he was a figure of authority; to the villagers he was a nobody. His first attempts were a complete fiasco. All the way back to Vinnitsa he analysed the reasons for his failure. Finally he decided not to give up, to try again, perhaps in a different way. "And so every Friday, after a working week in the hospital, I used to make up some credible excuse to leave work early and set off to some unknown place to give a lecture and practise my act. I was shaken around in a dirty bus, overflowing with people returning home after a trip to Vinnitsa to stock up on groceries; the roads were unmade and there was no guarantee of anywhere to spend the night. But none of this could stop me. These trips became an integral part of my life."

Years spent in the town of Vinnitsa had made him forget what life was like in the countryside. He, like others, never took propaganda seriously when the media claimed an improvement in the living standards of the Soviet people. But such facts as hundred-percent literacy and the absence of dire poverty were taken for granted. "Real life shook me to the bottom of my soul. I was struck by the poverty and wildness of villages, by the illiteracy of the rural people. When I talked to them I realized that we all had the same problems: a lack of accommodation, food and medicine. The supplies of the city were a little better, so often my fellow travellers were coming home loaded with packs of food products and even bread which they could not buy in their village shops. And my own life was not much better. For a long time the responsibility for getting food for the family lay solely on me."

Although certain goods and appliances became more readily available, improvements in housing and the food supply were slight. Shortages of consumer goods encouraged pilfering of government property and the growth of the black market. Vodka, however, remained readily available. The truth was never discussed on television or radio; censorship was tight. But on his travels Kashpirovsky saw life in its true colours.

"Most of all I was struck by the way people took their torment for granted," says Kashpirovsky, "and they didn't even seem to notice being treated like slaves." Whether they liked it or not Soviet people believed that their system was the best in the world and that life would soon get better.

He was particularly shocked by the rampant alcoholism, especially in the countryside. This was, indeed, one of the major causes of death during the 1970s, especially among the male population. Although Kashpirovsky did sometimes come across alchoholics in the hospital, they deeply affronted his puritanism and asceticism. He considered alcoholism and drug addiction not as diseases but as moral weakness. "I never tried alcohol myself until I was thirty years old," he used to say to his audiences. When people asked him to influence their husbands or wives to stop drinking, he was reluctant: patients had to show that they really wanted to stop.

Out on the road every weekend his performances were beginning to take shape. "At first my appearances took no particular form. Each was impromptu, because each audience was so different. And again and again I had to prove my ability to subordinate another's will to my own. I realized that a person becomes subordinate only when he witnesses the inexplicable. Often the task seemed too much. How can one make a 'miracle' happen in a village club, where there was neither light nor music at hand, and where the audience themselves were a sorry sight? As a rule, people came to my lectures at the end of a working day and usually tipsy. And this was the audience I had to captivate. And I did. How?

"First, I told them about psychotherapy, about scientists such as Sechenov and Pavlov, how I had met Platonov and the significance of his book *The Word as a Physiological and Therapeutic Factor*. Then as the audience demanded it, I would put on a show for them.

"Once when I came to perform in a small village, people could not calm down. They came to my performance right after work in the fields and continued to talk and laugh. Most of all I was wound up by a big lump, the local jack-the-lad, who did not listen to anybody. He came out onto the dusty stage. I could see that he was half drunk and in a belligerent mood.

"I decided to take a huge risk. It could easily have ended in disaster. I wasn't at all sure I could pull it off. What if he didn't respond? Disaster! Suddenly, I had a feeling of certainty, a conviction of triumph. I knew that I'd make him listen to me. I said: 'Look at him! He will fall down.' Just a wave of my hand, and he fell flat on his back, without bending. The audience did not understand what had happened. They thought I had hit him. His friends came on stage ready to fight. But another gesture and all of them were on the floor, and I did not even touch them. People were stunned, no one moved, their mouths wide open with amazement. After that, I could say or do anything I wanted."

This method of rapid hypnosis, used much more by stage hypnotists than by psychologists in their laboratories, can be extremely dramatic. The stage hypnotist has no time for subtle preparation but works with a direct, domineering, frontal attack. In his book *Using Hypnotism*, G. H. Eastabrooks remarks that "such an approach is highly unpleasant to most people and awakens strong emotion, closely akin to fear and anger. This, of course, plays directly into the hypnotist's hands. The emotion 'sensitizes' the brain so that his suggestions then become irresistible." Researchers in this field like Weizenhoffer (*General Techniques of Hypnotism*) and Harry Arons (*Techniques of Speed Hypnosis*) note that with a suggestible subject, a simple snap of the fingers or wave of the hand in front of the eyes, coupled with a sharp and forceful command, can induce a hypnotic trance almost instantly, as if by reflex.

Of course, this didn't always work and Kashpirovsky soon learned that he could be duped. Once, when performing in the town of Korosten, a gypsy in his audience demonstrated a remarkable degree of subordination to Kashpirovsky's will. He sang, he danced, he did acrobatic tricks. He allowed his palms to be burnt and pierced with needles without any signs of feeling pain. The performance was a great success. But later, Kashpirovsky received a photograph as a gift. He looked at it and suddenly felt sick. He understood that his favourite gypsy had been playing tricks on him all along. He had been made a fool of. The picture showed that the gypsy had just been pretending: he had an enigmatic Giaconda smile on his face.

Gradually Kashpirovsky's technique improved and he worked out how to make the performances more convincing and interesting. He came to understand that his own behaviour had to be attractive, and that he had to include some amazing tricks to impress people and win them over. No one wanted just to listen to his philosophical discussions. He created an aura of the magician for himself, powerful, self-contained, with great charismatic charge. He would entrance people by his presence.

"I've been to performances by Wolf Messing. He was a rather old, small man with a mane of wiry hair which he combed straight back. And it was hard to believe that this man dazzled Stalin, accurately predicted the end of World War II, and impressed audiences all over the Soviet Union with his powers. He claimed he could see others' thoughts as images in his mind. I remember when he was blindfolded, walking in the hall holding someone by the hand and saying: 'You do not think; you must think. When you think which way to go, right or left, I'll read your mind and find the person who gave me his watch. Now, think hard!' But, to my mind, he in fact subconsciously received tiny muscle movements that aided him in his 'reading'. I decided I could do the same."

No one taught him any of this. Having seen an act he wished to emulate, he worked it out for himself and developed it. The audience would sit there, mesmerized, not moving a muscle, while he, with a blindfold, would confidently come down from the stage and in the middle of the rows of seats would find a ring which had been hidden and would put it on his finger, or find the page in a book and a word on a page that someone had marked. He amazed them with his tricks: piercing peoples' flesh with needles or persuading them that a pencil held to their hands was, in fact, a lighted cigarette. He often talks of a "feeling of triumph", a strange intuition, a certainty that suffused his whole being when he knew that he was able to exercise such control.

In the coal city of Donetsk, Kashpirovsky performed for the miners with great success. Not long before Kashpirovsky's visit, three psychotherapists from Moscow had been to the Pochenkov mine there. They were Tabachnikov, Filatov and Rozhnov. The mine's administration had invited Moscow scientists to come and see the working conditions there and give their recommendations. Rozhnov and his colleagues put miners' overalls on and went down. "We could not walk and had to crawl along the narrow passage. Most of all we were suffering from the heat. We spent just a few hours there, but imagine working under such conditions!"

As a result of their visit, the mines were equipped with "special rooms for psycho-emotional stress relief, where miners would go after a working day," Vladimir Rozhnov wrote in his report. "The miners sit in comfortable armchairs and listen to classical music and try to induce the hypnoid state, repeating to themselves that they are not tired, they feel well. Such group sessions were organized for ten to twelve people at a time. Those who need help are cared for by psychotherapists who induce longer sleep-relaxation with the help of direct hypnotism. Such treatment helped to avoid somatic diseases like high blood-pressure, ulcers and other disorders." Typically, no one seems to have thought of actually trying to improve conditions down in the mines.

Such rooms appeared not only at mines but at other industrial plants where working conditions were no better. Local managers did not hesitate to spend money on these stress-relief centres. "I was impressed by the fantasy and imagination of the decorators. Imagine that you are on the deck of a sailing ship. You sit in an armchair and in front of you, you can see the waves of the Black Sea behind the Crimean shoreline. Your chair is moving as if rocking in the waves of the sea. You can hear comforting music." Rozhnov liked the way his ideas were implemented. "Or you are in a tropical forest with palms and flowers. You can hear the singing of the birds ... Or suddenly you find yourself in the centre of Russia with steppes, forests and groves and the spreading Volga river. In other words, you can see everything that is dear to your heart, the beloved motherland that you have known since early childhood. Being in such an environment, you are happy; you want to be a healthy, active, useful member of society. You feel happy that you are part of a great cause, the cause of your people, of your country."

With this terrifying vision Vladimir Rozhnov seduced the Soviet authorities, who supported him enthusiastically. Kashpirovsky disliked these Soviet tricks and one begins to understand his contempt for Rozhnov and his ilk.

His own performances attracted many miners who did not share the enthusiasm of the leading psychotherapist from Moscow. Of course, the relaxation rooms were useless and did not help them to forget their problems; they were looked upon as a bad joke.

To find out what a miner's job was like, Kashpirovsky too went down a mine. "At a depth of one kilometre and one hundred metres, with coal, dust and dirt in my eyes, where it was impossible to move in the narrow passages, I realized what 'convict labour' was; it wasn't just a brash journalistic cliché. Just for a moment I imagined that over me was a kilometre of earth and I felt scared. But these miners are spending their lives in such conditions! And they are our own Soviet people! That same evening, during a performance, I told the audience what I had seen down the mine. 'Dear miners' wives,' I said at the end, 'take better care of your husbands! Their work is so tough and dangerous!' The newspapers were full of talk about cosmonauts, about their journeys into space. But why was there nothing about miners? I can't say that their work is any less heroic." Later, when the Donetsk miners began a series of strikes demanding better pay from Gorbachev's government, Kashpirovsky supported them wholeheartedly: he considered that they, more than any other part of the population, had grounds for protest.

Wherever he performed, whether to miners and other workers or to simple peasants, he was always amazed to see how impressed and excited everyone seemed at his hypnotic demonstrations. In spite of the materialistic foundations of Soviet science, hypnosis was always a subject of great fascination and interest and had been deeply researched by Soviet scientists, sometimes with the rather sinister backing of the KGB and Soviet military who had their own agenda here.

As Kashpirovsky often claimed that he did not "hypnotize" people but that he was a simple psychotherapist, both words need some elucidation before confusion arises. Psychotherapy is usually thought of as a means of helping people with neuroses, phobias and other mental problems. Kashpirovsky calls himself a psychotherapist, but has little to do with these; he is interested in curing physical ailments. So, although he insists on calling himself a psychotherapist, he uses the word in a particular way, a way which was not recognized by doctors of clinical medicine.

It is important too to stress the centrality of hypnosis in psychotherapeutic practice in the former Soviet Union. It is perfectly possible to read a book on psychotherapy by an American or Western European and never find a mention of the word hypnosis—for example, Gerald Amada's *A Guide to Psychotherapy*. However, at the first major conference on psychotherapy in Moscow after World War II, the use of hypnosis and hypnotherapy dominated all discussions. Constantin Platonov said there that "hypnosis is without doubt the core of psychotherapy." Pavlov, who in the West is particularly associated with his research into reflex behaviour, most famously his salivating dogs, was the ultimate authority in Soviet psychology (ironically, as he himself was a passionate opponent of Soviet communism). In his work during the 1930s, he was a great pioneer of hypnosis. His word was law, the Bible of official medical research in this field. The confusion that arises in understanding Kashpirovsky's later claim that he was not a hypnotist stems from this complete belief in Pavlov and all his works. Pavlov, it was said, asserted that hypnosis took place only in a sleeping state, that hypnosis was sleep, as in the "you are feeling sleepy, sleepy ..." school of hypnotism. We now know that hypnotism and sleep are totally distinct. This has been conclusively proved by measurements of brainwave activity during both states.

Kashpirovsky saw quite plainly that he was perfectly able to influence people without making them go to sleep. Instead of challenging Pavlov's definition, he decided that what he was doing could not be said to be hypnosis, that hypnosis was too narrow a definition of his approach. When belittled by his detractors as a "mere hypnotist", Kashpirovsky would retort that "*Hypnos* in Greek means sleep. The fathers of Soviet psychotherapy, Pavlov and Bekhterev, have built their own theories based on the assumption that hypnosis is sleep. But my patients are never asleep: they are aware of everything that is going on around them." In fact, Pavlov's theories had been oversimplified. He was more subtle than has subsequently been allowed. He defined hypnosis as a state of somnolence, or near-sleep, but with an alert "monitoring point" in the cortex of the brain which allows rapport to be maintained and suggestions made.

So, the absolute respect that Pavlov's ideas, or what was understood of them, commanded in Soviet science and, more practically, the law which banned hypnosis in public, eventually led Kashpirovsky to formulate a theory based on his own understanding of his daily practice. He used the word *ustanovka* to describe his activities, particularly later on when his performances had developed into mass healing sessions and he had left behind the hypnotist's tricks of his early career. This word was first proposed by a famous Georgian psychologist, Dmitri Uznadze, in his investigations into human consciousness. He defined it as the "psychic preparedness" of the mind towards certain types of action. One could characterize it as a "mental set" which predisposes a person to suggestion. This concept was further confused by the use of the word in everyday Russian to mean a "directive" or "order". For the Soviet people, used to directives of all kinds, the words "Kashpirovsky gives *ustanovka*" became an idiomatic expression with a totalitarian connotation meaning basically "Kashpirovsky gives an order." Because of this, Kashpirovsky eventually began to replace this word also with the word "information". He claimed that he gave out certain "information" which people could intuit directly at a level which bypassed the conscious mind—that in his healing he was helping people to access within themselves those hidden regenerative powers which lead to recovery and health.

Nobody really knows precisely what hypnotism is, nor yet the actual mechanisms by which it works. Many are still reluctant to believe that it really does work. Generally people accept that hypnotherapy for smoking or weight-loss may be helpful, but not perhaps that any more profound changes take place; certainly not that hypnosis can be extensively used to cure physical ailments. This mistrust is partly due to the bad reputation of hoaxers and fakers in the field, but also to an image of the hypnotist personified most famously by Svengali, the sinister stage hypnotist in George du Maurier's novel *Trilby*, who could put people under his power and do with them whatever awful things he wanted.

Perhaps greater than all of this is the difficulty in allowing that the mind—insubstantial, incorporeal—can directly influence the body in the way Kashpirovsky and others claim. There is, however, an overwhelming amount of evidence and scientific literature which says just this, from Mesmer and James Braid, the Scottish doctor who coined the word "hypnosis", to the present day. There are, for example, on record, "thousands of cases of major operations such as amputations having been successfully performed with hypnosis as the only anaesthetic" (Robert Temple, *Open to Suggestion: The Uses and Abuses of Hypnosis*). Such was the difficulty that this presented to the understanding, particularly of the medical establishment, that early pioneers like Dr John Elliotson, a London physician who used hypnosis extensively, suffered the most outrageous persecution. He was forced to leave his post at University College Hospital, vilified as a madman and a threat to public order and sanity (rather like Kashpirovsky more than a hundred years later). John Esdaile, a surgeon working in India in the 1840s, performed over three thousand operations using only hypnosis as an anaesthetic. Then ether was discovered and the whole medical apparatus of anaesthesia followed. There are innumerable more modern instances of hypnosis being successfully used in surgery.

The literature is also full of reports of "physiological alteration through hypnosis" (Robert Temple). Accounts abound of the usefulness of hypnosis in counteracting all manner of diseases—not merely those that can easily be tagged "psychosomatic"—including, interestingly, the use of hypnosis in helping patients with haemophilia. As Kashpirovsky has so often been compared to Rasputin, it is worth remembering that this infamous Russian was able to stop the little Tsarevich Alexis from bleeding when all the greatest court doctors had failed completely. The evidence is there, for those who wish to pursue it.

3

The Travelling Hypnotist

*Russia is baffling to the mind,
Not subject to the common measure.
Her ways—of a peculiar kind ...
One only can have faith in Russia.*

(Fyodor Tyutchev 1866)

Kashpirovsky's early travels with the Znanie society went some way to assuaging his inner restlessness but so far they had been confined to a fairly small area. He wanted to explore his vast country, to fly off to its farthest corners. He began to dream of travelling to the East, to Sakhalin, though it was virtually impossible to get permission to go there. It was a place of exile and was covered in military bases.

"One of my patients told me that Sakhalin was the most beautiful and amazing place on earth. 'It's like being on Mars,' he used to say and this despite having spent ten years there, sentenced to forced labour just for saying to someone that an American Studebaker was better than a Soviet Zil. He had to work on railway construction with other convicts."

Kashpirovsky tried to remember what he had been taught at school about the island. Not much. He remembered that Gennady Nevelskoy, the admiral and explorer of the Far East, had explored the island, that Sakhalin was known as a place of exile and that Anton Chekhov had been there. He had gone to Sakhalin as a census-taker and described the zone of prison camps and the horrible conditions of prisoners' lives.

Sakhalin was a frontier, so it was closed to visitors, and even relatives of residents needed a special permit to go there. It remained closed until 1989 when it was opened for foreigners and non-resident Soviet citizens. "Nowadays it's easier to get to America than it was to get to Sakhalin. One had to have an invitation."

But he found a way. "At the Znanie they told me I could get an assignment to go to Sakhalin as a lecturer. But still I would have to wait several months to get the papers, the usual bureaucracy! But I did not want to wait. I decided to go there and to sort it out somehow when I arrived. In April 1971, I took a plane and flew to Sakhalin. It was amazing to speed across ten time zones, towards the stars. The further east I travelled, the more oriental faces I came across. The plane stopped in the Siberian cities of Chelyabinsk, Krasnoyarsk, Chita and Khabarovsk. Everywhere the airports were packed with passengers, waiting for their flights because of the weather or lack of fuel. Often passengers had to spend several days there. At night they had to lie on the floor, even women and children. I was struck by the dirt and the atmosphere of neglect. No one seemed to care about these people.

I arrived in Yuzhno-Sakhalinsk, the local centre, at midnight. The KGB border guards came straight to the plane and began to check everyone's documents. I knew that mine weren't in order but when the guard turned to me and requested my pass, I looked at him with an air of authority and gave him my lecturer's *putevka*. Surprisingly enough he let me through."

The whole island was covered with concrete guard shacks which later all collapsed in the terrible earthquake of 1995. Border guards were everywhere, as there were several military installations. Wherever he went, Kashpirovsky was taken first to the commandant's office for his documents to be checked. Sometimes guards with automatic weapons got onto ordinary buses. One would stand blocking the bus door while the others checked that everything was in order.

"When I got off the plane I felt like Neil Armstrong landing on the moon. Much of Sakhalin seemed uninhabited and gave the impression that no human foot had ever trod the land. Nowhere ever made a bigger impression on me, although I subsequently travelled widely. Even American skyscrapers did not impress me as much as the gigantic plants in Sakhalin. The burdocks were enormous, the size of a small house; grass grows six metres high."

He also liked the air there, full of the smell of wood from the timber processing factories. "Once I'd been there, I began to respect Chekhov. I always loved Gorky and Tolstoy, but I never appreciated Chekhov's works—maybe because of how his works had been taught at school. I could not read or watch his plays, *The Three Sisters* or *The Cherry Orchard*. I found them too boring. They lacked any sort of courageous spirit. But after, I could value him in a different way: he had been to all these places and described everything there.

Kashpirovsky went to Sakhalin three times: in 1971, 1972 and 1974, and travelled just about the entire length and breadth of it, giving lectures and demonstrating his hypnotic powers, sticking needles in people, knocking them over, making them think they were dogs or chickens, the usual stage-hypnotist tricks. Most of his audiences were Russian contractors: fishermen, miners, woodcutters, oil workers, who used to come to his lectures after work, tired but happy that they could meet someone from the mainland, as they called Russia. They asked him what was happening there because they had no information and letters took months to come. Because of the severe climate and harsh working conditions, some were paid bonuses, but nothing could compensate for their miserable lives.

David Remnick, author of *Lenin's Tomb*, visited Sakhalin in 1989 and described the mine:

> It was worse than anything I'd seen in Siberia, Ukraine or Kazakhstan. The mine was a horror. There were no elevators, and the shafts were brutal and tight. It took some of the miners two hours of sliding and creeping along stone just to get to their work stations. Later, my back and legs were covered with bruises and I was more sore than I would have been if I'd run ten miles. Until the strike, the miners had not been paid for this "commuting" time; they tore themselves up, four hours every day, for free.

As a foreigner, he was shown the best mine of all those existing there. "In others, water runs down your back all day," said Kashpirovsky.

People knew nothing could be done to improve their lives without a directive from the Party. Local Party authorities explained that they could do nothing without a command from Moscow. And Moscow was six thousand miles away. Kashpirovsky listened to their stories and thought it all sounded familiar, the same arbitrary rule as everywhere else.

Later on, in May 1988, Sakhalin became the centre of attention in the Soviet Union. National TV reported that the first signs of perestroika had reached the edges of Russia when hundreds of people gathered outside the Chekhov Drama Theatre in Yuzhno-Sakhalinsk and blamed their First Party Secretary of the *Obkom*, the regional party committee, for doling out apartments to his relatives and generally lining his own pocket. The police and KGB circled the small demonstration but were too stunned, too confused, to act. The Party tried to wish it all away. To acknowledge the demonstration would have been "a situation". That was impermissible, unthinkable. The next morning, the official papers made the requisite noise about "a handful of extremists" and then ignored the issue entirely.

But soon, as if sensing Moscow's breath at their backs, the local democrats staged even bigger demonstrations in the squares and streets of Yuzhno-Sakhalinsk. The island's Party leadership was suddenly on the defensive. A triumphant banner appeared over Lenin Avenue: "Get Rid of the Bureaucrats and Give Them a Shovel." Tretyakov, the Party chief, would have fought back if he could, but he got no support from Moscow. He was fired by the Central Committee, fled Sakhalin to Moscow on a military transport jet, and never returned.

Despite all the problems, Kashpirovsky revelled in the fabulous feeling of travelling: "I don't know why, but Znanie always planned my trips to start in the south of Yuzhno-Sakhalinsk in the direction of Japan. I moved along the eastern coast, along Aniva Bay, visited towns like Kholmsk, Nevelsk, and Shebunino. I loved the names—they were music to my ears. I even went as far as the Strait of Laperuz and saw Japan through binoculars. I'll never forget the beautiful view onto the Tatar Gulf, which separates the island from the continent, where at high tide water covers the road. There are three *sopka*s (little hills) in the sea, called Three Brothers—you can see them in full only at low tide.

"I came to the port of Alexandrovsk and stayed overnight in Mgachi, a small settlement where coal miners live. That same night there was a typhoon. I couldn't believe my eyes when I saw that as a result of the typhoon, a little *sopka* had slipped towards the gulf and blocked the road to all vehicles. Military tractors were sent to clear the road, but even they couldn't cope with the obstruction. They told me I would have to wait for a couple of days for transport. But I was rushing to the airport and simply couldn't wait. There was only one solution, to walk. But there was no road, nor path, so I would have to go through the woods and swamps. And so I walked for a whole day. I managed twenty-four kilometres, jumping from hillock to hillock and going through thickets which seemed never to have been visited by humans before.

"My daughter, Lena, asked me to bring her a bear cub from Sakhalin. So in Alexandrovsk airport I asked the girls who worked there to let me know if there would be a bear hunt. I was so busy that I completely forgot about it, but they called me to say that there were two bear cubs at the frontier post and to pick one up I had to fly six hundred kilometres. So I had no choice, I had to go. There is nothing I won't do for my daughter. The bear cub turned out to be so sweet, so defenceless, although he had already bitten a guard's finger. It was so funny to watch him move around. He was small, just about thirty centimetres. I put him into a plastic bag and brought him into the hotel. He immediately got under my bed and stayed there the rest of the evening. At night when he got hungry, he started squeaking. I gave him some milk and put him under my blanket. He fell asleep at once and never disturbed me anymore.

"In the morning I left some milk for him and went out. In the evening when I opened the door of my room I could not believe my eyes. It was such a mess. The bear cub had torn down everything he could reach. To complete the picture he destroyed my pillows and the feathers were flying in the air. I had to take him back. What would I do with him when he became big?"

The northern part of the island attracted him most of all. "I was born to live in the north. When it snows, in cold and stormy weather, I am aware of what life really is. Only then do I have the feeling that I am truly alive. I went there by train along the road that connected

Okha and Kotangli. I spent eight hours on the train looking around, on a railway line built by a patient of mine. The train was moving slowly, not more than twenty kilometres an hour. I was the only passenger. I watched a herd of reindeer which was moving in front of our train and we just couldn't overtake it. The railway went across the tundra, which consists of permafrost, its vegetation limited to grass, moss and lichens. No one seemed to live here and there was a sense of amazing stillness, although occasionally something dived in a lake or there was the sound of birdsong.

"The train made some stops: Dagi with the geysers, Nysh, Kotangli, Molochnye Kotiki, which means baby seals. There I was invited to take part in a hunt for baby seals. I'll never forget how a three-month-old seal was shot in the eye. The hunter hit him with an oar and threw him into the boat. The baby seal cried with pain till it died."

In the remote villages sledges pulled by dog teams were the only means of transportation. In the 1930s people were promised by the local Party administrators that Soviet power would change their lives and build roads so they could drive cars around and would no longer need dogs. As a result, thousands of dogs were shot in a barbaric manner. But the promises were never fulfilled, so it took a long time to re-establish the breeds of draft dog. Dogs are both shepherds and hunters. Sometimes a bitch's milk fed both puppies and human young. "When I was driving the sledge, I loved watching the dogs, especially the leader of the pack, who led six or seven dogs behind him. I imagined myself as a character out of Jack London's novels."

In Rybatchy settlement Kashpirovsky met a tribal people, the Nivkhi (Gilyaks). "I'd never heard of them, never knew they existed. The whole village came to my performance. They were short, stocky people with flat, rectangular faces and dark hair and beards. When they laughed I noticed many of them lacked teeth, even some girls, who looked no more than twenty years old. After the performance the Nivkhi invited me to be their guest. 'We are descendants of the semi-legendary Tonchi, the earliest neolithic inhabitants of this region,' a young Nivkhi told me. 'But now only three to five thousand of us are left. We are fishermen and fur trappers.' "

They were very hospitable and friendly. But Kashpirovsky noticed that though the men talked and laughed, the women just looked at him stealthily. "Yes, patriarchy reigns in family relations," continued his new friend. Until the twentieth century the Nivkhi retained a form of group marriage. Although converts to Russian Orthodoxy existed by 1917, most Nivkhi remained shamanistic. Today younger Nivkhi are abandoning the old ways for opportunities in the city. More than half of them speak Russian, but few intermarry with Russians. "I liked them a lot," said Kashpirovsky. "They were naive and open like children. But one thing I did not like was their alcoholism."

When Kashpirovsky moved to the south of Sakhalin, he met the Koreans who lived in the area which had become part of the Soviet Union after Japan's defeat in 1945. The Koreans were shipped there and then abandoned by the Japanese at the end of the war. Now about thirty-seven thousand Koreans live in Sakhalin. "The Koreans were always friendly and polite, especially the women. I liked them. When they talk to you, it seems that they are totally in love with you."

According to his assignment, he had to visit a party of geologists who could be reached only by freight helicopter. "I was seated on some lead container. All the while I was trying to guess what it might be. Then the pilot told me that it contained radioactive material! The helicopter landed in the Val settlement in the middle of the *taiga*, but there was no one to meet me. The pilot waved his hand in some direction and was gone. I was left alone not knowing what to do, where to go. Finally the geologists came, apologizing for being late." He received a warm welcome from them and all his performances there were a great success.

Once because of pouring rain, the railway was washed out, so the only way to travel was by air. "But it turned out that Okha airport in the north of the island was closed due to severe weather and I had to spend six days there, waiting for the plane to Yuzhno-Sakhalinsk. The rain changed to snow and the temperature dropped to below zero. The locals immediately unpacked their fur coats, hats, warm boots made of reindeer fur, and I was the only one left still wearing his raincoat and Indian sandals. People just thought I was an eccentric.

"At last I got help. The local Party secretary invited me to join him on board a military plane. The plane was big and empty—we were the only passengers. It had no heat, so the temperature dropped down to minus thirty. The Party secretary, who was dressed in a sheepskin coat and Japanese high fur boots, froze and started running up and down the aisle trying to warm up. I remained seated, convincing myself that I did not feel cold."

Sakhalin impressed him with its natural beauty and the diversity of its people. Despite the squat, shabby apartment blocks and the dreary collective farms, the island retained its magic for him, even while performing before prisoners at one of the camps at Zonalnoe. These were no longer Stalin's awful murder camps, but they were still fearful places.

"In Sakhalin I met a company of touring 'lilliputians' and got to like them a lot. One of them, Sasha, became a friend. They performed in the circus, so after performances we would sit together and talk and talk about everything. I never realized how hard their life really was. They told me they could not buy clothes, shoes, even furniture. It was as if they never existed, nobody cared about them. But in spite of all their problems, they liked to have fun."

As he travelled, his reputation grew. Sometimes he felt embarrassed seeing such naive faith in his "supernatural" powers. It reminded him of the situation with Mesmer, the founder of hypnosis, when people believed that he could mesmerize a tree, and that if they touched it, they would be healed. Confident in his own powers, he was still amazed at the absolute credulity of many in his audience.

"During that first trip I unexpectedly earned a lot of money. I had real money for the first time in my life; for sixty-four lectures they paid three thousand roubles! I came to collect my fee, and I felt awkward in front of the cashiers who were getting literally next to nothing. I have always experienced that kind of feeling for being paid for my performances. I never considered it to be real work that deserves to be paid. The cashiers probably felt the same. They could not believe that 'lectures' could be paid so well. They gave me the register, where I had to find my name and sign for the money. I looked at the names and saw that others were paid fifty or sixty roubles. Then I saw my name on the list, and I could not believe my eyes—I thought it was a mistake, too many zeros. The cashiers wanted to see my reaction and got their own back by giving me what was a huge sum at the time, three thousand roubles, all in single-rouble notes.

"I began to stuff the wads into my pockets, but they wouldn't fit and began to fall on the floor. To try to smooth over the increasing sense of awkwardness, I rushed into a shop and bought the girls some expensive sweets and champagne, but I still felt guilty."

From Sakhalin Kashpirovsky flew on to the Far East and carried on his performances in the Maritime Krai in far eastern Siberia. He went to Vladivostok, the capital, a major seaport on the Pacific coast. He was most impressed by the beauty of the city, which lies in a picturesque amphitheatre around a narrow, deep bay known as the Golden Horn.

"I had already got used to some success, but in Vladivostok I had my first taste of real fame and adulation. At my first performance at the Lenin Palace of Culture there were not more than two hundred people, but on the following day something unbelievable happened! People were so excited after what they had witnessed at the first performance that, evidently, rumours had spread about 'miracles'. Next day there were so many people gathered in front of the entrance that I could hardly squeeze into the sailors' club. The ecstatic audience wanted to touch me and tore at my clothes!"

He always performed in black: black trousers and a black poloneck, nothing superfluous in either attire or behaviour. He created for himself the image of a resolute, courageous ascetic, well trained, appropriately tough, unsmiling, not playing with the public. He never changed this image. If there was a mysterious element about him which drew the audience, it was accentuated by their sense of his independence, his absence of fear in being his own man. People respected this and accepted him without reservation because they saw a social equal in him, not some pretentious intellectual. They saw that he knew their life, that he had travelled and understood.

The penetrating gaze of his dark eyes also worked for him; people thought he could see through them and they were frightened. But they also loved him, especially women, who would always occupy the front seats in the hope of catching his healing gaze. After the performances they would come to the stage in order to touch his hand. They telephoned him non-stop, wrote love letters and would sit by the entrance to his hotel all night long begging for a meeting to share their problems and misfortunes.

In Nakhodka one woman came and asked in tears: "I know that my request might sound strange. But could you bring my daughter back to life? She died eight months ago." Kashpirovsky tried to comfort her. "I understood that she asked me just in case I could do something. I came to understand that although human faith has no boundaries, the potential to satisfy it is unfortunately limited and one should always think of this in order not to give empty promises.

"There I met a diver, Gena Kichigin, who was interested in yoga, bodybuilding and psychotherapy. He became a great fan of mine and offered to help me organize my performances. Of course I needed someone because people recognized me on the street and walking around town became a problem." His fans and those who heard about his "miracles" could approach him anywhere with their problems. "They could come up to me in a restaurant with their haemorrhoids, ready to demonstrate right on the spot. I remember how in a restaurant, where every night they arranged festivities in my honour, some drunk, who was perhaps their boss, told me, 'You, sucker, your hypnosis won't work on me.' People looked at me expecting my reaction. But I made no move. He was laughing and swearing, but nobody wanted to interfere and stop him. I continued to eat, watching attentively his every mood. When he was off his guard, I came up to him and tapped him on his forehead. In a split second he shut up, his face lying in his plate. I turned to the people. Everybody was silent, avoiding my eyes."

The city administrators tried to please him. "I was given a book of coupons for taxis. I saw there were so many that they'd last me the rest of my life. So I had two taxis waiting for me round the clock in front of the hotel. This was a kind of tradition, kept by captains who liked to squander money after long voyages abroad. Even for a trip from the hotel to the restaurant, no more than a mile, they would go by two or three cars. The first car would carry the captain's cap, the second had his case, and the captain himself would ride in the third. By the number of cars people could tell a person's importance. And I, who had never had any money to spend, behaved like one of them. It amused me, and honestly, I really enjoyed myself being treated like a VIP." It seemed everyone wanted to see him.

"I arrived in Nakhodka late at night. I woke up the next morning and looked out of the window. I was stunned. Our hotel was on top of the hill and had a wonderful view onto America Bay. I saw two rocks called the Brother and the Sister and thousands of ships. It was so still and quiet that I held my breath in admiration. Here and in other sea ports, like Iman and Suchan, which were closed to visitors, I was invited to perform aboard military ships. I was never asked for an official pass—something impossible to imagine in that time of secrecy and suspicion. Everywhere I went there was great interest in what hypnosis was about. But of course many had the wrong idea, thinking it was something supernatural, mystical. They looked upon me as if I were a superman with extraordinary powers.

"I was allowed into the International Sailor's Club, which was closed to my countrymen. In order to impress the foreigners, I demonstrated a cataleptic bridge. I hypnotized a huge black sailor. He was lying in the air with his head on one chair and his heels on another. The audience, sailors from all over the world, burst out laughing when, on his stomach, as a joke, I sat a Russian beauty with a huge bottom! And although they didn't understand a word, the success of the performance was colossal!"

He also performed on board merchant ships and the whaling ship *Sovetskaya Rossia*. "These sailors had experienced everything; they feared neither God nor the devil and at first looked at me with scepticism. Seventy people gathered in the passenger lounge and in the beginning refused to participate in the tricks, but after some time they too swallowed the bait and danced to my tune.

"Once, when I was on the Chinese border, I performed at the *Krasny Ugolok* (Red Corner), the place for political education, where soldiers were brainwashed. I went there with my wife Valentina. She was sent to keep watch while I put the whole frontier post into a trance on the floor. At that moment there was an alarm signal! Valentina came down the observation platform to let us know that some Chinese barge was approaching the border. The sergeant was left sitting on a chair under Brezhnev's portrait. Because of his rank, I had not put him into trance in front of his soldiers. He blanched with horror and became the colour of his baby's nappies—the baby was there too! Everyone had to be brought round quickly and I gave the command to set about protecting the state's border!

"This border post was really ridiculous. Once Valentina and I went for a walk and got lost. It became dark but we were still trying to find our way back to the frontier post, wandering backwards and forwards. When we returned, we were told there was a red alert. 'Someone,' they said, 'has crossed our state border five times!'"

The eastern edge of the Soviet Union always remained Kashpirovsky's favourite part of the world. He toured there seven times in twenty years. But just before his second tour he had a bad fall while training on the horizontal bars. "Usually I can endure any pain, but that time the pain was unbearable and I was brought to the hospital in a critical condition." The doctors thought he had ruptured his stomach and offered to operate, but he refused. A pain-killing injection was suggested and he agreed as he couldn't stand the pain any longer. "I was lying on the operating table and the doctor drew out the needle, as long as a knitting needle, and gave me the injection under the kidney. Suddenly I was overcome by a dreadful feeling of weakness and began to lose consciousness. It turned out I was allergic to novocaine and all night the doctors fought for my life. I didn't come round until the next morning. They moved me into a ward and put me onto a bed where the night before a young fellow had died of food poisoning.

"I was in hospital for a month, and gradually began to feel better. I discharged myself from the hospital and went off to perform in the Khmelnitsky region. But it turned out I hadn't fully recovered, and again I had nineteen attacks of unbearable pain which lasted five, six hours. As a result I ended up in hospital once more, a different one this time, the Vinnitsa railway hospital. I was diagnosed as having cancer. Our famous surgeon Sardak insisted on an immediate operation, but I refused. I'm sure that it was the right decision."

Valentina, Kashpirovsky's wife's cousin and namesake, was in hospital at the same time, waiting to have her tonsils removed. Anatoly knew she couldn't stand medical anaesthesia and, moreover, she was pregnant. She had previously sought his help before going to the dentist. A tooth was one thing but this was an operation, and Anatoly himself could hardly stand up because of the pain. But she asked him to help her and he agreed, although he realized that it was hardest of all to deal with relatives in such situations, since they do not necessarily regard one with quite such awe. Valentina Klepach lives in Canada now. Reminiscing about this incident, she said: "Against all the existing rules and regulations, Anatoly told them I shouldn't be tied to the chair. 'Close your eyes and do not be afraid!' he said. 'When you open them, everything will be over.' But I opened my eyes in the middle of the operation. I felt no pain but I was frightened to see so many doctors around me. For a minute I thought that I was dying or something serious was happening to me. Anatoly said: 'Do not worry! These doctors are simply watching how I'm anaesthetizing you. Now, close your eyes!' When I came to myself, I was in the ward and felt fine. I could already swallow without any pain on the day after the operation. Usually patients can't even think about eating for three or four days after surgery. But I dreamt about cabbage with sausage." The doctors were amazed.

The day after the operation, Kashpirovsky had a visitor. It was Dr Semyon Shlaen, head of the ear, nose and throat department. "He came to see me after learning about the operation. He sat on my bed and I could hardly bear the sharp pain as my bed bent under his weight. I never liked him. He was bald, bespectacled and rather slippery. But he carried out successful operations and was a good ENT specialist. I thought he would be angry with me for not asking his permission to operate without standard anaesthesia. But instead he offered me a partnership. He said he could find patients who were allergic to drugs and who would be prepared to undergo non-medicinal anaesthesia. Of course, individual cases of the use of hypnosis during surgery had already been heard about, but here was an opportunity to conduct such operations on a conveyor belt. I agreed. I wanted to test myself.

"We began to work together, and I enjoyed it. I got carried away seeing such excellent results, and we performed seventeen operations. The patients were aged between twelve and forty. The day before the operation, Dr Shlaen would warn me to be prepared. I stood by the table, clutching my side and bathed in sweat because I was so weak, and I worked. I had no idea who was going to be my patient. Some patients were very suggestible. They would fall asleep at once. Others stayed awake and still did not feel any pain.

"One patient told me: 'You know, doctor,' he said, 'your hypnosis did not work on me.' I asked him why he thought so. 'Because I was awake and heard everything.' 'Did you feel any pain?' I asked him. 'No, I did not. But maybe you gave me some medicine to anaesthetize me?' In fact, we did not. For many, hypnosis is associated with sleep. And in cases when they were not asleep, they believed that they were not hypnotized. On the whole, anaesthesia for operations involving the upper respiratory passages is very complicated, since it is connected to respiration and blood supply to the nasopharynx. Nonetheless I was able to cope with all this. Dr Shlaen, as he promised, gave a report about these operations to the medical board of the hospital. But his colleagues were sceptical; they simply didn't believe him.

"Meanwhile, time went by, and I myself was getting no better. I was lying in bed thinking: how have I become so sick? I never poisoned my heart, liver or other organs with alcohol or tobacco, never spoiled myself by overeating and idleness. So, what can I do to cure myself? I realized that I needed to mobilize all my resources. So I decided to help myself in a fairly exotic way. I decided to go one more time to Sakhalin Island, to see those *sopka*s again." So he applied to the Znanie and was given an itinerary.

Of course, those at home considered this decision to be madness, and didn't want to let him go. But he managed to cut himself loose and left. There was no direct flight to Sakhalin, so he had to fly to Moscow to take a flight to Khabarovsk, and there to change for the flight to the island. "I boarded the plane with a bag containing sixty biscuits baked by my mother." He decided this would be enough for two months if he were to eat one or two a day. Biscuits were the only thing he could eat at the time. He also had a syringe with alcohol and some anti-spasmodics in case of further attacks.

In those days, passengers were served food during the long flight to Khabarovsk. "It smelt so tempting and I couldn't resist it and decided to have a bite. The consequences of this were not slow in coming: when I got to Khabarovsk, I felt so weak that in spite of the cold, sweat was streaming down me. And here I gave up. I thought I wouldn't manage to get as far as Sakhalin and decided to return home. But there were no tickets at the Aeroflot office for the next two weeks, and the Sakhalin flight was leaving in half an hour. The only choice was to take it. The forty-five-minute flight seemed to last forever. I was sitting on my fists and counting the seconds, thinking I would not make it. A friend came to meet me. I said, 'Get me to the hotel, quickly, or I'll die.' I wasn't able to breathe properly until I arrived at the hotel and had an injection of relaxants and painkillers."

Again he had to go to distant settlements by helicopter or along impassable forest tracks, getting stuck in the snow—and this when he could not walk properly because of the pain. After a month in Sakhalin he still could not eat or drink. He looked dreadful, pale and thin, but didn't cancel a single performance, which always lasted for at least three hours.

"When I came to the north, it was already winter. Nothing had changed since my last visit. The Korean girls were giggling with their boyfriends under the statue of Lenin in the town's main square. I went for a walk and went into a food store in order to warm up and to smell my favourite smoked fish. My head began to swim because of hunger. Some dogs were sitting by the door. I thought they were hungry and threw them a couple of biscuits. But when I went out, I saw they did not even touch them—they were waiting for some sausage. I felt ashamed but couldn't help it: I looked around to be sure no one saw me and picked up the biscuits.

"My diet did not help me. I still had awful pain. So I changed my treatment. When we were driving along the Sea of Okhotsk, I would ask my companions to stop the jeep and tell them to move ahead. I would find a puddle, break the ice and then lap the water like a dog to make myself sick and clear my system. The water smelled of oil and tasted terrible. I would repeat the same procedure several times. After that I felt a little better. I noticed that Koreans drink a lot of water while they eat. I started doing the same. The most difficult thing was trying to stay on a diet when everywhere I went people tried to treat me with something tasty. After performances everyone wanted me to be their guest. I was tired of having to explain that I couldn't eat anything."

In the city of Nevelsk an acquaintance, Yuhvana, a Korean, saw that Kashpirovsky was seriously ill. "I can help you," he said. "My aunt is a healer. She wanted you to come."

"I went to her without much trust, expecting to see some kind of shaman dressed in a coat with bells on it and holding a tambourine.

But my illness was so acute that I was ready for anything. The aunt, however, turned out to be a perfectly ordinary woman. She welcomed me warmly and invited us to eat. As usual with Koreans, the table was low and we had to sit on the floor. On the table was a bottle of vodka, a carafe of water, *kimchi*, a fiery Korean cabbage, and mushrooms which grow on trees. There was also some *pense*, piquant noodles several metres long. When she invited me to try these delicacies, I thanked her but refused on account of my indisposition. 'Well, that can be helped,' she said, and came up to me. She ran her fingers down my spine. Then suddenly she pressed a point on it with her finger and a piercing pain shot through me. 'Now,' she said, in an authoritative voice, 'you can eat anything that's on this table.' I ate properly for the first time in ages.

"After that they asked if I wanted to try their national delicacy, dogmeat. I was so overcome by the absence of pain that I agreed to try it without thinking. She went out and brought a bucket covered with gauze. She signalled to me to take a look. Under the gauze I saw a dog's head lying on top of some meat.

"The aunt sent us to the mountains after supper to look for some roots which I was to take in case of pain. Later I gave them to one of my colleagues and she complained that she could not leave the bathroom for a week. The roots were laxative and worked fine. Then Yuhvana walked me back to my hotel. It seemed that all the dogs in town came out to bark at us, as if they knew what we'd eaten. I expected the onset of an attack. But it never happened. I began to eat whatever I wanted. I left Sakhalin feeling quite healthy." The pain never returned.

His experience with the Korean healer left a profound impression. Perhaps she had used some form of acupressure to relieve his pain, or maybe he had responded deeply to her powers of suggestion. She had done what he was trying to do: her 'authoritative voice' was her *ustanovka*.

Kashpirovsky had hoped that in Sakhalin, under pressure, the mechanisms for self-regulation would start working. He wanted to harness the inner resources of his organism. "It seems to me that evolution has provided us with huge regenerative powers. We do not use our internal resources to anything like their full extent. I'm sure that the medicine of the future will be based on them and not on chemistry."

He arrived back in Vinnitsa to discover that his daughter had fallen ill. He took her to see Dr Shlaen, who diagnosed chronic tonsillitis and recommended an operation. Lena was five, so her father stayed with her all the time in the hospital so that she wouldn't be frightened. "I wasn't going to hypnotize her; I just hoped my presence would help her cope with the operation more easily. But I wasn't allowed into the operating theatre—surgeon's orders, I was told. Suddenly I heard a heart-rending scream: 'Papa, papa, save me!' I could not control myself. I began to kick at the door, demanding to be let in. Lena was crying but I was helpless. They just wouldn't open the door to the theatre. I didn't see my daughter until after the operation was over, when she was brought into the ward in a state of semi-shock. Then it turned out that Dr Shlaen had made a mess of the operation: he had torn part of her soft palate." Shlaen justified his refusal to let Kashpirovsky into the operating theatre by saying that he hadn't wanted him to watch his daughter's operation. Kashpirovsky thought this wasn't the only reason. "I broke up with Dr Shlaen when I was told he had demanded money for our operations." A feud sprang up between them. Shlaen later claimed that Kashpirovsky had not, in fact, been completely effective in his anaesthesia. It seems quite impossible to get to the bottom of this story after so many years. What is left is only their mutual antagonism.

Each time Kashpirovsky returned, he found that in Vinnitsa he was treated as nothing special, as a common doctor. His fame here was limited to a circle of friends and relatives. There was no popularity, no crowds of fans. Coming home meant coming back to his usual routine at work where nothing had changed. He was coming back to the same hateful case-records, which he never had time to fill out, to duties at home, as father, husband and son. He always felt happy returning home to his family, but after a time he became impatient and everything irritated him. He knew that he had to leave, to go anywhere if only for a weekend.

"I led this kind of life for more than twenty years, without rest, without Saturdays and Sundays. My colleagues thought I was after money. But I used to go not so much for money, but out of curiosity.

I wanted to meet new people, to learn about new places, to test myself. I used to travel mainly during annual leave. And if I needed more time, I asked the hospital administration to provide me with a leave of absence. Thus I could get a month and a half or two months. When I finished my performances, I would come back to the hospital to my usual routine. They would say, 'Anatoly Mikhailovich, we've got a patient with epilepsy, and today it is your turn to register him.' I was so frustrated, thinking I was wasting my entire life. I felt I was capable of more. My intuition told me I was on the brink of understanding something profound about the laws and mechanisms which regulate our lives. However, I fulfilled my obligations, doing the daily grind which did not excite me in the least, but it gave me experience, taught me to be patient, to control myself.

"In fact I was meeting interesting people even among the patients of the psychiatric hospital. I never ignored an opportunity to learn something new, something that would give me some stimulus. Once I had a patient, a former pilot, a colonel, who happened to be in our hospital because of obsessive jealousy. He was madly in love with his wife. Aleksandr was a tall, blue-eyed and very handsome man. He could be seen reading books all the time and he told amazing stories. I really liked him, and we spent hours together just talking, discussing different problems. Our friendship attracted the attention of a young boy, who hung around us. At times I took him with me to the gym. Sasha could see me doing my squatting exercises with two hundred kilos on my shoulders ten times.

"Sasha became obsessed with self-perfection. He started reading, studying a lot. They were both released from the hospital and I always thought of them with warm feelings. Eight years later, I learned from a Yampol doctor that Sasha went to Kishinev to study there. Once, when he went to see his girlfriend, he witnessed a burglary and tried to interfere, but they killed him. He was found many days later down a manhole."

Kashpirovsky himself never belonged to the ranks of the dissidents. Like the majority of his fellow countrymen, he just wasn't interested. Neither was he interested in the Ukrainian nationalist movement although he had lived all his life in the western part of the Ukraine. However, in the hospital he had a reputation for fierce independence. He would never kowtow to the bosses and he was punished for this by the Party organization in his hospital. They refused to admit him as a Party member. This was a serious setback to his career and blocked all possibility of promotion.

In the West, Soviet psychiatric hospitals have a terrible reputation; everyone now knows about the horrors of treatment carried out on political dissidents in the appalling conditions of psychiatric wards that were really prison cells. At the end of the 1960s the Central Committee of the Soviet Communist Party developed a plan for a network of special psychiatric hospitals to be used in the battle against the dissident threat to the Soviet state and the social order. Whereas regular psychiatric hospitals fell under the jurisdiction of the ministry of health, these "special" hospitals were under the direct control of the MVD (ministry of internal affairs). A "dissident" could be sentenced, without the right of appeal, to compulsory psychiatric treatment. People ended up in these psychiatric hospitals for many reasons: for "anti-Soviet propaganda and agitation"; for the "circulation of fabrications known to be false that defame the Soviet state and social system"; for the "betrayal of the motherland"; or for "illegally leaving or illegally entering the USSR." A chief of staff of one of Moscow's psychiatric hospitals declared, quite sincerely, that "only a mentally abnormal person could be dissatisfied with life in the Soviet Union." Brains were put right with aminazine and other dangerous drugs.

Although Kashpirovsky never worked in one of those "special" psychiatric hospitals, he did come across many examples of people on the edge of a society which was itself half mad. Many suffered from persecution complexes and the "spy mania" which was a product of Soviet propaganda. Others believed they were Brezhnev himself, a sort of Soviet version of the Napoleon complex. Kashpirovsky vividly remembers one patient who had dyed his eyebrows black in order to look like the leader. Ironically, many years later in the early 1990s there were reports of a sudden influx of patients who believed they were Anatoly Kashpirovsky.

One unfortunate man, the son of a KGB colonel, had tried to leave the country, a certain sign of madness, and was allowed no visitors except a rather sinister daily visit by the KGB. Although he was perfectly normal, he was put on sedatives and prescribed insulin. Kashpirovsky helped him to avoid this. "I showed him how to increase his blood pressure simply by holding his breath so that he could be taken off the insulin. I did what I could to make his confinement easier, letting him out for walks or even down to the beach." Even this exposed him to considerable risk.

At that time Kashpirovsky began to think more and more about the nature of hypnosis, trying to understand the way it worked. He compared what he had read in textbooks on hypnosis with his practical experience. "I was taught by academics who wanted to explain any influence as an hypnotic state. They came to a point when they described almost any communication as hypnosis. But clearly when I want to say I love you, I do not need to put my wife to sleep first so she can understand it better.

"A friend came to me with a toothache. 'I can't bear the pain. Hypnotize me, please,' he asked me. 'What do you think hypnosis is about?' I replied. 'Hypnosis is a sleep,' he said and wanted me to put him to sleep in order to get rid of the pain. 'Didn't you have a good night's sleep?' I insisted. 'Why does your tooth still ache then?' There is so much confusion about all this. Most of all I hate it when doctors divide their patients into the suggestible and non-suggestible. They say that about ten percent of people are very suggestible, easily hypnotized, and ten percent are not. And what about the rest? The eighty percent? How does one make them more suggestible to the use of hypnosis?

"In Kharkov I had attended lectures by Professor Maria Teleshevskaya, who proposed using drugs to depress the activity of the brain in order to make patients more susceptible to hypnotic suggestion, so-called narcopsychotherapy." This can help with patients who are difficult to hypnotize. Its main use is in neurotic disorders. "When the patient is semi-conscious, the psychotherapist starts making suggestions such as: 'You are not stuttering anymore, your obsessive state is gone, you are no longer impotent' and so on. Many people were given drugs for nothing. People called them 'drunk shots' because they felt so tipsy. All these narcotics are completely unnecessary." In fact Professor Teleshevskaya is highly respected. She gives low doses of drugs to help patients into a relaxed state before hypnosis. But Kashpirovsky has no time for academics.

"I cannot trust scientists who do their research in institutes and research centres. They have never seen real life like I have. So why do they think they can teach me something? Why don't they get out of the cloistered world of academe and move on into the real world, get out to the people and help them solve their problems? Our psychotherapy is completely impotent.

"The only method these 'Rozhnovs' advocate is autogenous training, which has never achieved the results I have. The German psychiatrist J. H. Schultz went to India to study yoga and demonstrated that it was possible by suggestion to bring about physical effects such as changes in the pulse rate. He elucidated, rather pedantically, a hundred and forty-four different formulas for relaxation. And this technique was then offered to Soviet dairymaids, who did not know what to do with it. People laughed at it. They could not make themselves repeat that their legs and hands were warm or cold or that they were feeling better and better.

"I came to the conclusion that there is no such thing as hypnosis or suggestion. They don't exist. They have been made up by scientists who simply repeated these words without thinking. When I talk to a person, I give him information. I can give it anywhere and anyhow. There is no need for me to induce a so-called hypnotic state or trance so he can understand what I want. There is no need even for words; sometimes silence says much more than words.

"The main thing is the *ustanovka*, the power and direction of my will over a person. I discovered later on that the famous Georgian psychologist, Uznadze, had written about this, but I came to these conclusions by an empirical route.

"More than once, as a result of my *ustanovka*, I managed to bring out a hidden talent, perhaps even genius, in people who were not even aware that they possessed such talents. This had been done before me by other psychotherapists or hypnotists like Vladimir Raikov in Moscow and Pavel Bul in Leningrad, but unlike them I did not put people into a trance.

"Once I visited the town of Ussuriysk, an important railway junction in the south of Maritime Krai. My lectures were held in the local cinema. I paid attention to a small red-haired girl. Her face was totally covered with freckles, her legs were so short that she did not touch the floor. I noticed that her eyes were restless as if she had encephalitis. I came up to her and said: 'You are a poet!' Her eyes started moving faster from side to side. It looked as though she was composing a poem and sure enough, in a minute she was ready with it. It sounded good to me, but I was not sure if it was hers. I gave her some topics like Ussuriisk, love, spring, high boots, sausage and other things, choosing words at random. The audience was listening with interest and then exploded with applause when she recited her poem.

"You know, Olga became a real poetess. She used to send me her poems. I don't know how, but she always knew where to find me. Once when I was stuck at the airport because of the weather for several days, I was rudely awakened in the middle of the night by a militiaman who kicked me with his boot several times. 'Are you Kashpirovsky?' he asked. 'There's a call for you.' I was so angry, but went to answer the telephone, stepping over the bodies of sleeping passengers who like me had no other place to sleep. 'It's me, Olga!' she said. 'I have written a poem about you. *You are not a gypsy, but the road is calling you.*' I could hardly hear her voice, but I immediately memorized the words. Since then it has always been my favourite."

Kashpirovsky continued to move around the country. His performances attracted people in Siberia and the Baltic republics, in the Caucasus and the Far East. And it did not matter to him whether he went to a major city or a small village as long as he was among the people who wanted and needed him. Very often he travelled alone, but sometimes he preferred to take his children with him so that they too could see how huge and varied the Soviet Union was.

He developed a tradition that wherever he went, he had to go for a swim. "I dreamed of taking a dip in Lake Baikal, the largest freshwater lake in the world where the water is so transparent that you can see the bottom. Baikal is fed by more than three hundred rivers and streams. Its only outlet, however, is the Angara River which flows past Irkutsk, where I was invited to perform.

"After the performance in the Irkutsk Palace of Culture, we went to the sauna. The semi-drunken sauna owner, a local fishwife, brought us a bottle of vodka and the local delicacy, a fish called *omul*, which is eaten raw. It can be found only in Lake Baikal. After the sauna, we decided to take a dip in the lake. It was late November and the lake was beginning to freeze over. I jumped in. The water was freezing cold and I could not breathe. I jumped out like a bullet and ran to the sauna. On the second try, I could stay in longer. I was swimming in this enormous lake looking at the stars and feeling great. After the swim I decided to play a joke. People used to watch Alan Chumak on television. He was a healer who would 'charge' water that the viewers placed in a bowl in front of the TV set. By drinking this charged water, he claimed they would recover from all manner of ills. Remembering this, I wrote on a wall of the sauna: 'Kashpirovsky was here. Lake Baikal is now charged for the next thousand years!' Next day the sauna burned down!"

All the while he worked on his performance, changing it, improving it, honing his skills. By the end of the 1970s he had given hundreds of shows. He learned how to sense the mood of an audience and how to manipulate it. A stage performer has to work fast, with absolute confidence. Nevertheless he had to learn some hard lessons. "I got used to success. I forgot that I should be careful. In Dnepropetrovsk I had an accident: during a performance a woman fell from the stage into the orchestra pit. I usually performed rather risky experiments before saying goodbye to the audience. On this occasion five girls were on the stage and at my command they were to return to their seats and await my signal to rush to me, ready to carry out my commands. In order to excite the audience a little bit, I said: 'As soon as I click my fingers they will run on stage and kiss me.' I already knew that even under hypnosis, people would never do anything they did not want to do. In front of the stage was the usual orchestra pit, over three metres deep. When I sent the girls back into the hall I did not notice that one more girl was standing behind me. She was in a trance, so instead of going back with the others, via the steps which led down from the stage, she moved straight ahead towards the edge.

"The audience made themselves comfortable, anticipating an interesting spectacle and thought that all was going according to plan. Only when the girl reached the very edge and put her foot into the pit did everyone gasp with horror. I turned sharply in her direction, but realized instantly that I would not be able to stop her. There was a crash. The poor girl was gripped by convulsions, but then fell silent when she lost consciousness. She was carried backstage, and the audience believed me when I said that everything was fine. They demanded that I continue with the kisses. There was nothing to be done. I had to go through with that too. But I didn't hang about saying farewell to my fans. I rushed to casualty. When I saw her, lying there pale and immobile, I thought she was dead. Suddenly she opened her eyes. 'Are you OK?' I asked her. 'Yes, I'm fine,' she said, 'but why do you ask? Is something wrong? Where am I? Where is my mother?' and she tried to get up but a grimace of pain appeared on her face. Her collarbone was broken. I looked at her mother. 'Please, forgive me,' I said. 'I know I deserve to be sent to prison. If you need anything, money, I'll do anything you say.' The girl's mother didn't want revenge, nor did she ask for any help. She just said: 'I understand that it was an accident. I hope we can be friends.'"

It was then that Kashpirovsky realized the full weight of his responsibilities. He knew he had been lucky this time and swore to himself that he would never allow such a thing to happen again. Danger lurked around every corner. Among his audiences there were sometimes mentally ill people for whom public performances were clearly not a good idea. Once a schizophrenic attacked him with a knife.

More and more it occurred to him that his talents and capabilities were underused. He began to think he was working in too narrow a way and to no great effect. Giving lectures, demonstrating what he could do, all this was no doubt interesting, but he was missing out on life, on the chance to make his mark. He had a desperate sense of needing to expand his horizons, to make some quantum leap, to use all those extraordinary resources he felt within him.

4

From Vinnitsa to Moscow

Should you love, be it a furnace
Should you threaten, be in earnest
Should you swear, then make it hot
Should you strike, give all you've got!

Should you argue, speak not coldly
Should you punish, lay on boldly
Should you spare, hold nothing back
Should you feast, let nothing lack!

(Alexei Tolstoy, 1850–51)

*I*n 1980 the country went mad preparing for the Olympic Games. Socialist propaganda had always claimed that only the Communist bloc had preserved the high ideals of the Games and that politics and sporting success were inextricably linked. That summer Moscow turned into a real Potyemkin village. (Potyemkin was famous in Russian history as the adviser to Catherine the Great who built a whole series of fake ideal villages to impress the empress on her travels through the country.) The city was cleaned up in every sense: prostitutes, tramps, alcoholics and dissidents were moved elsewhere in order not to besmirch the pure image of the socialist capital. Entry to the city was restricted, business trips and even visits to relatives were cancelled. Goods were brought into the shops so that foreigners could witness the prosperity and well-being of Muscovites—who were delighted by it all. The Moscow Olympics are still remembered as a shoppers' Eldorado, a time of well-stocked shelves and smiling assistants. It even became possible to talk freely with foreigners, although the police and KGB whipped up an atmosphere of fear about them, with scare stories about sinister Westerners with poisoned chewing-gum. Muscovite children were moved out of Moscow for so-called safety reasons.

Under socialism, money spent on sport was no object. The budget deficit for the Games was a hundred and twenty billion roubles. Those who could jump the furthest obviously had the best political system. It is no secret that Soviet sport, developed in hothouse conditions, was actually not amateur at all, but professional. The Party took winning extremely seriously. The defeat of the Soviet ice-hockey team by Czechoslovakia in 1978, the year of the tenth anniversary of the invasion of Czechoslovakia, the so-called "fraternal help", was considered an unimaginable disgrace and was discussed in the Politburo.

The country inherited this reverential attitude towards sport from Stalinist times. Sports parades and military parades were a favourite spectacle of the great leader, the *Velikii Uchitel*, demonstrating that the spirit and health of the whole nation was strong. In these parades of the 1930s any mess-up in the coordination of the well-rehearsed march could cost the guilty parties and the organizers their heads.

Once the Moscow Architectural Institute dragged a globe the size of a two-storey house across Red Square, and on top of this globe the most muscular architecture student was using a hammer to break the papier-maché chains, symbol of imperialism, which bound the planet. As his stooping fellow students bore this epic composition past the Mausoleum, the student on top, in a rush of enthusiasm inspired by the sight of the Leader of the People, swiped at the chains so violently that he broke the Earthly sphere and disappeared inside, howling. The Leader reacted with dissatisfaction, but the other participants continued to march on their healthy legs as though nothing had happened and bore the broken symbol from the square.

The unlucky athlete, it seems, was pardoned. About twenty years later, in the same square, during a routine anniversary celebration, there was another famous fiasco, greatly enjoyed by Muscovites. The best horsemen were to demonstrate the wonders of their equestrianism. Towards nightfall the veterinary gave the horses a laxative so that they would open their bowels in their stalls and not before the shocked eyes of the government leaders. He didn't get the dose quite right, because the horses polluted the sacred square. "That's a rather strange riding trick," remarked the Generalissimo, and his son, who was quite a young general at the time, rushed off to the barracks to shoot the veterinary. And if the veterinary had not drunk himself unconscious—so terrified was he by what had happened—Stalin's offspring would have emptied his pistol into him. The unfortunate vet was saved from reprisal only because each time Stalin junior tried to stand him against the wall, he slithered down again.

After the war, special sports schools were set up to train future Olympic competitors. In order to get into these schools, children had to be very gifted in sports, had to pass exams and had to be well connected. Kashpirovsky, even though he spent so much time training in physical fitness and weightlifting, could not hope to go to such a special school because he was a mere village boy. However, he had always seen himself as a sportsman, a sporting hero in the Soviet tradition, and as a boy would avidly watch sporting parades on documentary newsreels, which were usually shown before feature films started at the cinema. He admired the trained bodies with their rippling muscles and pushed himself hard to become like them.

Even though the Moscow Games were no real Olympics because the Americans did not come, in protest against the invasion of Afghanistan, grandiose spectacles of the opening and closing ceremonies were broadcast on television all over the world as if nothing was wrong.

Brezhnev was wheeled out to wave at the crowds, although everyone knew that he was terminally ill. He had never fully recovered from his stroke in the 1970s. Nobody felt any sympathy for him; they just wanted to know when he would die. "In power was a man who was unable to make a realistic evaluation of either the political situation or his own actions," said Academician Yevgeny Chazov, his doctor. "Brezhnev differed from the Lenin of 1923 only in that he was still able to speak, although of course he didn't understand what he was saying." The world, watching with alarm what was going on in Moscow, realized that a system which was fatally sick itself was headed by a terminally ill man.

However rotten at its core, Moscow held the key to everything in the Soviet Union. It was the new Babylon. Kashpirovsky knew that in order to advance his career, he had to get there, though control was strict and permission to perform more difficult to come by. Eventually his opportunity came. He was invited to perform at the Moscow Institute of Industrial Transport in the beginning of the 1980s, at a time when public demonstrations of hypnosis were not allowed. He persuaded the officials in charge that he could make people do things without putting them into a trance. Permission was granted and he was allowed to deliver a lecture on hypnosis and suggestion.

The tight control over hypnosis was a typical example of Party paranoia and had come to a head two years before at the Karpov–Korchnoi match for the world chess title. The "defector" Korchnoi, whom the Soviet press labelled a traitor, claimed that he had been defeated under the influence of hypnosis. From what the Soviet press said, one could have formed the impression that Korchnoi had just gone mad. It was as if everyone had forgotten that in 1972 during the Fisher–Spassky match, the Soviet side had protested on the grounds that Fisher or one of his team was undermining Spassky by means of hypnosis. If one looks at the film of the Karpov–Korchnoi match, however, it is extraordinary how Zuchar, the hypnotist that Brezhnev's beloved Karpov brought along, quite plainly and openly sat staring fixedly at Korchnoi throughout the matches, in the most unnerving fashion. After the tournament, rumours persistently circulated that the General Secretary himself had become terrified of being hypnotized by his enemies. Just in case, Soviet bureaucrats took extra precautions, and control over public performances was tightened.

Kashpirovsky knew that this was a crucial moment for him: "At first my audiences in Moscow looked down on me, as if to say 'who on earth are you, you country bumpkin from Vinnitsa? What can you teach us? You'll have to show us what you're capable of.' But they were just like the ordinary fishermen, miners and geologists on Sakhalin or in other cities around the country. They weren't any different at all. I could make them laugh, sing or do anything I wanted them to do!"

He soon received more invitations to other places, for the most part to "P.O. boxes"—so called because these special industrial plants run by the military were so secret they had no addresses. But there, as a rule, greater freedoms were allowed. It was considered that the workers there could know and see more than ordinary mortals. "I was once invited to the *Sokol* military academy, known as the Soviet Pentagon. In spite of its strict procedures, not only did I manage to get in without a pass but I managed to carry a huge tape-recorder past the guards. They did not even stop me. Later there was a terrible scandal and other performers had difficulty getting in."

Kashpirovsky's popularity grew and he was invited to Moscow more and more often. But at home in Vinnitsa he still lived in a state flat, which he didn't get until he was forty—the children had grown and the three small rooms were cramped and uncomfortable. "People came from all over, in need of help, but I couldn't invite them home. I was afraid that if they saw the conditions I lived in, it would affect my authority and be reflected in the results of my work. People approached me wherever I went. Sometimes I met my patients in the park, sometimes just at a tram stop. Sometimes people just needed someone to talk to. My work was really psychotherapeutic listening. After that they got better and went back home full of their miraculous recoveries."

Vinnitsa had only very basic provision for such counselling and psychotherapy. At the beginning of the 1980s Kashpirovsky was finally transferred to the psychotherapy department in the hospital and was depressed by what he saw. He shared the surgery with another doctor who had his own approach to treatment: a hunchback who seemed angry at the world and was sharp and unsympathetic to his patients. Kashpirovsky could not understand why this man had chosen the profession of doctor. He himself had always felt sympathy with the needy. Although he cultivated the image of a macho man, he was deeply disturbed by the lack of proper treatment the hospital could offer.

According to instructions from the ministry of health, the psychotherapeutic surgery was supposed to be as comfortable and bright and welcoming as possible, to encourage patients to feel confident and relaxed. "But local administrators did not look upon my work as something serious. The room was tiny and dark. I was receiving patients and plaster was falling down on our heads. They explained that there were no funds to do the repairs. Nobody seemed to care that people could not get proper treatment in these conditions. But still I found my work interesting and enjoyable. They wanted me to provide individual therapy; but from the very beginning I understood that people have the same problems, so why waste time? I found it much more effective to give group therapy. The room was in the basement, the so-called hypnotarium. But here I was happy because I felt I was really able to help people."

He started group therapy sessions for the overweight, for those who wanted to stop smoking, and had great success with stutterers and sufferers from chronic enuresis, using hypnosis as the major tool of his therapy. Over the years his experiences as a performer had sharpened his technique to such an extent that he was able to induce a trance-like state in almost all his patients extremely quickly. His sense of excitement at the possibilities this suggested for psychotherapeutic, or hypnotherapeutic, treatment of all kinds of illness grew almost daily. But the lack of acknowledgement and the meagre support he received from those in charge frustrated him terribly. He felt that all his ideas, all the results of the good work he was doing, were likely to be buried there in the basement in Vinnitsa. So he began to cast around for ways of breaking out. He formulated a plan: he would write to offer his services to the highest in the land, to the head of state himself.

For years Brezhnev had looked as though he was on his last legs. When the radio played symphonic music for longer than usual, people came to a standstill, expecting a government announcement. On public holidays people would gather at their television sets to see who was standing on the Mausoleum, but year in year out Brezhnev would be dragged on, even though it was obvious that each time it was more and more difficult for him. People even began to feel sorry for this feeble old man, forced to stand freezing in the cold for three or four hours at a time.

Suddenly everyone noticed that Brezhnev had got younger and

started to move about better. The extraordinary Georgian, Dzhuna Davitashvili, then the current queen of extrasensory healing, had been treating him. (Later she was to treat Boris Yeltsin.) Under Brezhnev's protection, she had moved from Tbilisi to Moscow. Despite the ban on studying and disseminating parapsychological phenomena, which had become stricter again during Brezhnev's era, she was allowed to practise. Members of the Politburo, other bureaucrats and eminent people also resorted to her for help. For a time Brezhnev seemed to benefit, though, in the end, she too turned out to be powerless against the natural ageing process. To paraphrase the famous slogan of the communists, "Lenin is dead, but his cause lives on," people used to say about Brezhnev: "Brezhnev is dead, but his body lives on."

Encouraged by the example of Davitashvili, Kashpirovsky contacted Gennady Smertin, the stage hypnotist from Odessa who had helped him get started on the lecture trail. Together they concocted a letter. Some days later Kashpirovsky received a phone call from the KGB in Vinnitsa: "We need to talk to you, Anatoly Mikhailovich. Please come down to our office. How serious are your intentions to treat Comrade Brezhnev?" the KGB major asked him. Kashpirovsky replied: "I realize that he is getting the best medical treatment possible in the country. But maybe Gennady Smertin and I could offer something else. Why not try?" The KGB major took him seriously and promised to see that the letter was delivered to the Kremlin.

Some time later Kashpirovsky was summoned by the head physician of their hospital. He had received a telephone call from the USSR ministry of health in Moscow asking him how exactly Kashpirovsky was intending to treat Brezhnev. But matters were taken out of his hands before he could get to Moscow. His services were not required. Brezhnev had died.

Some years later, in 1991, Brezhnev's daughter, Galina, became a great fan and attended many of Kashpirovsky's seances. She used to sit in the front row, looking just like her father. During the first seance she "switched off" to such an extent that it took two hours to restore her to what passed for her normal state. Afterwards, during a long conversation with Kashpirovsky, she told him her father had never received his letter. Perhaps it was just as well that the scheme had come to nothing. Brezhnev's death heralded a more propitious time for Kashpirovsky and marked a watershed for the Soviet people.

The beginning of Andropov's rule was a pleasant surprise. That famous barometer of prosperity, the sausage, appeared in the shops. The government promised to introduce order and the people approved, though the intelligentsia were terribly alarmed. Perhaps Andropov has been underestimated. Although his years as KGB chief made him deeply suspect to most Western commentators, his influence on events was decisive. He started corruption proceedings against Brezhnev's old supporters and it was he who brought Ryzhkov and Gorbachev to the Politburo.

After Andropov came Chernenko and he soon died too. People gave these frequent deaths the sardonic title of "the hearse race", and regaled each other with volleys of new jokes: "Today the General Secretary of the Party's Central Committee, Konstantin Ustinovich Chernenko, set about his duties without regaining consciousness." Despite the endless tedious films on television celebrating Soviet productivity, the defects of the system were all too obvious and even Andropov's sausages were little consolation for the endless shortages. One of the best-loved comedians of the time, Mikhail Zhvanetsky, created an act which had his audience weeping with laughter and falling out of their seats. It was, quite simply, the recipe for a salad. No one had eaten such a salad for a very long time. He would read it very slowly: "Take two kilos of meat, some caviar, cut a cucumber and some fresh tomatoes ..." The KGB eventually banned it.

Initially Gorbachev's accession to power in 1985 did not arouse much enthusiasm. He was considered a Party leader who would behave exactly like his predecessors. When Andropov was immobilized by a fatal kidney illness, Gorbachev became his agent in state and Party business. The first hints of his proposed perestroika and glasnost were accepted without particular excitement. Gorbachev's programme, launched on the country at the April 1985 Plenum of the Communist Party Central Committee, was criticized and christened "a routine propaganda hoax." But Gorbachev was much younger than the rest and had a great deal of self-confidence. He really wanted to be seen as a great reformer. For the first time here was a Communist leader thinking about serious change to the system.

The ideas of perestroika and glasnost were approved by the Twenty-Seventh Party Congress of February 1986. Afterwards these concepts came to have a broader meaning. Though at first glasnost was applied to cultural life and the press, it quickly came to mean everyone's right to information and freedom of discussion. Later it invaded politics and history, enabling the Soviet people to know what was going on in the country and the world.

The West reacted seriously to statements from the new Soviet leadership. He was especially popular with Margaret Thatcher. After her meeting with him in London in 1984, she concluded that he was, famously, a man with whom she could "do business." This definitely strengthened his authority both in Europe and in America. In Russia his popularity began to grow too, and not just among the intelligentsia. Television helped to create the image of a world leader. It emphasized the striking contrast between Gorbachev and the senile old men who had come before.

Kashpirovsky remembers watching his visit to Leningrad. It made a great impression on everyone. Gorbachev arrived in the northern capital, like a democrat, without the usual irritating escort, and did the unimaginable. He got out of his car, left the stunned bodyguards and walked towards the people standing in the street. Everyone froze. No one knew how to react; before Gorbachev, no government leaders had done walkabouts. Standing shoulder to shoulder with mere mortals, he began to chat with them in an ordinary way, but they were so bewildered they didn't know how to reply. *Vremya*, the evening television news programme, showed what had happened, and the whole country, enraptured, watched this new appearance of Christ to the people.

"At the beginning, like everyone else, I liked Gorbachev," said Kashpirovsky, "but people expected concrete improvements. They didn't understand his intellectual explanations: glasnost and perestroika. It was too abstract for them. What's glasnost to those who have nothing to say? What's freedom for if there is nothing to drink?"

However, perestroika was of the greatest significance for Kashpirovsky and made all his later success possible. The authorities now took a much more relaxed attitude to public performances of all kinds and he was invited to give a performance in Moscow in 1986 at the Palace of Sports. Through his old weightlifting friends he became involved with the organizers of bodybuilding competitions, a new phenomenon in the Soviet Union. After the competitors had shown off their muscles, he would get on stage with them and do his tricks. The audience loved to see these huge men falling flat on their backs at his command.

Because of the publicity that this gave him and, again, through his connections with the Ukrainian weightlifting team, in the autumn of 1987 he was invited to work with the Soviet team on the eve of world and European championships. "After my performances in Luzhniki with the bodybuilders, I became the talk of the town. When in Vinnitsa they found out where I was going and why, they gave me the kind of send-off they would have given someone going into outer space." This was a hugely prestigious appointment given the high profile of the sport in the USSR. He was no longer just a doctor from the provinces who did some tricks, but the psychologist to the national team.

"I was invited by David Rigert, the chief trainer of the national team and famous Olympic and world champion. He was wearing a cap and marine T-shirt. I liked his face, turned-up nose and decisive chin. I felt great respect for him. I watched his performances with great admiration. When he set a world record, he would not, like others, throw the dumb-bell down, but he would kiss it first and then lay it down carefully. He was a real artist.

"At first my son Seryozha and I went to Feodosia to meet the team. The centre was a two-storey house on the seashore used for training sessions. When I stepped into the gym and saw my idols, Yury Zakharevich, Anatoly Pisarenko and Anatoly Khrapaty, whom everybody knew as the strongest men on the planet, I immediately felt in my element. I had, after all, given fifteen years of my life to this kind of sport." And although it was years before that Kashpirovsky had stopped his training as a weightlifter, he still did physical exercises to keep in good shape.

"I'm so used to morning exercises that if I don't do them for some reason, I get the feeling that I forgot to brush my teeth or did not iron my shirt. To be in good shape is one of the requirements of my profession. When a patient meets a psychotherapist who is fat, untidy and smokes, he thinks, 'What can you teach me?' He won't feel trust and there will be no rapport, the most important part of communication.

"David Rigert came to us with a smile. 'I'm glad to see you, Anatoly. I'm sure we'll work well together!' Straightaway there was the problem of what exactly I should do with the team, how to inspire them to lift more." Psychotherapists were invited to help athletes to diminish stress and be better prepared for competitions. There were advanced techniques of visualizing or imaging:

> Trainers have their students and athletes lie down and listen to calming music, especially the largo movements of baroque instrumental music, with their strong, regular bass rhythms of about sixty beats per minute. After a few minutes, the listener's heartbeat becomes synchronized with the beat of the music, producing deep relaxation. Then the athlete visualizes, in full colour and complete detail, a winning performance. This is repeated until the physical act becomes merely a duplication of a mental act that had already been successfully visualized. Soviet research indicated that athletes who spend as much as three-quarters of their time on mental training do better than those who place more emphasis on physical preparation.
> (*Love, Medicine and Miracles*, Bernie Segal)

But Kashpirovsky did not like such time-consuming methods, neither did he want to teach them how to use autogenous training, which was popular in those days.

"The athletes told me, laughing, how they had been taught to concentrate their thoughts. They had to repeat to themselves about twenty to thirty times phrases like 'every day I feel better and better' or 'my arm is becoming warmer and warmer, heavier and heavier.' But why would they need to think about their arms becoming heavier when they had to concentrate on lifting record weights? The lads just thought it all a joke, they couldn't concentrate; such training was a waste of time. When I was introduced to them, they looked on me as another charlatan, but I showed them who I was. I told them to line up and then laid them out on the floor in one go. That really impressed them and from then on they believed that I could help them."

Then he began to work with them, helping them to switch off.

"Before a competition, a sportsman gets nervous, doesn't sleep properly; he is bothered by the feeling that millions will be watching him. This traumatizes his mind. When competing, it is essential that he should be able to cut himself off from earthly things. He must not hear conversations or noise in the hall, he must know that he is alone with the block of metal and, moreover, be confident of lifting the weight.

"I liked to work with them. They were honoured champions and at the same time very down-to-earth and simple. They had their training sessions twice a day. They worked hard and during short breaks liked to play practical jokes on each other, especially on Vasya Alekseyev. An extraordinary weightlifter, who won the Olympic Games superheavyweight class twice, he paid no attention to them. He was so friendly, open and modest, though he had won eight consecutive world championships and set eighty world records. He was on a pension after a poor performance at the 1980 Moscow Olympics, but he used to come to the training sessions to share his experiences. I liked him a lot. We used to dine together and became good friends." Then when Vasya Alekseyev became a team coach, he invited Kashpirovsky to go with the team to Barcelona, but by that time Anatoly was too busy to accept the invitation.

"After the trainers' council I'd have my seance for the whole team, athletes and trainers included. Some responded better than others. Zhenya Sypko, a giant over two metres tall, for example, reacted instantly. It was sufficient to tap him on the forehead for him to fall into a trance. Yurik Sarkisyan suffered from insomnia. He asked me to help him. One gesture, one glance and Yurik instantly fell asleep until the morning without even changing position. And he woke up fresh and robust, his strength renewed. He had tried to use autogenous training before, but without success.

"I also helped Khafiz Suleimanov, who was eighteen years old and became the champion of the Soviet Union and then the world champion. After a tournament in Greece in 1989, he decided to defect. Perhaps it was Vitaly Stabrov, the team masseur, who persuaded him not to return to the Soviet Union. They both went to the Turkish embassy and asked for political asylum—and this in 1989 when everybody was allowed to leave the country. It was so stupid I could not believe it. In 1987 they used to play and fight with Seryozha, who was just twelve years old. There was not much difference between them. His father, Delavar Suleimanov, went to Greece to see him at the Turkish embassy and tried to talk him out of it. But Khafiz said, 'I will not return home, they will shoot me down there.' He cried but insisted that he did not want to return to the Soviet Union.

"After Feodosia the whole team moved to Podolsk, near Moscow, where they have a training centre in a very beautiful place by a river. There I met Yury Vlasov, the Olympic champion. At the time he was the president of the Federation of Athletic Physical Training. But he never looked like a typical athlete; he wore glasses and was nicknamed 'the professor of weightlifting'. His harmonious physique and versatile talents won him the love of countless fans. He was elegant and extraordinarily well-built, and to watch his performance was a joy for all. During his sporting career Vlasov set several dozen records but he has remained in the memory of sports lovers as the Olympic champion, the strongest man on the planet. He won the hearts of millions not only because he could lift what at that time were fantastic weights, but because they saw in him the embodiment of the athlete of the future: a man of great physical strength and powerful intellect."

Vlasov began a serious interest in weightlifting when he was a student at the Military Air Academy: "I grew up in a cadet school, among strong and healthy lads. Strength and courage were greatly prized qualities. We went in for wrestling, boxing, all track and field events. Our minds were fed on stories of struggle and victory, our bodies shaped by hard training and sports." Vlasov and Kashpirovsky had much in common and quickly became friends.

"Yury was stunned when I demonstrated how Zhenya Sypko could be 'switched off.' He couldn't believe his eyes." Vlasov at that time was in bad shape himself, very thin and weak and could hardly walk. He had been badly injured, had damaged his spine and now took to writing books about his athletic past. Everyone believed the state looked after athletes after their careers were over, and people were really shocked by Vlasov's plight and the revelations in his writings.

His short stories and novels have been highly praised both by readers and critics. At that time he was working on the book *Goryachi Krest* (Burning Cross). Kashpirovsky called it "the Bible of the Soviet state". "Yury Vlasov was the first athlete to tell the truth about the Soviet sporting machine. After his accident in Tokyo, he was paralysed and got no support from the Sports Federation. He could hardly move but he forced himself to continue his exercises. He never gave up hope of getting back to active life again. He kept a diary and later published it. For many it became a good example of how to survive in a hopeless situation." Now Vlasov has become a symbol of extreme Russian nationalism.

The two friends performed together in the Ukraine Sports Centre in Kiev, in front of four thousand people. Vlasov talked about his experiences in sport, and then Kashpirovsky would perform. The money they received they gave to the Kiev orphanage. Yury Vlasov encouraged Kashpirovsky to use his seances to help people as much as possible and to emphasize the importance of kindness, justice and respect towards others in a healthy society.

Working with the team, Kashpirovsky had unquestionable success. "Pavel Kuznetsov, a talented weightlifter considered too old for any real hope of winning, set the world record in Arkhangelsk. He responded very quickly to suggestion. He fell asleep at once. I would just call 'Pasha!', and he would fall into a trance. During training, when he tried a weight of a hundred and eighty kilos, it was enough for me to say: 'He won't lift this!' and Kuznetsov would fail to lift it. But at the next approach, I would say: 'He will lift it now,' though another five kilos had been added. Pavel tried to ignore my words, because weightlifters try to be independent, they pay no attention to anybody. But each time I was proved right."

Everyone was impressed by this. Weightlifters are superstitious in general, keep all sorts of lucky charms and have their own little private rituals before competitions. They thought Kashpirovsky possessed supernatural powers. He could control the whole team of strong men completely. They were considered the strongest men on earth, but they obeyed his every gesture and they fell as if their feet had been cut from under them. Moreover, this could happen anywhere at all, even while out walking in a park. "I would go out for a walk and see them sitting on a bench with a girl. It was enough for them just to glance at me, and in a minute they were 'switched off'. Imagine, a giant of over a hundred kilos like Kuznetsov, but helpless like a child in my presence. So, in order to hide himself away from me, he would pull his coat over his head. To tease him a little I'd say, 'You'd better hide under her skirt and then I won't get you!' "

Team members constantly took dope, twenty or thirty tablets twice a day, and they had no scruples about injections either. Anabolics, vitamins, enzymes, salts—all became an integral part of their diet. They had all become used to this and considered it normal and essential. Kashpirovsky also considered it part of international practice and did not protest about it.

Meanwhile David Rigert was replaced. Aleksei Medvedev was elected chief trainer during a training session in Arkhangelsk, and things went differently. "The trainer plays a very important role in this kind of sport, especially from the psychological point of view. He is constantly with the sportsman, supervising his movements. He fixes the weight for him, says when he must limber up, what to start with, brings the liquid ammonia, coffee, gives massages. He watches the way the competitor moves and sees what weight the opponent goes for first. He decides how much you should lift, suggests how to correct mistakes. He controls absolutely everything: all the sportsman has to do is to walk up to the weight and lift it! Weightlifting is a very complex kind of sport and much depends on technique, on little tricks." Aleksei Medvedev and Kashpirovsky did not get on. Medvedev couldn't accept Kashpirovsky's role within the team and finally dismissed him.

However, Kashpirovsky remained almost lyrical about his time with the team: "I liked to watch the training of Yury Zakharevich, the Olympic champion. To my mind he is the most talented weightlifter of our time. He had his own way of preparing for a competition. He knew how to save energy, to relax and concentrate his attention. During warm-ups he pretended he could not care less. He laughed, joked, pulled faces, made remarks. When he made his attempt to lift a record weight, the people in the gym came to a standstill. There was complete silence. Zakharevich would walk to the platform and limp jokingly as if he were an invalid, making everybody roar with laughter. But then he touched the dumb-bell and started to concentrate. Again silence would fall and all eyes were fixed on him. Yury slowly lifted his head and suddenly put out his tongue. And then, 'hop', the dumb-bell was in the air, above his head. He needed no help from anybody, because he could control himself. That is why it was very interesting for me as a psychotherapist to work with those guys. I learned a lot from them."

While Kashpirovsky lived with the team in the town of Podolsk, he often visited Moscow and gave more performances in the Palace of Sports in Luzhniki and in Izmailovky before thousands of people. These performances were called "Athletic and Psychological Training for the Harmony of Body and Mind." In the first half of the show came performances from bodybuilders (a novelty at the time), and Kashpirovsky performed in the second half.

"I like some of their exercises. I saw once how Yury Zakharevich did the cataleptic bridge: his head and feet were placed on chairs while three people stood on his body. He was smoking a cigarette as if nothing was going on. I also tried to demonstrate the same thing to my colleagues. I was laid out between two chairs and asked somebody to climb on me, but they stood back. Then one woman, who weighed as much as three men, climbed on top of me. Unfortunately she put her foot right onto my throat. And while she smiled and bowed before the audience, I was having a hard time breathing. She was enjoying herself so much that she did not want to get off or move her huge feet. I was suffocating and could hardly move my lips to ask her to lift her foot off my throat. Luckily she did not hear the precise words that I was using at that moment.

"Despite being busy with my work, performances and other things, I was also interested in martial arts. Bruce Lee became my idol. Later when I had a chance to read his book, I understood we had very much in common. But at that time martial arts were forbidden by law, so Seryozha and I attended underground clubs where self-taught instructors promised to teach us. It was soon evident that these amateurs did not know what they were doing."

In their book *Russia and the Commonwealth A–Z*, Andrew Wilson and Nina Bachkatov wrote:

> In 1986 underground clubs became nurseries for young hoodlums all over the country, especially youths of the Moscow working-class suburb Lyubertsi, who took to descending on the

capital. Their violent physical attacks on "snob" Muscovites and "rubbish" punks, demonstrators, drunks and prostitutes caused fear and a public outrage. No longer illegal, these clubs now help train bodyguards for "businessmen" and politicians.

"When classes in martial arts were organized at the Vinnitsa militia's training centre, we attended three times a week. Most of all I enjoyed the warm-ups, which really taught you how to concentrate on your inner self and how to control yourself. At the age of forty-five I did a somersault for the first time in my life."

To make his Moscow performances more spectacular, Kashpirovsky would invite as many as a hundred and fifty volunteers onto the stage. The audience was both enraptured and terrified as these people began to fall as if they'd been mown down like a great swathe of grass. But he himself had had enough of this kind of show. He became obsessed by the idea of using television to reach a wider audience, and not just for hypnotists' tricks but for a real therapeutic purpose. He felt he had the power to help huge numbers of people. He wanted to "heal the nation". "Why should we have so many sanatoria, knowing they will never be sufficient to help all, when the treatment I offer can benefit everyone?" His fans supported his idea with great enthusiasm.

"I sincerely believed my proposal would interest the people in charge of the health of the nation, and that it would not meet with any opposition. But I was wrong. It turned out that I needed the support of highly placed people." Someone mentioned the name of Academician Konstantin Frolov, the vice-president of the Academy of Sciences, holy of holies of Soviet science. Though Frolov had nothing to do with psychotherapy, getting his support would mean a great deal.

Until the break-up of 1991, the Soviet Academy of Sciences continued to play a central role in Union scientific, industrial, economic and social matters. In the second half of the 1980s reforms were made with a view to ending political manipulation within the Soviet Academy, rejuvenating its membership and making it more useful to the nation. In October 1986 a secret ballot (the first in its history) resulted in the replacement of the eighty-three-year-old president, Anatoly Alexandrov, with Gury Marchuk, twenty years younger. In 1990 a presidential decree made the academy independent of the state, gave it ownership of many state-owned facilities, increased its budget and allowed it to work with institutions abroad, although this last change caused a brain drain, as specialists on foreign assignment, particularly mathematicians and computer experts, showed a reluctance to return home.

"I hoped that Academician Frolov could help me get permission to broadcast my seances on national TV. But it appeared that despite all the new changes, without connections or *blat* it was impossible to reach him. He was well protected by his assistants, secretaries and advisers. But I was lucky. One of my acquaintances who had a master's degree in medicine but worked as a groundskeeper for Frolov, promised to introduce me. I thought that fortune favours the brave and decided to go to his dacha in Podmoskovye."

So, on a sunny day unusually warm for autumn, they climbed into an old Zaporozhets car and set off. "I introduced myself to Frolov but he took no notice of me, and when his wife came out they began to talk to my acquaintance about fixing a hole in the fence. I understood that I wasn't expected, that my acquaintance, evidently, hadn't warned them that I was coming or told them who I was. I felt offended. I said: 'If you have any problems, let's discuss them right now. Otherwise I have to return to Podolsk, eighty miles away.'

"They looked at each other in bewilderment and said they had no problems. 'Nor have I,' I replied, not very politely. 'The only one is getting back.' My independent behaviour caught the academician's attention. Moreover at this point my acquaintance finally had the wit to explain who I was. He explained it so clearly that the academician's wife asked: 'So, you can pass through walls?'

"'Yes, I can. I will pass through your fence, which has a plank missing.' They laughed, and the academician's wife, also his personal secretary, began to ask questions. I realized that a lot depended on her. So I tried to explain my plans for getting onto national television with my healing seances."

As an example, he told her how he had tried once before, in Alma Ata, the capital of Kazakhstan, in 1986. There he had managed to record a session where he healed enuresis at the Kazakh television studio. Although all the children who took part in the programme were cured, his hope that the programme would be broadcast in Alma Ata came to nothing.

"Perhaps I impressed his wife, and she made a signal to her husband to listen to what I had to say. I tried to condense my theory to the minimum. I talked to him about the potential for self-healing that the human organism possesses and how psychotherapy can release this potential. I knew that scientists were already working in this area and had found such substances as lidase and interferon. However, all the experiments were conducted in static situations. My second point was that psychotherapy or hypnotherapy on television should not be considered as something new. It had always existed on some level in the form of speeches by our leaders and other subtle but pervasive methods of influence. All information broadcast on TV has psychotherapeutic properties. My suggestion to use television as a means of healing enuresis could help an enormous number of children.

"I also told him that psychotherapy could be used in the training of special forces carrying out complex and dangerous missions. At this Academician Frolov apparently became interested. During my speech he was digging small holes in the sand and after each proposal, he would fill them up. I counted five such holes before I finished. 'I find your ideas worth pursuing. I would like you to stay in Moscow to develop them further.' 'No, no,' I said, 'I must return to Vinnitsa. I have many patients waiting for me there.' I wanted him to insist on my staying, and give me a more substantial offer. But he did not." Academician Frolov told Kashpirovsky that he should first set all his ideas down on paper and promised to give the help he needed. Anatoly went back to Podolsk, pleased with the turn of events and anticipating his imminent appearance on television.

However, things didn't turn out as he had hoped. Work, performances, crowds of people with various requests, family problems—all this didn't leave him a minute to set out on paper what he had explained to the academician. Besides, Kashpirovsky hated paperwork. So, instead of writing a report immediately, he found any excuse to put it off. For three months he struggled with his report for Academician Frolov, which was thirteen pages long. At last he sent it off to the Academy of Sciences and waited for a reply.

"Three months later I was invited to the Moscow Radio Electronics Institute. It turned out that my report had been sent to the director of that institute, Academician Pavel Gulyaev." In the mid-1960s, at the time of the Thaw, Dr Pavel Gulyaev, who was Vasiliyev's disciple and successor at the University of Leningrad, had developed, it was claimed, a device that could detect and record the human aura and the auras of animals and even insects. According to the Soviet press release, "The aura Gulyaev found is a complex electric field around the body, a sort of ghostly second self." They hoped to use this "electrical aura" to diagnose illness. Gulyaev's laboratory also spent years studying topics such as telepathy between twins and telepathic hypnosis.

Pavel Gulyaev was a handsome man with nice manners. "I have heard so much about your talents," he said to Kashpirovsky. They had breakfast together and chatted away and then went to Gulyaev's office. Here he was amazed to find himself the subject of an experiment. "We would like to measure your electro-auragram. We have just measured Dzhuna Davitashvili."

"When I heard this proposal, I could hardly control my indignation: 'You haven't got a clue about me. I'm a certified medical doctor, not a charlatan. Dzhuna claims that she puts out some sort of biological current, a special energy field or God knows what else. She says that she uses ESP when she treats her patients. I am not anything like her at all. I am a normal person. There is nothing supernatural about me. Instead of measuring my energies, you should help me to study my patients during my seances.' I was disappointed. I realized that I was in the wrong place. Psychotherapy has nothing to do with such things."

On his return to Vinnitsa, he was given an opportunity to further his ideas. Lyubov Grabovskaya, a nurse who worked with him in the hospital, came up to him in tears. "'Anatoly Mikhailovich, help me. I've got a tumour and I need an operation. But I won't survive it. You know my problem.' She was upset because she could not stand even the smell of novocaine. Twice she had reacted so badly to it that she nearly died. I told her to go to her doctors and tell them I would anaesthetize her. But they refused to do the operation—they did not believe it was possible and called me a charlatan. I got angry with those doctors and decided to prove that I could do it. I called my friend, Nikolai Bondar, a doctor in Kiev, and he offered his support. I said, 'Listen, Kolya, let's *show it on television*. After all, it would be a wonderful advertisement for my idea about the TV treatment of enuresis. It would convince all those blockheads in Vinnitsa.' Kashpirovsky wanted to anaesthetize Lyubov via a TV monitor set up in the operating theatre while he remained in the studio in Kiev. But Lyubov would not at first agree to be anaesthetized *via television*. She was too afraid.

"Meanwhile, Anatoly Pisarenko, the Olympic champion weightlifter whom I'd met in Podolsk, introduced me to Valentin Sherbachev, the editor of Kiev television's sports programmes. He was also known as a football commentator. Through him at last, came a breakthrough! My performances in the Kiev Palaces of Culture were broadcast on Kiev TV. This wasn't exactly what I'd had in mind because, again, they were more interested in my tricks than in the sort of healing sessions I had been proposing. But at least it was television." Although he now became well known in Kiev, the problem of how to get onto national television remained.

From the end of the 1980s, because of perestroika and glasnost, a tidal wave of new information swamped newspapers, magazines and television. However, glasnost was never as strong in television as in the press. All programmes were still controlled by the Central Party Committee in Moscow, new ways of presenting material needed permission from Yakovlev (in charge of ideology and propaganda) or from Gorbachev himself. Despite this, one real innovation was the sudden flurry of live discussion programmes and international telebridges, *telemost*, on national TV. These 'telebridges' linked people by satellite across the USSR and with other countries. Vladimir Pozner and Phil Donaghue, for example, started programmes in which Soviet and American citizens could meet on the air.

"At my performance in the Luzhniki sports stadium in Moscow in 1988 I noticed people with TV cameras. After the performance they came up to the stage. One of them introduced himself as Vadim Belozerov and said he was from the TV programme *Vzglyad*. My heart missed a beat. He said: 'We liked your performance here. Very impressive. I'm sure television viewers would like it, don't you think? Could you perform the same tricks on television? Would it work? What would you say to the idea of performing on a Kiev–Moscow telebridge? We are just trying to set one up.' I jumped at the idea. It was exactly what I needed. *Vzglyad* was considered the best programme on national TV."

As a rule *Vzglyad* finished long after midnight: its sensational subjects and their daring treatment held the audience's attention until two or three in the morning. Young presenters without any fear interviewed major political and government figures, discussed the spread of Aids in the USSR, the catastrophic state of orphanages and health care. No other programme could compete with the extraordinary nature of their reporting. To be a participant on the show became a mark of considerable prestige. With a helping hand from Belozerov—who was interested in anything unusual—folk healers, witch doctors and parapsychologists appeared on television. Witnesses of UFOs told their stories, and hunters of the abominable snowman. Previously such things were mentioned only in rare publications or lectures; people had never expected to hear about them on television.

Belozerov at once liked the terse doctor from Vinnitsa. He realized his tricks would interest the viewer. "I wasn't keen on my demonstration being considered as a show, but I didn't have much choice. The main thing was that I no longer felt alone; I was surrounded by friends. My team was taking shape. Sherbachev took it on himself to solve the problems with Kiev television, and Belozerov took care of national television." As a result the Kiev–Moscow telebridge took place in March 1988. The following day this appeared in the newspapers:

> It was already late, but any feeling of sleepiness disappeared as if by magic. What was shown yesterday on *Vzglyad* didn't fit in with any notions of the believable. This time the hosts were linked with Kiev, the capital of the Ukraine. The opening did not portend anything out of the ordinary. But all of a sudden Vadim Belozerov, who hosted the show, pierced his hand with a needle. The smile on his face showed that he felt no pain. Someone else took a glass of boiling water in his bare hand. Then on a command from Kiev,

participants on the show in the Moscow studio started falling over. What was going on? We would have called it hypnosis if the hypnotist had been present in the Moscow studio. The hypnotist or whatever he was gave commands via the studio monitor. He was introduced to us as Dr Anatoly Kashpirovsky, a psychotherapist from Vinnitsa.

Kashpirovsky remembers it vividly: "They gathered a group of ten or twelve people in the studio, and I was in Kiev. Little by little I started influencing them. The programme lasted for three hours. Among the group was a sixteen-year-old girl who had a problem with enuresis. I told her that from now on she wouldn't suffer. Two weeks later, when I came to Moscow, this girl and I met at the Pushkin monument. She kissed me with gratitude."

Despite the late hour of the broadcast, the following day everyone avidly discussed what they had seen. They could not understand what it was about. For many, Kashpirovsky was just a hypnotist with a number of funny tricks. But some people wanted to know more about him. And in Vinnitsa the attitude to him changed after his appearance on *Vzglyad*.

"Of course, the Kiev–Moscow telebridge made me famous, but with fame came other problems. People thought I was like any other stage hypnotist, but I had outgrown those theatrical tricks. My penetration was much deeper than hypnosis," Kashpirovsky explained later.

Then Lyubov Grabovskaya, whose tumour was growing, decided to accept his offer and to appear on TV. She became convinced that everything would be fine after she had learned about the girl who had been cured of enuresis during the recent telelink. Kashpirovsky was excited that this operation would prove his abilities to do what had never been done before. He received an invitation from another TV programme, *Before and After Midnight*. "They wanted to broadcast the operation, but then they changed their minds. Someone from the Kiev Institute of Neurosurgery told them it would be a great risk, because in the course of the operation they would need to remove the muscles and three or four ribs. They were sure I would never manage to anaesthetize the patient, being in another city, so far away from her."

In spite of this, and with some doubts of his own, Vadim Belozerov was determined to fulfil his promise to broadcast the operation. But the hospital administration also raised problems. Four times the director of the medical institute refused permission for the broadcast. Four times the poor woman had to be taken off the table. Staff even removed the broadcast equipment from the roof of the institute, but finally the moment came. "She looked into my eyes. In a split second she felt no pain and the operation began."

On April 1, Belozerov went on the air: "On March 31, 1988, a unique operation was carried out in the USSR. Lyubov Grabovskaya, aged thirty-eight, a medical nurse and mother of two, went into the Kiev Radiology and Cancer Institute. She needed an urgent operation to remove a breast tumour. Dr Vladimir Korolyov, one of the Ukraine's most prominent surgeons, was to conduct the operation. Lyubov was allergic to anaesthetics, so she asked Dr Anatoly Kashpirovsky to anaesthetize her. Nikolai Bondar, a friend of Kashpirovsky's from student days, from the Kiev Institute of Radiology and Cancer, managed to persuade the administration of his clinic to go ahead with the operation. A TV monitor was set up in the operating theatre above the patient's head."

The viewers and the patient could see Kashpirovsky's face on the TV screen installed in the theatre. The patient listened to his voice on earphones: "I'll give the order when to start the operation. Look me in the eyes, Lyuba. Can you see me now? She must see me all the time." In a calm and measured voice he told her she would remain fully aware of everything but feel as if someone else, not she, were on the operating table. "Now she is ready. One, two, three. Let's go."

Dr Korolyov stood at the patient's side and seemed reluctant to start the operation. At last he made the incision and the surgery proceeded like any other. One could see how the tumour was excised. It was sent to the laboratory for analysis. When asked after the operation, Dr Korolyov said: "I wasn't aware of any difference between the anaesthesia used and a general anaesthetic. The patient was absolutely anaesthetized."

Belozerov concluded the broadcast: "We congratulate Lyubov Grabovskaya. The tumour proved non-malignant. She was released from hospital the same day, bought some sausage and returned home to Vinnitsa, although after such surgery the patient usually stays in hospital for at least two weeks. In the post-operative period there was no pain."

In such circumstances one usually says: "The next day he woke up famous." It can't be said that the majority of viewers really understood what was going on, but they did realize that they were seeing something very unusual. Moreover, Kashpirovsky claimed that his method of anaesthesia had no relationship to traditional hypnosis:

"What I do has nothing to do with hypnosis. I hypnotize patients only in exceptional cases." To the question: "If it isn't hypnosis, then what is it all about?" he offered the following explanation: "Verbal and visual suggestions can stimulate the human body to synthesize complex organic compounds far more effective than the most advanced medicinal painkillers. The body is the best of all possible pharmacies. It produces hundreds of curative and protective substances, many still unknown to science. Of course, you have heard about traumatic shock, an immediate response to unbearable pain. And you must have heard stories of people who have jumped over fences many times their own height or lifted unbelievable weights when aware of mortal danger.

"All of this supports my hypothesis that under extreme conditions the body produces stimulants or narcotic substances. Pharmacology will take a giant leap forward when we have identified all those substances and studied them well enough to manufacture them on an industrial scale."

In the press there was much excitement. Opinion ranged from acknowledgment of Kashpirovsky's unique abilities to accusations of charlatanism. Vladimir Rozhnov immediately reacted in his article *Hypnosis Without Miracles*, in which he said he saw nothing unusual in such anaesthesia, particularly because the doctor and the patient had known each other well and there was an established rapport between them.

"I responded with an article *Miracles Without Hypnosis* but it was not published," said Kashpirovsky. "That we knew each other proves nothing. If I sleep with my wife under the same blanket for years, it does not mean that I am able to anaesthetize her. I cannot anaesthetize myself! In fact, after the operation, I did try to anaesthetize her before she went to the dentist. It did not work. Why doesn't he try to do it himself? I'd like him to imagine Lyubov's feelings before the operation, knowing that I was so far away from her and that instead of novocaine she had only a TV screen."

Valentin Sherbachev, who covered the nationwide television broadcast from the operating room, tried to make things clear. "Before the operation began, I overheard someone from an emergency anaesthesiology team saying: 'Kashpirovsky is nothing but a quack!' The surgeon looked apprehensive too. Lyubov Grabovskaya was the only person who looked serene and optimistic. Twenty-five minutes before the operation, I asked her: 'How do you feel about what's going to happen to you? Even the doctors are dubious.' She replied: 'Of course they have their doubts, because this has never been done before; no one has ever seen it or heard of it. I have no doubts. I believe it can be done.'

"In my opinion," said Sherbachev, "many people, especially physicians, think that all psychotherapists are charlatans. Kashpirovsky encountered stiff resistance when he announced that his method worked with neuroses, ulcers, asthma and obesity, and could be used as a form of surgical anaesthesia. No local doctor in Vinnitsa agreed to test his radical new method, so Kashpirovsky turned to surgeons in Kiev. When I learned about his discoveries, I became his ardent supporter and did my best to provide him with ample television coverage. Together we arrived at the idea of such a long-distance experiment in anaesthesia. This operation was not a publicity stunt; Kashpirovsky was searching for a way to help many patients at the same time. Television seems perfectly designed for this purpose."

Kashpirovsky became a national hero. "My life immediately became a mess. On each landing of our twelve-storey building were thirty to forty people waiting for me. They drank wine and vodka and soon our clean sweet-smelling home was turned into a public toilet. My family nearly went mad."

A barrage of letters arrived at the television studios demanding information about Kashpirovsky. People wanted to know where he lived and worked, whether they could go to him for treatment. Many sceptics didn't understand why the operation had to be shown on television. Newspapers carried more interviews with Kashpirovsky, but the main aim of getting healing sessions on television had still not been achieved. The television bosses had yet to be convinced.

A journalist from the magazine *Smena* wrote:

> I arrived at the Yushchenko psychiatric hospital in Vinnitsa at eight-thirty in the morning. So many people were waiting for Dr Kashpirovsky that he had a hard time getting through to his office. He came to the door and announced: "I won't see anyone. Come back here in about two months when the problem of space has been solved." The crowd thinned out, but not by much. Kashpirovsky entered his tiny office, but people were already there. Polina Stepanovna, his nurse, answered the telephone, which was ringing non-stop.
>
> Kashpirovsky turned to an old man, who was suffering from asthma: "Have you been suffering for a long time?" Kashpirovsky asked him. "Yes, quite a long time." The asthmatic strained himself for each breath. "I was six years in remission. Then last January, after a nervous breakdown, the asthma returned." "I'll help you. Polina Stepanovna, take his name." Then he turned to another patient: "What's your problem?" "Epilepsy," replied the patient. "I don't deal with epilepsy." "But I came all the way from Tashkent to see you," pleaded the patient. "I can't help you. You need treatment with drugs." At this moment a crying woman with a girl burst into his office: "Doctor, please, help her! She won't survive another operation, if you don't help her." Noise, cries, people, coming in and out. It did not look like an ordinary doctor's office. People demanded to be cured by him and only him.
>
> At eleven o'clock Kashpirovsky started his seance at the hypnotarium, which is nothing special, just an ordinary room with two windows, full of people. All thirty armchairs were occupied. I was given a chair next to the door. Anatoly Mikhailovich walked along the front row, looking over each patient. "Make yourselves comfortable. Put your arms on the armrests!" And for the first time I saw a quick smile on his face, but it was enough to put everybody at ease.
>
> "Who will be the first one? How are you feeling, Igor?" A boy about ten years old drowned in a large armchair lifted his sad eyes and replied: "I feel well, thank you." "Are you sure? You won't stutter anymore." Then he came to a woman. "And what about you, Nina Ivanovna?" "I feel well, but have occasional headaches. Maybe it's a sign of coming rain?" A woman sitting next to me whispered

into my ear, "This Nina Ivanovna couldn't say a word just two weeks ago; she could only growl." "Quiet! You are disturbing me." Anatoly Mikhailovich approached my neighbour and lightly touched her forehead with his palm. She fell back in her chair and I could see that she was in a trance.

In a few minutes everybody quietened down. They were not sleeping but it was as if they had been turned off. Kashpirovsky walked from patient to patient, touching some with his hand. He took a young woman's arm, lifted it up high and threw it down. Her arm hit the armrest and she showed no reaction. My attention was drawn to a fourteen-year-old girl, thin as a rake. Just a week ago she was transported here from the Siberian town of Chelyabinsk directly to intensive care. She had difficulty breathing and kept passing out. She started to attend Dr Kashpirovsky's seances and today was her third. She still had problems with her breathing. "How are you feeling?" asked Kashpirovsky. "Thank you, doctor. I slept well for the last two nights," she replied, trying to give him a smile.

"All thirty patients are unaware of what is going on around them. They can hear everything but their attention is focused on their own illness," said Kashpirovsky. "Ordinarily the healing of asthma, enuresis, stuttering, neurosis or obesity requires several seances, usually five or six, in some cases more." "But you have so many patients. How can you help all of them?" I could not help asking him.

"There are many ways to help these poor people. One of the possibilities is to videotape some seances to heal bed-wetting. A child would need to spend five or six hours watching the tape in order to be healed. Such a tape could be used at other hospitals as well. I've tried this already in Alma Ata. We received letters confirming good results. And this was after a single seance. I placed children in front of a television monitor in the studios and just talked to them, nothing specific, did not even mention their disease. But the results were amazing. The funniest thing is that among them were two three-year-olds. I sent them out of the room. They could not see me at all, just heard my voice, but they also have been healed." "But why not start today? Where is the tape?" I asked him. "They say that special permission from Moscow is needed," he replied. Kashpirovsky also plans to make videocassettes for treating obesity—although in addition to watching videos he also advises a diet! But to start such treatments he needs approval from Moscow.

In his surgery people were already waiting for him. He was immediately attacked by two big women, typical Ukrainians. "Anatoly Mikhailovich, please, help us!" But his reaction was, mildly speaking, quite surprising. "I know you. You are from Vinnitsa, get out of here!" he said, recognizing one of them. "She needs an ear operation," said the one he recognized, ignoring his indignation. "I told you to leave!" Kashpirovsky seemed merciless. "She is allergic to anaesthetics. Help her, please. You are her only hope!" Kashpirovsky took the woman by the hand and seated her. "You are in a forest. Look around. Look at the flowers, pick them up!" The woman squatted down easily forgetting about her girth and started picking flowers off the floor. I thought she was too obedient, pretending to be in hypnosis in order to please the doctor, so he could not refuse to help her. Kashpirovsky read my mind and ordered her up and pierced her hand with a needle. Her face did not change. The woman did not react to pain. She really did seem to be hypnotized. He seated her on a chair and said: "Come around." But the woman continued to sway, having difficulty coming out of the trance. Eventually she returned to normal. Kashpirovsky talked to her: "I'll help you; you are a talented patient. But listen carefully. If this operation were to be performed abroad, for example in Tokyo, would you agree?" "I'll agree to anything. I don't want to be deaf." Kashpirovsky had in mind a proposal he had received from Japanese television to do a Moscow–Tokyo telebridge.

A month after the Grabovskaya operation, he performed another in Vinnitsa, his home town, by keeping his hand on the patient's forehead and talking to her while major surgery was performed on her feet. Galina Burovaya, allergic to anaesthetic, had come to Vinnitsa hospital from a remote village in the hope that Kashpirovsky would help. He knew that the coming operation could be very painful. Usually it is carried out under deep anaesthetic, because the bone is cut out and removed. Vadim Belozerov wanted the operation to be recorded, so he sent a television cameraman to Vinnitsa.

The surgeons Filonenko and Maiko were ready to start. They were supposed to operate on both feet at the same time. They looked at Kashpirovsky, to see if he was ready. "Hands on the table, look at me!" he said to the patient and struck her hand with a hefty bunch of keys. Her expression did not change. "She feels no pain! She is ready."

The surgeon began to apply the tourniquet. Galina started fidgeting. "Oh, it hurts!" she whispered to Kashpirovsky. Hoping the cameraman wouldn't notice, he thought she was just frightened and signalled to the surgeon to continue. "A-a-a, I can't bear it anymore! Stop it, please!" Galina shouted at the top of her voice. Clearly pain was being experienced even before the start! But he decided not to give up: "Cut!" he said.

"The surgeon made an incision at the base of the big toe on the right foot. The incision was tiny, just a centimetre. But how she yelled! I realized that this was it, that we couldn't go on. Besides there was that cameraman. Defeat. Knockout. I said, 'OK, I give in. You can go to the devil! I'm going home!' The surgeon and the patient froze. But something pushed me back to the operating table. 'Cut!' I ordered. And everything went well. They cut the patient's skin, chiselled the bones, drove a pin beneath the nail to fix the toe, and all this accompanied by jokes. 'Oh, now I feel fine!' Galina said. When the surgeon was preparing to chisel the bone, I decided to encourage the patient: 'What an attractive knee you have!' But I thought to myself: any moment now the blow will make the leg jump, and there might be an unpredictable reaction. 'Well then, Galochka, which shoes are we going to wear? Maybe Italian?' I asked when the surgeon took the chisel. She answered with a laugh: 'Any shoes, Anatoly Mikhailovich. I only wish I could walk.' The surgeon struck with his chisel. I think I felt the pain more than she did."

Appearing on national television made Kashpirovsky a hero. After the *Vzglyad* programme the whole of Moscow wanted to be healed by the "new Rasputin." High-ranking bureaucrats, diplomats, performers and sportsmen wanted to see if his powers would work on them. "Alla Pugachova, Yevgeny Yevtushenko, Aleksandr Rosenbaum and other Soviet luminaries approached me with appeals to help them with their insomnias, pains, smoking problems, disorders of all kinds."

His successful performances opened doors to the most prestigious offices of the capital. "I was driven up to the entrance of the Ministry of Foreign Affairs. I saw a crowd of people all dressed up and I thought: 'Are these snobs here to see me, a provincial doctor?' What was I going to do with them? I decided not to change anything in my usual routine." These Soviet diplomats and politicians were eager to take part in Kashpirovsky's psychological experiments and did just as they were told. The diplomats, who took a childlike delight in seeing their colleagues fall flat on their backs, found their smiles soon changed to tears. After taking part in the performance, not one was allowed to travel abroad: it was decided they were all too suggestible, a massive security risk!

Back in Vinnitsa Kashpirovsky, in the warm glow of the new capitalist dawn, set up a medical cooperative with the hospital—one of the first in the country. He could now use its facilities in return for cash and hold larger sessions on the premises. His wife Valentina organized everything. He had been so overwhelmed by persistent demands for hypnotherapeutic help from thousands of women trying to lose weight that he decided to arrange things properly. So, in the summer of 1988, overweight people from all over the Ukraine and from Moscow descended on Vinnitsa. The cooperative flourished.

They began with six groups of six hundred people, but demand far exceeded supply and so similar sessions had to be organized in Kiev and Moscow. Kashpirovsky's sessions attracted people who had already tried every diet that existed. Tales of happy patients who had achieved astronomical results such as losing thirty or forty kilos left people who heard about it sleepless and made them travel anywhere to get on the waiting list so they could at last become the owners of a magic ticket.

Crowds of excessively overweight women pursued Kashpirovsky from town to town. They all dreamt of individual treatment. He became the object of their adoration. Stories and jokes started to circulate: "Two women had come to be cured of obesity. They paid their entry fee, filled in some forms and were told to wait in a dark room. They'd been waiting for a long time and almost lost hope, but suddenly a familiar voice was heard. 'Oh, please, help us to lose weight!' they begged. 'Stop gorging yourself like pigs and you won't get fat!' was the answer. 'What shall we do?' said the bewildered women. 'Get out of here!' yelled Kashpirovsky. The women were so offended they nearly cried. But when they arrived home and started stuffing themselves with dumplings, they felt at once that they couldn't swallow a morsel. They couldn't look at food, let alone eat it. The slimming directive had begun to work."

Kashpirovsky's photograph was also said to be a powerful means of influence. It was usually placed on the fridge. Kashpirovsky would be looking crossly at them, as if saying: "Don't even think of it!"

"I received thousands of love letters. Women of all ages wrote to me to tell me they loved me and could not live without me. They wrote hundreds of poems and sent me their photos in different poses, sometimes nude, saying, 'Just give us a sign and we will come to you.' One woman sent me letters in which she described how I came to her every night, made love to her, kissed her and bit her. She claimed she had the bruises to prove it and that she had tried to lock her windows and doors but I would pass through and get her every night, even though she lived thousands of miles away."

It seemed to Kashpirovsky that expending his energies on the battle with the overweight was profitable but limited. Mass healing sessions on national television seemed an unattainable dream, although a steady flow of writers, film stars, and Party bureaucrats from Moscow visited him in Vinnitsa. They demanded his individual attention, even threatened him if he refused. But among them he made some useful contacts. Sergey Mikhalkov, First Secretary of the Writers' Union, famous for his poetry, his wealth and the fact that he had supported the repression of dissident writers like Solzhenitsyn, brought his wife to Vinnitsa for a private consultation.

"Mikhalkov had seen me on *Vzglyad* and believed in my abilities. His arrival instantly changed the Vinnitsa *Obkom*'s attitude towards me. Suddenly its functionaries and secretaries also needed to attend my sessions. The Second Secretary of *Obkom* and First Secretary of *Gorkom* (the city Party committee) sat in the hypnotarium with other Party bureaucrats. It was such fun to watch them. There followed an order from the *Obkom* that a new psychotherapy surgery be placed at my disposal immediately. And now, though the whole hospital had just been renovated, they began to build again, preparing a spacious office and three rooms for group sessions. They came to me to ask if I liked the changes they had made. I would say, 'No, it needs to be redone this or that way,' and they agreed to anything I said without comment.

"I liked Mikhalkov and was thankful to him for what he had done for me. I asked his advice on how to reach people who could help me to promote my ideas on treating enuresis on national television. 'I can help you reach Gorbachev himself. I'm sure he would appreciate your work and your concern for the masses,' Mikhalkov said." He took a videocassette of the operation and a letter that set out Kashpirovsky's proposal for healing the nation and restated the ideas he had written down for Frolov.

Mikhalkov confirmed that he had handed the package over to Ligachev, who had assured him that he would pass it on to Gorbachev. Mikhalkov told Kashpirovsky that much interest had been shown and that now all he had to do was wait.

So Kashpirovsky waited. "Naively I expected an immediate summons to the Kremlin. In reply all I got was silence."

5

Healing the Nation

Of course, before we know he is a saint, there will have to be miracles.
(Graham Greene)

Only what is possible happens.
All that happens is possible.
(Spinoza)

Though the Kremlin remained silent, Kashpirovsky's new-found fame bore immediate practical results. He was given a large flat in Kiev, capital of the Ukraine. He was able to jump the long waiting lists only through the personal intervention of Vladimir Shcherbitsky, First Party Secretary of the Ukraine, whose long tenure was noted for its cultural sterility, political stagnation and the disaster at the Chernobyl nuclear plant in 1986.

"I was given a flat in a twelve-storey block which belonged to the Central Party Committee, in the best part of the city. The flat was the pinnacle of my desires: three large rooms, a hall that was big and spacious unlike the narrow corridors in typical Soviet flats, two balconies. I could never have dreamed of having a flat like this. It was on the sixth, most prestigious, floor. My neighbours were ministers and high-ranking bureaucrats. When I stepped into the building I was amazed to see such cleanliness and order."

A reception at the Central Committee offices on his arrival in Kiev was followed by receptions at other places and an invitation to the Ukrainian ministry of health. "I was received by the deputy minister, Serdyuk, who happened to be a very nice and understanding person and a neighbour. He facilitated my appointment as head of the republic's psychotherapy centre at the Pavlov Psychiatric Hospital in Kiev." Kashpirovsky was told at the Central Party Committee of Ukraine: "You can rely on the support and understanding of the Party." Now many doors opened for him; people were eager to help. He became busier than ever.

"In the hospital I was allotted a block of ten rooms instead of the four which had been suggested. And even this was not enough to satisfy everyone who wanted treatment. My arrival destroyed the hospital's peaceful life. Instead of four hundred patients a month, there were now two or three thousand a day."

A crowd gathered early every morning in an effort to get to the surgery. People came from all over the Ukraine and from other parts of the Soviet Union. The atmosphere often became heated. People stood, pinned together, waiting for hours. A young nurse with pencil and notebook took down the names of prospective patients. The waiting list stretched on for three years! Everybody was anxious, insisting they had to be seen by the doctor immediately. Kashpirovsky would open his door and ask them all to stay calm, promising to work without a break. But this did not reassure the crowd.

In November 1988 a notice was put up announcing that a preliminary waiting list was being prepared. About thirty thousand people gathered in one of Kiev's parks and, although cold weather had already set in, they camped there and were prepared to wait as long as necessary. Camp kitchens and canteens were set up. The scene was almost biblical, a parallel which escaped neither the priesthood nor Kashpirovsky and did nothing to endear him to the church.

"I gave sessions daily. Hundreds of people came to me with referrals from the ministry of health, the Central Committee or MVD or other places, asking—demanding—that I receive them. Everyone thought I was having a blissful time, that I had attained fame and fortune, that all my trials were behind me. Rumours said I had three cars, that I did not know what to do with all my money. In fact, I did not even need a car of my own because I was offered the use of the cars of the ministry of internal affairs! People said I was a millionaire, but I was happy when I managed to get building materials and finish work on my new flat. There were also stories about me being master of a harem, that I had a dozen wives and so on.

"Once a sixty-year-old woman came from Israel. She insisted on meeting me in person. She introduced herself to everyone as my wife. I was in Moscow, so she said she would not leave Kiev until I came. She spent two weeks living in the garden nearby and finally got into our block and managed somehow to slip into my neighbours' flat. She locked herself in their bathroom. After twenty-four hours of sitting in the tub, she finally gave up.

"I was not really prepared for all this. There were difficulties and inconveniences in my life which I hadn't had to deal with before. People waited round the clock on every floor of the block I lived in. They wrote their addresses and telephone numbers on the walls, hoping I would contact them. The two telephones in the flat rang every second. Simultaneously the doorbell would be ringing and downstairs someone would be speaking through the intercom. Invalids in their wheelchairs gathered speed in the corridor and crashed into our door, frustrated after sitting there for days and losing hope of getting my attention. I never had enough sleep and walked about like a man possessed. Although I kept saying everywhere I went that I wouldn't see people at home, there was no question of being left in peace. They brought their sick children with them. It was horrible. I could not stand it. And I did not know what to do."

This obsession with getting through to national television and being given time to do healing sessions was clearly now not only a private ambition but a real necessity.

"Anatoly Pisarenko, a friend, suggested I try the football stadia in Kiev and Lvov, which could seat tens of thousands of people. He volunteered to help me obtain permission—which would have been quite impossible before Gorbachev. We agreed to share the profits. According to our agreement Valentin Sherbachev and Anatoly Pisarenko were supposed to get ten percent each, about seven and a half thousand roubles. My share of the money, ten thousand roubles, I would transfer into an account for veterans of the Afghan war." This was at the time a huge sum, and Kashpirovsky felt this was a crucial gesture. He had to demonstrate that he was not merely exploiting the desperate and the gullible, an accusation that still enrages him. However, as with so much that surrounds this complex man, his financial affairs remain rather mysterious.

On the day of his performance in the Kiev stadium, which had eighteen thousand seats, they still couldn't fit everyone in. Kashpirovsky entered the field to the accompaniment of his favourite Vysotsky song. At his request about a hundred and fifty people rushed up to him to take part.

"I said: those who want to sing a song, come up here, please. I hardly had time to say a word, before people were prostrate on the ground. One woman, who claimed she had been unable to talk, grabbed the microphone and began to sing. Another who could not even stand was walking across the field offering spring flowers for sale. Elderly people started jumping around the field as if they were twenty years old, others danced and felt no embarrassment. Something unimaginable was happening in the stadium. It seemed that participants in the experiments would do anything." The onlookers, both interested and confused, watched in astonishment. A group of Germans began to fidget nervously in their seats: someone had said people were eating the grass at Kashpirovsky's command!

"The success was enormous," said Kashpirovsky. "Yet again I felt strongly the extraordinary need that people have for some kind of 'miracle', the need and desire to see proof that the incredible exists. Also the psychological importance of being freed from all inhibition, even if it meant making fools out of themselves. I know that people will obey a command only as long as they want to. If something goes wrong or they don't agree with it, they stop doing it. They are aware of everything. If they sing, it means they want to sing, perhaps subconsciously. One can be a super hypnotist of great power but if you order a woman to take off her pants, she would immediately come out of her trance and be outraged.

"At the stadium I was accompanied by the Kiev film director, Pavel Boon. I never really liked him, but he was so persuasive. Valentin Sherbachev introduced him to me and said they had found a millionaire from Toronto who agreed to sponsor a three-part film to be called *The Centre of the Cyclone*. So Boon was hanging around, filming me at my hospital, during seances, everywhere, and the film was a disaster, to my mind—a complete travesty.

"I began, also, to experience some of the problems associated with trying to organize such events. Valentin Sherbachev did not come to the seance at the stadium. He had had an argument with the chairman of the cooperative which organized the seance, and the man had refused to pay him. Valentin got very upset and even angry with me, although I had nothing to do with the financial arrangements. I did the performing. Still, afterwards he went with me to Lvov. He did what he was supposed to do, introduced me, helped me during the seance. So of course he got paid, though only two and a half thousand, much less than he was supposed to have received in Kiev. But he never forgot the Kiev stadium and held it against me."

There was no less of a rush at the Lvov stadium. "Many came forward with testimonials of the benefit they had received from previous seances. The performance was very impressive. But it nearly ended in tears, because after the seance a crowd of fanatics rushed after me. I did not know what to do. They were crazy. Trying to escape, we ran into the basement. Five militiamen were there to guard me. They stood in front of me trying to protect me, but the crowd cornered us and started to tear at my clothing. There were no less than three hundred people, so there was no air. I was suffocating and I had to react fast: 'I'll count to three,' I said, raising my voice above the crowd, 'and if you don't clear off at once, you'll all die of cancer!' The corridor instantly cleared. 'I'm removing the curse,' I yelled and rushed off.

"Soon after this two English journalists who had seen the Kiev–Moscow telebridge asked me to repeat some of the psychological experiments for a Kiev–Birmingham link. I agreed and they asked if I could influence the audience in Birmingham even though I had not met them before the performance. I said yes, of course I could. I wanted people to realize that I did not only use people I knew.

"The programme took place in the summer of 1988 and consisted of three parts. The first two parts talked about the war and about Kiev, and my performance began in the third part. I wanted to make it more spectacular and invited a young lad who had just recovered from a spinal fracture. I put him on the glass platform and lightly tapped him on the head. He fell flat on his back, without bending, like a tree. I wanted to demonstrate not only the depth of the trance but also that the boy was quite safe, that the body would look after itself. But immediately after his fall, something terrible happened. The English audience was on its feet. One psychotherapist was demanding that the performance be stopped. He said he would not allow people like me to cross the border! I paid no attention to their reaction and calmly poked the lad's hand with a needle, to demonstrate the anaesthetic effect. But worst of all was their reaction to my offer to do the same thing there, via the telelink, as agreed. They went for me like wild beasts. There was no trace of English restraint. They declared that my patients behaved like robots, that my performance was a farce and had nothing to do with medicine. They were indignant, you see, because according to their etiquette a person shouldn't fall down in front of everyone and shouldn't be touched unless he has given his assent. Everything must be handed to a person wrapped in a napkin. But I was doing only what we had signed for in our agreement, nothing more! I believe they were simply jealous of my success. They use psychoanalysis and cannot demonstrate any results; patients go on for years without getting any better. I behaved as a representative of the Soviet Union should, otherwise I would have told them all to go to hell."

The cultural divide had proved too great. Kashpirovsky was absolutely convinced that everyone concerned was either malicious or a fool. "And, of course, it was the fault of Sherbachev, who had not arranged it properly. He did other things which at the time seemed insignificant but had unfortunate consequences."

However, this failure did not dampen the ardour of his enraptured devotees, who wrote to newspapers and television, demanding more information about him. Negative reactions to him were rare at this time and, amid the powerful eulogistic chorus, sounded sharply dissonant. "I myself don't really like conducting such experiments," explained Kashpirovsky to journalists, "poking needles into peoples' palms, making them feel no pain when they hold a glass of boiling water in their hand, making whole crowds of them sing songs and whirl around in an Indian war-dance and so on. But there is no other way of proving what is possible. Something dramatic is needed. To get television seances going, my 'farcical performances' are essential, otherwise no one would take any notice of me."

Nevertheless, he had enough experience to know that public acclaim could backfire. He feared, rightly, that aspersions cast in his direction could reduce to nought his efforts of many years. The only thing reassuring him was that the number of people wanting to attend his seances kept on growing. An ironic article had appeared in the Tbilisi newspaper *Zarya Vostoka* in September 1988, in which the author claimed that when he had taken part in Kashpirovsky's psychological experiments, he had not for one moment been under his influence but had just simulated all the required actions. Despite this, Georgians continued their pilgrimage to see Kashpirovsky: a weekly charter flight flew into Kiev from Tbilisi.

"At the end of 1988, I met with the management of Kiev television. Valeriya Vrublevskaya, who had introduced me to Shcherbitsky, organized five television seances there, starting in November, to heal children suffering from enuresis."

These television seances caused some sensation. It all seemed so unusual, incomprehensible and mystical. In fact Kashpirovsky did nothing very different from the performances he used to give in clubs around the country. "We had a girl, the TV presenter, who read out letters and telegrams from the viewers. I wanted everyone to hear about the positive results that others had obtained. Later I was criticized for using these testimonials as a form of self-advertisement. But I could not allow any hint of possible failure; that would spoil everything. My treatment of enuresis is very simple. I induce sleep and then I say, 'This is the way you sleep at night. Now, you need to wake up. Wake up and go and pee. After that go back to bed.' You see, the problem is that kids cannot wake up at the right moment. So I tell them how to do it. That is all. It is extremely successful.

"We named the seances *Glaza v Glaza*, Eye to Eye. But the first seance was a bit of a disaster. Sherbachev had not advised me properly. Cameras were filming me from every angle, and this was not nearly so effective. So I suggested that the cameramen should work, basically, in close-ups." This achieved the effect of Kashpirovsky's eyes being almost constantly fixed on the audience. This was just right.

Even the presenter, who was reading from the script, slipped from her chair at the end of the programme, completely numb. She had to be brought round. Kashpirovsky was pleased: now people would believe that it was possible to achieve the required pitch of influence on television too.

These teleseances increased his popularity in the Ukraine to such an extent that it became quite impossible for him to appear on the streets of Kiev. "I had to wear a wig and a false moustache. I could no longer sit in the passenger section of an aeroplane. I had to fly with the pilot."

After the fifth and final seance it became clear that the people of the Ukraine had got used to their weekly treatment from Kashpirovsky and they were insistent that they should not be deprived of this free medical care. Soviet citizens, accustomed to seeing dirty tricks behind everything, simply could not believe that nobody was squeezing Kashpirovsky, that it was his decision to stick at the given number of programmes. Rumours went around that the teleseances were being cut on the orders of the ministry of health, frightened, it was claimed, by Kashpirovsky's popularity.

In response to the programmes, about fifty thousand highly complimentary letters were received by the television company over a period of one and a half months. Seventy-two percent of the people claimed that they had been cured, and not only from enuresis but from many other things. "For the first time I realized fully that I should not name any particular disease in my healing. People with all manner of different problems would be ready to respond at the same time. I just had to show them that I was willing to help, that I was there for them. And, of course, the power of television made all this possible."

Letters to the Kiev television studios continued to pour in: "As we all know, our health service is not first rate, especially in the countryside. It's almost impossible to get to see a decent doctor. We live in a village with a population of five thousand and we have only two doctors. We rely mainly on Dr Kashpirovsky's teleseances. We're working people and we beg you to continue with them," wrote the members of the Virishalny *kolkhoz* (collective farm) in the Lokhvitsky region of Poltava, with three hundred and forty-two signatures on the letter. "We've started to feel better; tiredness and headaches are disappearing. Many children who suffered from bed-wetting have been cured. Your programmes have given us hope." This came from workers on the Chernorudka state farm (Ruzhinsky district, Zhitomir), with a hundred and fifty signatures. "Millions of people need your help. We're not exaggerating this figure," claimed workers from the Institute of Mechanics, Soviet Academy of Sciences of Ukraine, with two hundred and twenty-six signatures. There were prayers for help in almost every letter: "You are my last hope, Anatoly Mikhailovich. I am relying on your compassion! For Christ's sake, for the sake of my children, help me!"

There were letters claiming fantastic evidence of the healing of diseases such as diabetes, rheumatoid arthritis, multiple sclerosis, mastitis, psoriasis, bronchial asthma and allergies of all kinds. Many official testimonials came from dentists, confirming that their patients insisted that they needed no anaesthetic after having watched the seances, that they felt no pain. "It turned out that, as I had suggested, television healing was more effective than direct contact," said Kashpirovsky.

"I went to Tbilisi to perform and Georgian television came to broadcast the session. One of the journalists, Mark Rivkin, showed great interest in making a special programme about me. I mentioned that I would like to do another telebridge, maybe this time to connect Tbilisi and Kiev and show something interesting live." Rivkin responded enthusiastically and proposed doing "one better than Moscow". Kashpirovsky suggested two operations at once. They agreed on the spot, and Rivkin promised to come to Kiev in November to make a preliminary recording.

"On my return to Kiev, I had millions of other things to do and I forgot about the agreement with Tbilisi. But the journalists from Tbilisi came to Kiev as promised, to shoot some material. During a seance, in the presence of eight hundred people, I asked: 'Who wants to participate in a Kiev–Tbilisi telelink and allow their arms and legs to be cut off without feeling any pain?' About twenty-five people raised their hands and I started choosing the candidates for the operation. 'What is your problem?' I would ask, 'I have haemorrhoids.' 'I don't think that is very suitable. Next.' 'I have varicose veins'. 'That's not very exciting.' And so I continued, with lots of jokes, but in the end I selected two women: Olga Ignatova with a hernia, and Valentina Bondar with a womb to be removed. Both were serious cases needing immediate attention.

"But just one day before the agreed date of the programme (March 1, 1989) a telephone call came from Tbilisi and I was told that because of the different nature of the two operations, they had to be performed in two different locations and there wasn't enough television equipment to shoot from two places at the same time. I was asked to choose two identical cases. So I started calling potential candidates from the list. Lesya Yershova was first. She was always in a state of depression, cried a lot, was very emotional and fearful. I was not sure I wanted to take her, and she was not sure she really wanted to go. However, she was allergic to all anaesthetic and badly needed an operation. So I called Mark Rivkin and said: 'I will have two patients needing hernia operations, Olga Ignatova and Lesya Yershova.'"

Olga and Lesya had started coming together to his healing seances in 1988. As a result, Ignatova had lost an incredible amount of weight, got rid of her mastitis and gout in her foot, and Yershova got rid of her lymphocytosis and osteoarthritis. Lesya, particularly, had had serious problems which Kashpirovsky had managed to help.

"Both patients hoped they would be sent off to Tbilisi like martyrs or heroines, with flowers and music and cameras flashing. But I said firmly: 'No journalists, no special activities, just set off like any Soviet people.' I knew the most important thing had already been achieved. If they were prepared to go, they were ready for anything. And I could picture their thoughts: 'If he sends us off there like this, he must be sure of success; there will be no pain. We know him well. He would not perform an operation in front of television cameras unless he were absolutely certain of success. Then the people in the TV studios would not risk their careers unless they too trusted him, so we must trust him. If he says there will be no pain, there will be no pain.'"

It turned out, though, that many people already knew about the forthcoming operations in Tbilisi. "We're the centre of everyone's attention now," said Lesya to Mark Rivkin, who interviewed both patients before the operation. "People keep coming up to us and

*The hypnotic gaze of
Anatoly Mikhailovich Kashpirovsky*

2 *Participants floored by Kashpirovsky at a seance in the Kiev football stadium,*

3 The extraordinary effect of Dr Kashpirovsky (Kiev, 1989)

4 Adoring fans in Bratislava reach out

5 *Kashpirovsky at work with the sick and the lame*

6 *Kashpirovsky on stage: another admirer under the influence*

7 A Moscow audience showing support after the ministry of health had threatened to ban Kashpirovsky's appearances

8. Demonstrators demand
TV healing sessions:
"Stop the nation's tears!
Put Kashpirovsky on TV!"

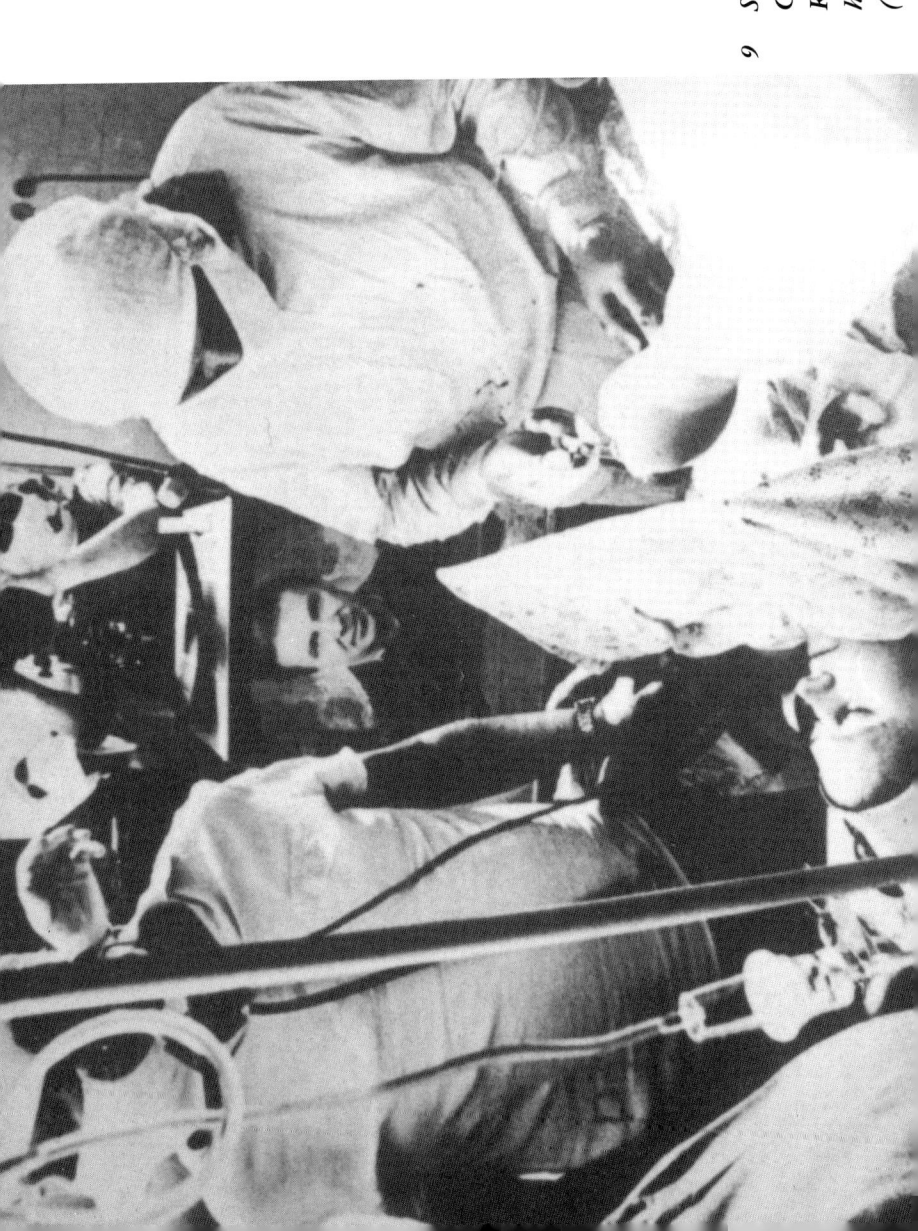

9 Surgeons remove Lyubov Grabovskaya's tumour while Kashpirovsky anaesthetizes her via the TV monitor (Photo by Sergei Kivrin)

10 *With Lech Walensa and interpreter in Poland*

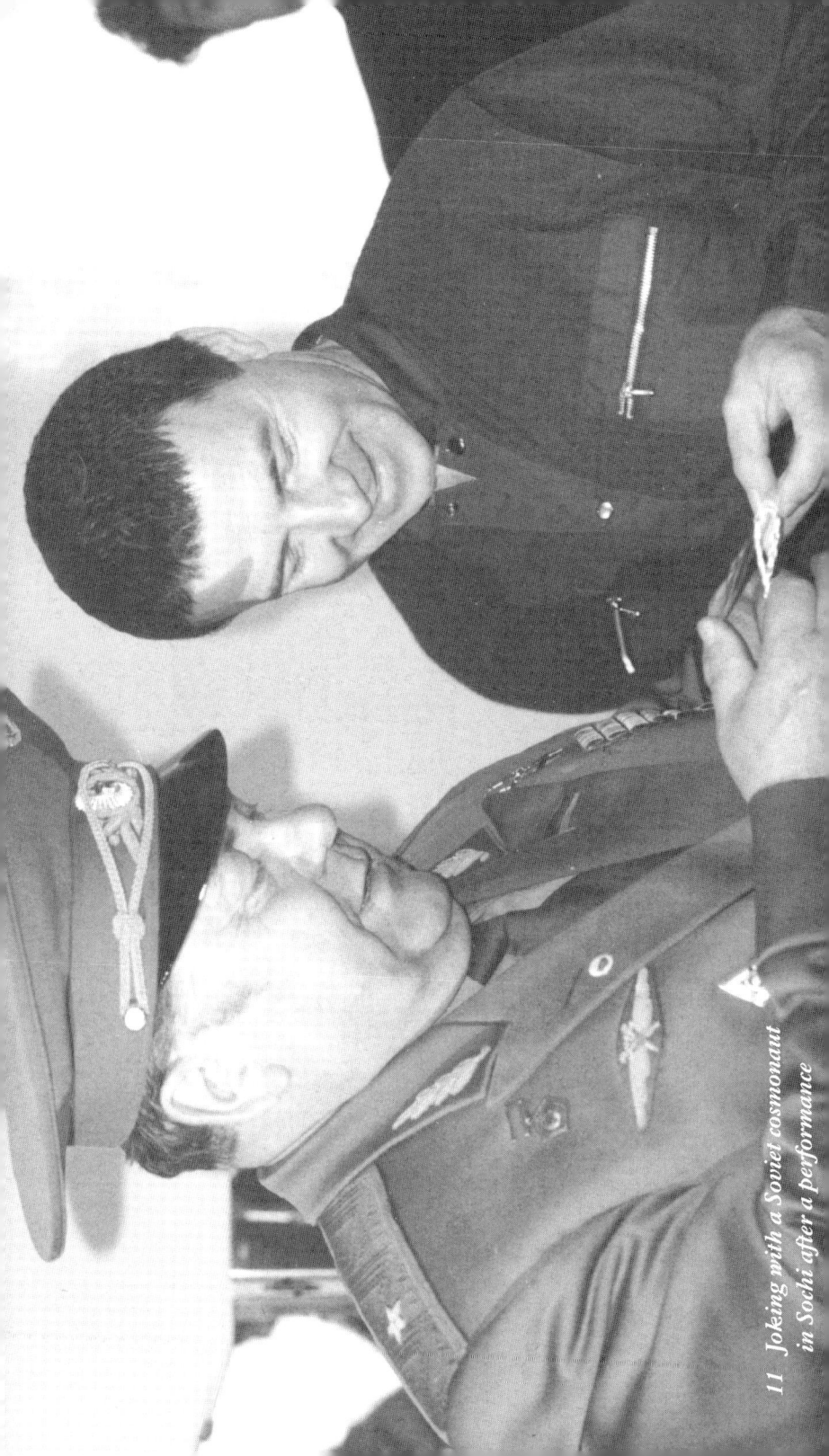

11   Joking with a Soviet cosmonaut in Sochi after a performance

Анатолий Кашпировский –
ВЧЕРА, СЕГОДНЯ, ЗАВТРА

Kashpirovsky the Dark Force:
"Yesterday, Today, Tomorrow"

13 *With Mohammed Ali—which Kashpirovsky considered the highlight of his American tour*

14 At the United Nations press conference on Chernobyl with the Kiev Green party (New York, 1992)

15 *"Who Are You Anyway, Doctor Kashpirovsky?"*

16 *"Kashpirovsky for President"* on the cover of a Polish magazine

КТО ЖЕ ВЫ, НАКОНЕЦ, ДОКТОР КАШПИРОВСКИЙ...

17 *Kashpirovsky with the author, Galina Vinogradova*

prodding us. They want to know if he has 'kashpified' us. One woman pinched my hand today and said, 'I've been on your trail for ages. Now I can see that you do feel pain.'"

The Kiev–Tbilisi telebridge took place on the appointed night. Two republics, the Ukraine and Georgia, watched this unusual broadcast live. Horror and curiosity kept everyone glued to their sets. The Georgians knew the operations would be performed by famous Georgian surgeons, one of whom was Ioseliani, the respected academician, a member of the Georgian Academy of Sciences. Viewers could see two operating tables set up in the Tbilisi Institute of Clinical and Experimental Surgery. A monitor stood in front of each table. Music was playing, though the volume had to be changed later at Kashpirovsky's command. The curious came rushing from all round the clinic and settled themselves on stairs and landings.

Kashpirovsky recalls: "I came to the studio at midnight in a bad mood. 'Oh, just problems at home,' I said to Nikolai Bondar, who assisted me during the experiment. My mood got worse and worse as I saw that the cameraman was drunk and could not set up the camera properly. Nothing seemed to be in working order. I had no audience to inspire me."

In Tbilisi the patients were brought into the theatre. They lay on the operating tables like queens, fully made-up and wearing earrings and rings on their fingers, their hair done and decorated with hair-slides! Hospital staff would never have allowed this under normal circumstances, and Kashpirovsky was dismayed to see it now. They were dressed for the cameras. Valeriya Vrublevskaya, a devoted friend, was with them in the theatre to give moral support.

Kashpirovsky appeared on screen and greeted them. They smiled. "Oh, we missed you so much! What is the weather like in Kiev now?" asked the patients. "The weather in Kiev is wonderful. Today is the first day of spring. Look, girls, millions of people are watching you, now!" And then, turning to the operator: "Show me their stomachs! And at that point I got their stomachs mixed up. Which was whose? Then, thank goodness, Lesya Yershova's face appeared on the screen."

"Oh, I can see my stomach on the screen," she said. Suddenly Kashpirovsky commanded: "Now, switch off!" Lesya obediently closed her eyes. Then she turned to the screen: "I am not switching off," she cried, "I can't do it." Things had begun to go wrong. Everyone froze and waited to see what would happen next.

"Oh, what the hell! Get on with it! Switch off!" ordered Kashpirovsky. But she didn't.

He decided to leave her alone and turned to Olga Ignatova. "Olya, close your eyes! You have no pain from your stomach to your spine!" His command was sharp, penetrating, and to the surgeons: "You can start the operation; you can pinch her or do everything you want. She won't feel anything now."

"Oh, my legs are shaking," came her plaintive voice. "No, they're not. Switch off! Cut!" shouted Kashpirovsky and banged his fist on the table. "I am as strong as the devil! Shut your eyes. Switch off!"

"The scalpel is blunt! Give me another one," said the surgeon, Zurab Megrelishvili. He finally made the primary incision on Olga ("To tell the truth I pricked her skin first, but there was no reaction," he admitted after the operation.) The operation had begun. Several times Kashpirovsky repeated: "Attention! None of the medical staff are to fall into a trance!"

"Show me the area you are going to operate on. I must see her face and that area all the time. All sensitivity is gone! Olya, you'll be hearing my voice clearly all the time! Nobody talk to her! Olya, the fear is gone! Look at me and close your eyes! You're floating! Everything is fine. You'll feel the instruments, but no pain. You are now as relaxed as if you were intoxicated."

One could hear the voices of the surgeons: "That's the umbilical hernia. We must slice it off."

Olga begged: "Don't take your eyes off me, please, Anatoly Mikhailovich, keep looking at me. I feel like something is burning inside!" But Kashpirovsky would not allow her to panic: "Oh, they are cauterizing your blood vessels, nothing to be afraid of! And after all, who would like their intestines twisted about! Even God can't make you avoid feeling some sensation, but there will be no pain. Have you ever been to the seaside? Now, you'll see the sea, OK? Turn your face to the sun! Do you feel a nice breeze?" (The voices of surgeons: "Bleeding ... Now start coagulation.") "A seagull is pecking me!" said Olga. Kashpirovsky comforted her: "Don't worry, we'll shoo it off! What would you like to talk to me about now?" "Let's talk about love!" she said and started smiling. But suddenly her face twitched in a grimace. She turned pale and her features became drawn.

"Are you all right, Olga?" asked the surgeon.

"I feel nauseous and dizzy," she replied.

The doctors: "It looks like shock. Blood pressure is falling sharply. Now it's eighty over forty. Maybe try caffeine?"

Kashpirovsky said calmly: "She doesn't need it. I'll get the pressure up. How much do you need?" Then he said to her: "Listen! You're going upstairs, carrying a bag of a hundred kilos. Run quickly up to the third floor!" The surgeons confirmed that her blood pressure was back to normal: a hundred and forty over ninety. "Olya, you can rest now!" The operation was coming to an end. At last Kashpirovsky said to Olga: "Now they are sewing you up tight, in a Georgian way. Artistically. You'll have the most beautiful navel." And then: "Well, now you'll be able to sleep peacefully, and things will start to heal quickly."

Mark Rivkin could now ask if she had felt any pain: "I didn't feel pain. It was like mosquito bites or a little pinching, although I was conscious all the time. I could hear what was going on. I remember how he said: 'Olya, you're swimming in the sea. It's a beautiful place!' And I really could see the mountains, the sea and a seagull seemed to be gently pecking me."

Mark Rivkin then asked Zurab Megrelishvili, the surgeon, if his patient had felt any pain: "The operation lasted fifty-eight minutes. My patient felt no pain at all. I could see that she was nervous at the beginning, but then everything went fine. We surgeons did not notice any unpleasant feelings. And hardly any blood was lost during the operation. The muscles did not quiver, although we made an incision of twenty-five centimetres." Olga's face appeared on screen for the last time and she happily winked at the viewers.

Then it was the turn of Lesya Yershova. She'd been in a light trance during the previous operation. Kashpirovsky turned to her with the question: "Lesya, are you going to stay on the table or get off?" "I'll do whatever you want." "We've got to get on with it. Close your eyes! Switch off!" And turning to the surgeons: "I'll do it differently with Lesya."

"Lesya, snap out of the trance! Talk to me! Look at me! Resist closing your eyes. Now you are floating! At the count of three, start the operation. One! Her skin and cellular tissue are anaesthetized! Two, three: let's start the operation!"

At this point the surgeon, Ioseliani, touched the patient's skin with the point of his scalpel before making the incision, testing her sensitivity. "You don't need to do that, professor! Work without testing!" burst out Kashpirovsky. The surgeon made an incision more than forty centimetres long. "Lesya, would you like me to read something?" She nodded her head approvingly, and he began reciting the prologue to *Quiet Flows the Don*, by Mikhail Sholokhov, with great feeling. But then something happened with the sound—there was static in the speaker. Lesya started nervously fidgeting. Then she dozed for a while and suddenly her sleeping face was distorted with pain. "What's wrong with you, Lesya?" asked Kashpirovsky.

"My stomach is pressing ... it hurts ..."

"Hold on ... We're halfway there."

"It's hard ... Ring my son ..."

"OK, we'll ring him straight away."

After that he said: "I'm going to suggest enjoyment to you. You're about to really enjoy yourself."

Lesya replied: "I thought at the beginning that I would. But now I have a strange feeling, like a ball lying on my stomach or something."

Kashpirovsky continued to watch her: "Do you see me? OK, I'll have a cup of coffee now. You look fine, much better than Olga. You know, she is so cranky, but kind. Your face is pink. Your pulse is normal: eighty beats per minute. How many times did they operate on you? Four times under general anaesthesia?"

Lesya: "After the first operation I was clinically dead. Each time the post-operative period was very difficult. I had a heavy cough."

Kashpirovsky: "This was a reaction to the anaesthetic. Why are you grimacing? Do you feel pain?"

Lesya Yershova: "No, I don't. I am all right now."

"How do you feel now?"

She opened her eyes and said: "Oh, I thought it would hurt, but I feel like singing and dancing."

"Perhaps you'd sing something for us, Lesya?"

"What would you like?" she replied.

"Something about love."

Lesya started to sing *Tbiliso* then a few more songs, and then she ended up with *Moscow Nights*. And after the last verse she said: "Oh, why do I have such a high voice today?"

Finally, the last stitch was finished and the operation ended at six o'clock in the morning to the applause of those present in both studios. They were singing along with Lesya Yershova and had the feeling that they were participating in some great discovery! They were happy and excited. They thought they had witnessed a miracle.

When asked his opinion about the operation, Professor Ioseliani said: "When the Georgian ministry of health proposed that I should take part in the experiment, I said I don't like circus tricks in medicine. But one of the patients turned out to be an especially difficult case—she had already undergone four operations on her abdominal cavity, had a serious case of peritonitis, had twice been pronounced clinically dead—so I considered it impossible to refuse. It is hard to describe my feelings when I made the first incision on the patient. She had not been given any anaesthetic, absolutely no medication at all. I felt a bit better about it when the operation on the first table had begun and proceeded without a single groan or shout. I could hear only Kashpirovsky's voice. He joked, told her how the operation was going, gave commands, and sometimes, it seemed, deepened his influence. My patient's condition was not at all simple: the tissue had become very thin, there were commissures and layers that had fused together. She had a hernia the size of a basketball. When the operation started, she dozed, then it was suggested that she should sing. I must admit that this didn't have a very good effect on me: she had a forty-centimetre incision, her stomach was wide open, she had a ventral hernia, commissures, and she opened her eyes and sang *Tbiliso*. But when she did, the organs being operated on relaxed, calmed down, which sometimes not even relaxing drugs can manage to do. After two and a half hours she was still on the operating table, singing *Moscow Nights*. I've been doing surgery for forty-five years and I've never seen anything like it."

The specialists were surprised that the intestines of both women were working. There is usually paralysis of the intestine for about three days after similar surgical intervention. With Kashpirovsky's permission, Lesya was to be given antibiotics, since she had previously suffered from peritonitis. Lesya and Olya felt so well that they were drinking champagne the day after the operation.

Kashpirovsky recalled, somewhat bitterly, that problems came later: "Then the convalescents went back to Kiev to finish their treatment. The first abdominal operation in the world conducted by television anaesthesia might have ended in tragedy. The local doctors were not in a hurry to give the patients the help and aftercare they needed. Olga's wound began to suppurate. And they didn't even want to give Lesya sick leave from work! I was openly called a charlatan and all sorts of other names."

Both patients were fine in the end but Kashpirovsky felt he had been called upon only to anaesthetize the patients, which he did successfully, and that post-operative care should happily have been left to others.

This remarkable programme had been watched by viewers only in the Ukraine and Tbilisi; people in Russia and other republics learned about it from newspapers and short pieces on news programmes. Opinions differed: some blamed him for risking the lives of his patients, but others believed the surgeons knew what they were doing and if the power of suggestion had weakened, they would have had time enough to give them anaesthesia anyway.

The whole operation had been so extraordinary that people were confused; they didn't know how to react. However, they were soon distracted by political events in the country. For the first time in seventy years, elections of deputies to the Congress of Soviets was taking place in an almost democratic manner. To start with, Gorbachev's summons to re-elect the highest legislative bodies were met with indifference by many people, who considered that everything would, as always, be falsified. No one really hoped that truly worthy candidates would be elected.

But it turned out that according to electoral law, the candidates had to present their programme, answer electors' questions and explain where their flats, cars and country houses had come from and what they intended to do once they were deputies in the Supreme Soviet. Meetings with voters were broadcast on television, and soon television debates became the most popular viewing. People were prepared to watch them until late into the night, and next morning they were hotly debated at work.

Although a third of the seats at the Congress were guaranteed to go to representatives of the Party, Komsomol, trade unions and other social organizations (and for this reason it is more correct to call these elections semi-democratic), there was a glimmer of a real possibility that people could express themselves freely.

Anatoly Kashpirovsky was also nominated as a candidate for election as a People's Deputy of the USSR for the Lenin district of Kiev, but he didn't get enough votes at the district meeting. This upset him, although he understood that because he was so busy he would not have been able to cope with the duties of a deputy. When asked if he intended to try for parliament in the future, he replied: "No! In any case, I think my main work will be of far greater benefit to people. I received so many vicious, poisonous letters during the campaign that anyone else in my place would have given up there and then. It was precisely at that moment that I lost any desire to run for election again."

On March 26 there were amazing scenes at the polling stations. Until only very recently, people felt little purpose in voting; now many came determined to blackball the Communists. The democrats' victory was especially convincing in Leningrad and Moscow: the Party apparatchiks of these cities were totally wiped out. For the first time in the history of the Soviet state, people had expressed their real opinion. Although the elections were not taken seriously in the provinces, where they called it "the big show in Moscow", the victory at the elections was hailed as another revolution. The people of Leningrad exulted: they had got rid of the hated Solovyov (First Secretary of the regional committee) and the mayor, Khodyrev. Boris Yeltsin won in Moscow, quite unexpectedly.

In April 1989 Kashpirovsky set off for Tbilisi, where a press conference was to be held. He had not chosen a good time for this. The capital of Georgia was plunged into mourning. Witnesses told Kashpirovsky how on the night of April 9 a peaceful demonstration by students and others, demanding the restoration of independence to Georgia, had been dispersed. This event had shaken the whole republic. Rumours about bitter reprisals on unarmed citizens were going around. It was said that tanks and armoured cars had been turned on them. Sixteen people had been killed, mostly young women; students had been beaten with combat shields and spades. Casualties began to appear in Tbilisi's hospitals shortly afterwards. Rumours, later substantiated, said there were many victims of poison gas, including children, which the troops had used to disperse the demonstration and to terrorize the city. The whole of Tbilisi was in deep shock.

Kashpirovsky went to Tbilisi with his son, Seryozha, and a writer from Kiev, Vladimir Sidorenko, who was going to write a book about him. "I consider Vladimir Sidorenko a talented writer. He has written several books in the Ukrainian language, but he did me a favour I could have done without. We stopped at a hotel—it belonged to the Institute of Geology—with a splendid view onto the sacred mountain, Tatsminda. I went out for a walk and when I returned to the hotel, Sidorenko introduced me to a priest, who had come to the hotel to see me. 'I've been dreaming about this meeting with you for a long time! I'm sure your noble mission to help the suffering is similar to the work of Biblical prophets. Your name will be renowned for ever and ever!'

"I was pleased to meet him. He was so nice and educated, and I asked him to tell me about himself: 'I've become a priest only recently. Before that I was one of Shevardnadze's aides. I speak five languages and I liked my job very much. But one day everything changed. I was involved in an accident and died. For two days I lay in the morgue and on the third day, when they started the autopsy, opening my chest, I opened my eyes. They were terrified. They couldn't believe it. Yes, I was alive! Before I came round, I had a vision of God, who told me that I had to devote myself to the service of the church, helping the poor and needy. He told me about the difficulties of being a priest, an educated man among poorly educated clergy. He said something about religion with which I totally agree. He said that religion must constantly evolve otherwise it becomes a dogma. Man should constantly strive for the Truth.' This meeting was to cause problems later."

On the evening of the same day a reception was organized in Kashpirovsky's honour in the Tbilisi television studios. There were many guests and lots of flowers, music, speeches, congratulations, journalists with cameras. Mark Rivkin showed the videotape of the operations. Kashpirovsky, Ioseliani, Olga and Lesya were given a standing ovation.

Both patients looked healthy and happy. They answered questions, emphasizing that they had not felt any kind of pain. Professor Ioseliani said: "I am a confirmed realist, but I am confused. We must develop Kashpirovsky's method as a matter of priority. This is both an opportunity to help patients who cannot tolerate anaesthetics, and also to ease the post-operative period. How universal, how widely applicable is this method? Only practice will answer that question, but my junior colleagues and I are ready to take part in the continuation of Kashpirovsky's experiments. When people ask about the level of risk during the operation, I reply: 'We reduced it to a minimum once we had thought through all the variants. So, if something unexpected had happened, we would not have been caught unawares.'"

And, of course, most of all there were questions for Kashpirovsky. "I decided to do operations on television," he replied, "in order to break people's stereotypical way of thinking. I wanted to prove convincingly yet again the effectiveness of psychotherapy, so as to bring psychotherapy out into the open at last, to give it a chance to help millions of people simultaneously by means of television. There is so much demand from the population for help. Even now there is not one modern, well-equipped psychotherapy centre in our country, whereas, for example, there are hundreds in the USA. So television psychotherapy might relieve this deficit to a certain extent. And it isn't essential to be near the patient. I think I have proved that it is possible to conduct anaesthesia at a distance. All you need is preliminary contact. The patient must know that at the time of the operation I will be suggesting the absence of pain."

The whole of Georgia watched the press conference. Viewers rang the television studio and asked how to get to one of Kashpirovsky's surgeries. At the end of the programme Vladimir Sidorenko spoke about the popularity of Kashpirovsky in the Ukraine and added: "But now I know that he is also famous and popular in Georgia. Today a Georgian priest visited Anatoly Mikhailovich and said that Kashpirovsky's name will be blessed." The meeting closed with a standing ovation.

These words, however, were to land Kashpirovsky in deep water. The Patriarch of Georgia was told that Sidorenko had been referring to him, and he did not like it. And that moment during the operation when Kashpirovsky mentioned the devil ("I'm as strong as the devil"—an odd thing to say, but typical of Kashpirovsky) led to several priests calling his healing satanic.

Next day Kashpirovsky visited hospitals, accompanied by the Georgian health and justice ministers, to see the victims of the poison gas. "I believe this bloodbath was Gorbachev's fault," said Kashpirovsky later. "I sincerely wanted to help the victims of the incident." The previous evening the whole Soviet Union had watched an interview with a doctor from one of the Tbilisi hospitals. He had confirmed that many symptoms of those recovering from the attack corresponded with the effects of poisonous gas. This information contributed more to the atmosphere of horror and the hopelessness, anger and frustration of the Georgian people. But Kashpirovsky, like some others, thought many of the victims were really suffering from shock and mass hysteria, so, the Georgians felt, underplaying the real horror of what had happened. He told his companions that it was a psychic epidemic, and if they gave him two hours on television, he would solve the problem.

In the evening of the same day Kashpirovsky and his son Seryozha went on television. But the atmosphere was completely different. Instead of flowers and speeches full of praise, Kashpirovsky was left to face a group of infuriated young Georgians. Instead of five hundred people, there were three times that number. All were shouting in Georgian and waving their national flag. In the front row was a group of four in cassocks. Kashpirovsky believes that they were not real priests, that he was being victimized. A red-haired Georgian priest jumped up on the stage and shouted: "If you believe in God, say a prayer." Kashpirovsky yelled back: "Who do you think you are, ordering me around? I am the one round here who does the suggesting and the ordering!" Then the priest turned to the audience and shouted something to them. The audience sprang to their feet.

"I looked back and saw about twenty Georgians behind me. They climbed up on stage. Their looks left no doubt. They were there to kill me. They saw that I was watching them, that I was on my guard. I jumped onto the table and was standing there ready to fight back. Here my sports training came in handy. I looked around but I could not find any of my friends. I was left alone with the lot of them. Seryozha sat on the balcony filming the whole mess on an amateur videocamera.

"At that moment Badry, my contact on Georgian television, pushed his way through the crowd and announced that there would be a break. We managed to escape to a dressing room. He told me I had to leave because they could not guarantee my safety. Someone started knocking on the door, threatening to kill me. I realized there was no other way and managed to get out through a back door."

This fracas was broadcast throughout Georgia. The fans of Kashpirovsky and other people called the television studio, militia, KGB, other officers, in protest. Kashpirovsky left Tbilisi with some pride at the daring he had shown and with an undiminished belief in his own rectitude. He felt he had been a victim of anti-Russian feeling in the republic. He did not understand all the complexities of the situation.

Back in Moscow at the opening of the Congress of People's Deputies on May 25, 1989, Andrei Sakharov and his supporters appealed to Gorbachev to sort out what had happened in Georgia. Why hadn't he used his authority to stop General Rodionov, the commander of the Transcaucasian military district, from confronting the demonstrators and allowing his troops to react with such violence? A commission was set up to investigate the situation in Georgia, and the full truth has yet to be told.

Observing Gorbachev's behaviour during the Congress, people started to note signs of the old authoritarian attitudes: an impatience towards the opinions of others, a wish to get his own way. Gorbachev's behaviour towards Andrei Sakharov made people especially indignant. Right-wing forces accused Sakharov of treachery and of hatred of the Army which had fought with valour in Afghanistan. Sakharov paid no attention to the hissing and booing which erupted and continued to speak against the invasion of Afghanistan. He said he had struggled not with the people who had fought, but against the people who had sent them to fight. But Gorbachev did not defend him against the attacks of the hard-liners.

Now Gorbachev no longer gave the appearance of such a kind and understanding democrat. It became clear that he was friends with Yazov, Ligachev and Lukyanov, and that he hated Yeltsin, whose popularity was growing daily. In Moscow demonstrations were taking place and the deputies reported back to the voters with an account of what was going on at the Congress. Gradually joy in "democratic victory" faded. The work of the Congress ended in mid-June.

Television screens were then filled by a man who appeared every week on the morning news programme *120 Minutes*. He claimed he could cure diseases and he "charged" water and creams with his mysterious energizing power. This was not Dr Kashpirovsky, but the journalist Alan Chumak. Chumak asked viewers to close their eyes while he moved his hands around in magical gestures in complete silence. Chumak suggested nothing to anyone and used no words but, it turned out, he too helped people. Sometimes his sessions of silent influence were broadcast on the radio! Even this seemed to help. People wondered what had happened to Kashpirovsky. Why were his sessions not being broadcast on television?

Kashpirovsky felt his position had weakened. "Belozerov arranged the appearances of Chumak to spite me. His seances leaned towards mysticism and parapsychology. They cast a shadow over my psychotherapeutic seances. I could not immediately show the Tbilisi operations nationwide, because Mark Rivkin left for Hungary or Czechoslovakia and it took him about eight months to edit the film. The fascination of my first appearance started fading, and people simply forgot about me."

When journalists asked his opinion about Chumak, his competitor on television, Kashpirovsky used to say: "There should be no question about competition. I like Chumak as a person. He has a nice face and cultured manners. But his explanations of his methodology confused many viewers. I'm a doctor. I use psychological techniques to treat people. Chumak is a journalist, but in the age of perestroika it has become possible for anybody to profess his ability to heal. He talks about bioenergy, cosmic flows, energy-charging. His seances make people believe there are some extraterrestrial, uncontrolled, mystical forces that regulate the condition of our health. All this makes my work more difficult. I'm influencing the subconscious of people, getting them to tune in to their own subconscious, not to believe that some kind of extrasensory force is influencing them. Belozerov betrayed me by putting Chumak on television."

The background to this is somewhat opaque. But it seems Belozerov, the producer who had helped set up the Tbilisi–Kiev telebridge, had fallen out with Kashpirovsky over money. This, it has to be said, was rather the usual pattern in the doctor's business relationships. Kashpirovsky thought, wrongly, that Belozerov had decided to promote Alan Chumak, an extremely popular healer, and had arranged for him to broadcast his seances on national television from Moscow. As this was precisely what Kashpirovsky had been desperate to do for years, he felt particularly angry, frustrated and slighted.

However, at the end of July 1989, just on the eve of his fiftieth birthday, new friends from Moscow—Steve Shenkman, the editor of a very popular sports magazine, and Inessa Bubnova, a TV producer—arranged to broadcast a show called *A Meeting with Dr Kashpirovsky* where some of his devoted patients and fans came with him to the concert studio of Ostankino TV centre. The programme was sponsored by the sports studio, whose director Alexander Ivannitsky managed to get permission from the higher echelons of the TV directorate.

"I've been trying to reach you, my dear fellows, for twenty-seven years," the man on the screen spoke quietly with an Ukrainian accent. There was something compelling about him. Many well-known faces could be seen in the audience. He began to talk about his life: "For years I worked at a psychiatric hospital, moving around the country giving hundreds of lectures, meeting all sorts of people. I wanted to experience everything, to see everything, in order to understand something of what man is. I came to understand that man is capable of anything. Of course, there were ups and downs on this road to comprehension. I can't tell you what I've experienced in my life. But there is no need to tell you. My life is no different from yours. My appearance here before you became possible because of glasnost and perestroika. Only my closest friends know that I've been here in this studio once before, when in 1982 I was doing a seance for the workers of the Ostankino TV studio. At that time nobody could ever have imagined broadcasting my performance on TV. Now everything has changed, I hope, for the better. Today you will meet my friends and my patients who became my friends."

The presence of so many famous performers, sportsmen and cosmonauts helped to persuade people that Kashpirovsky was genuine and could be trusted. But, of course, the most amazing were the stories told by Lesya Yershova and Olga Ignatova. They were smiling now, but the fact that just six months before they had undergone such extraordinary operations made viewers feel creepy all over. "No, I did not feel any pain at all," Lesya Yershova told the stunned audience. "I'll never forget what you have done for me, Anatoly Mikhailovich! You saved my life! I'll be grateful to you for the rest of my days!" Other grateful patients gave their testimonies. It seemed that Dr Kashpirovsky could cure anything.

Next morning he woke up a superstar. The programme was broadcast three times and hardly a person in the whole Soviet Union did not see it. The months of July, August, September and October 1989 were the time of his absolute triumph. It was announced that six healing sessions with Dr Kashpirovsky were to be shown on national television.

Even at this stage this decision could not be freely made by TV executives alone. Kashpirovsky had to appear before the board of the ministry of health at two meetings specially devoted to him. With the support of Professor Raikov, a scientist well known for his experiments on hypnosis and suggestology, particularly his work on the teaching of foreign languages under hypnosis, the board was persuaded that Kashpirovsky should go on. Permission was granted for six broadcasts, and these were endlessly repeated.

When they were shown, Soviet citizens were able to improve their health by watching Alan Chumak in the morning and Kashpirovsky in the evening. Chumak, a white-haired, gentle-looking man, was given the soubriquet *Morning Star* and Kashpirovsky, with his rather stern appearance, dark eyes, black hair, black jacket and poloneck, was nicknamed *The Black Force*. More than three hundred million people watched these shows throughout the republics and eastern Europe—glued to their television screens. The streets were deserted. It seemed that all other problems were pushed to one side.

"I looked into the eye of the TV camera and I realized I was looking into the eyes of those three hundred million people. I thought at this moment people are looking at my face; some of them like it, and some of them don't. Some of them trust me and some despise me. I knew they would all be reacting differently, but for some of them the thirty minutes of my seance would be enough to change their lives, to avoid an operation, to heal themselves. I felt overwhelmed with happiness."

Articles on the "Kashpirovsky phenomenon" were published every day. His life was discussed and dissected: his work, the cases of cures under his influence, his loves and hates. The press wrote about the "Kashpirovization" of the country. In August 1989 *Izvestia* published a lengthy interview with an extremely well respected academician, P. Simonov, the director of the All-Union Institute of Neurophysiology, which enormously encouraged Kashpirovsky.

Simonov was asked if he was for or against Kashpirovsky. "Without any doubt I'm for Kashpirovsky," he replied. "Kashpirovsky is a bright figure. He is a highly qualified professional, and one should not equate him with other television healers who are not medical doctors. Kashpirovsky is a learned psychotherapist. He uses classical methods of suggestion and hypnosis and achieves good results."

"How can you be for him, when you are a well known opponent of parapsychology?" asked the correspondent.

"I'm for medicine. This is real healing and the ministry of health should pay Kashpirovsky a high salary. The reality of hypnosis no one can deny, though the mechanism of hypnosis is not yet known. But we cannot deny the existence of this phenomenon. Kashpirovsky does not put up a smokescreen, he does not pretend he is using bioenergy or telepathy. He explains that he obtains results by gesture and word. He is part of a great scientific tradition. All Kashpirovsky's predecessors practised in a closed atmosphere, in laboratories or in clinics. They treated individuals one-to-one. But Kashpirovsky speaks to the world. He has the television screen at his disposal.

"The effect of suggestion is impossible without a ritual, without a shaman's tambourine, and in our time the best tambourine is the TV. It's excellent that he is using it. It's very interesting to see how he has created a special method and adapted techniques to our modern times.

This multiplies the power of his influence. In fact, it really is only television which makes Kashpirovsky so very different from other psychotherapists. Many of them mastered hypnotic analgesia. There are volumes of medical books about it."

"You make it sound simple," said the journalist, "but Kashpirovsky does more than use words to talk someone out of pain. The woman on the operating table was singing! She was in an induced state of ecstasy."

Simonov replied: "Well, of course, he must have huge talent as a hypnotist in order so powerfully and, if you like, so dramatically to influence the threshold of pain. The master of this biochemical reaction is the subconscious and of course Kashpirovsky addresses his suggestion to the subconscious. Our science as yet knows very little about the brain and I will not attempt to translate the methodology of hypnotherapy into the language of the molecular biology of the future. It is, however, very important that such a talented doctor should be helped by the scientific establishment so that we can begin to understand this language better."

The correspondent continued: "Perhaps there is some element of the superman in the image that Kashpirovsky projects? A mixture of magic and sexual energy, like Rasputin. This causes submission in his patients and the ecstasy we see in the women who go to him."

Simonov replied: "The women in his seances act as accelerators because they infect the rest with their adoration and their desire and ability to be totally submissive. This irrational behaviour influences others. Imitational behaviour is a very ancient mechanism within the human psyche. Of course, one has to be careful with this."

"Are trance and suggestion not connected?" asked his interviewer. "Kashpirovsky did not seem to put his patients into a trance or to induce sleep."

"Good hypnosis does not require that," replied Simonov. "Even words are not needed to achieve it. Facial expressions, body language, gestures, the eyes—all are important. Kashpirovsky uses all this brilliantly. He is a clever professional with an artistic bent and a great sense of humour."

"But you totally deny the reality of the so-called bioenergy which other healers claim to be able to transmit via television?"

"In order to become a supporter, I need proof," replied Simonov. "Kashpirovsky's seances do not need any new theories to support them. They do not contradict classical psychology in any way."

So what went on at Kashpirovsky's healing seances? What form did they take? In 1990 he had a videotape made of a session at the Palace of Culture in Leningrad—with a label on the cover reading *Warning! In case of duplication this tape will lose its medical properties.* The tape begins:

> The theatre is packed. Kashpirovsky sits on stage at a table, looking very self-possessed, very serious. He greets his audience warmly and invites them to come to a microphone placed in the stalls. Many stand and wait in line for the opportunity to deliver their testimonials. Almost all have the same story to tell: they were ill, they saw him on TV or attended a session, now they are better. All give their name and address, so that they can be identified and not be accused of being a Kashpirovsky plant.
>
> A pretty girl in a red dress, in her early thirties, had severe problems with her bowels. She had not believed in him or trusted him. But after watching one session her problems have gone. An Afghanistan veteran, a young man covered in medals and obviously in a dreadful state, had been shot through the head. He had been paralysed and the doctors said he would never move again. He watched some seances and started to walk again. He even recovered movement in his right arm though his left arm still has problems and the nerve in his right eye is damaged. He wants to know if there is any chance it might recover. Kashpirovsky replies that he cannot guarantee it but that he has had patients with even worse problems who have recovered. He points out to the audience that he wants comments only about successful recovery, not about remaining problems. Then an epileptic comes to the microphone. He says he has had no fits for some time, and Kashpirovsky replies that he's glad the man feels better, though for him the case is not convincing enough. He stresses that he wants reports of really convincing cases.
>
> A woman of forty has had a lung removed and after watching the TV seances, the scar from the operation has almost completely disappeared. She tries to go on about this, but Kashpirovsky interrupts her and again says that no one should spoil the atmosphere, that he wants to hear only positive things. He says everyone has five or six diseases and he doesn't want to hear about the ones

that haven't been cured. A man in a red jumper, an artist from Warsaw, has seen six seances on TV and says the shape of his face has changed. Nobody laughs. The pains from his prostate operation have gone, the scar on his knee has disappeared, and his hair has darkened. He used to be blond! His wife's hair has also darkened! And a friend who had been paralysed stood up and went shopping after watching one seance in their flat. At this point there is laughter. Even Kashpirovsky smiles.

A fat lady in a patterned dress says she has great news. Her grandson's hernia has disappeared after five years of problems. Her own varicose veins have gone and her husband's hair has darkened. She says everyone must do what they can to help Kashpirovsky continue his work. Everyone claps.

Another woman had cancer. The previous September she had felt terrible; she had pains all over, and her arms were numb. After six sessions she now has no pain and the lumps in her breast have disappeared. As she's talking, her arms move and her head twists round. Kashpirovsky asks if these movements are really involuntary. She says they are and that it feels good. Whenever she hears his voice, she feels a sensation like little needles pricking the place where the pain used to be. Kashpirovsky stops her and tells her that these movements she shows are not necessary. She seems quite prepared to talk forever.

Still, queues of people wait for their turn at the microphone. An elderly lady in a pink dress says she had a stroke and problems with her circulation. Now she feels much better. She can stand and she can eat properly. She says they should all build him a clinic, but he warns them to be very careful and that it is not a good idea to collect money because this could be misinterpreted by his critics.

A singer appears on stage and sings a comic song about how they'd all get fat and start smoking if it wasn't for Kashpirovsky. What would they do without him? The audience laugh and clap. Kashpirovsky gives her a bouquet of flowers.

Another middle-aged woman points to her sick brother sitting next to her. He suffered terrible side-effects after a bout of flu and became paralysed. After watching Kashpirovsky, he started moving again. "He goes into a trance-like state and moves and walks about, although he had been paralysed for a year and a half. These trances sometimes last for a very long time—between two and nine hours—during which he keeps walking around the room." She is very unhappy about this but Kashpirovsky replies that perhaps he is happy being in a trance, that he prefers it. The woman agrees that he does like it, that he feels good. Kashpirovsky suggests that his body needs it and she says: "Yes, all right, but we have to follow him around for nine hours while he's moving, to make sure that he's OK." The brother is sitting there swaying his head from side to side. Kashpirovsky snaps his fingers and says: "He's out of it now. See, he's coming out. But he obviously likes his trances." He tells the young man to look at him and, indeed, he does sit up and appears suddenly alert. His head stops swaying. Kashpirovsky tells them they need not fear adverse reactions from his therapy, that no such thing is possible. They must banish all negative thoughts.

Eventually he calls a halt to the testimonials. Everyone sits down and he calls for music. The gentle sounds of a guitar drift across the stage. He tells them that though they might think that treatment is only now going to start, it began the moment they arrived. He talks very calmly and slowly.

"You can close your eyes and think about anything. Perhaps you want to think about your illness, perhaps not. Some of you have come out of curiosity, some because you have a real problem. A child sits on his mother's knee and thinks his childish thoughts and does what his mother tells him, innocently. Be like this. Don't try to guess anything, to solve the puzzle, to find the answer. Just let your mind drift. My words will just be an accompaniment to the music, to add to your sensations. Of course, you have some feelings. Perhaps you are in a lyrical mood. I like these lines of poetry: 'I feel that in my chest a string is plucked and my heart has started crying secretly. I see your eyes in front of me and I remember everything that has happened. All these memories provoke a bitter-sweet pain in my heart.'

"Some of you will think of your past. If you think about or feel something strange, unusual, don't be frightened. Accept it all in your different ways. Some will see images of loved ones or images of nature, far, far from here. They will almost seem real. You are in the mountains or at the North Pole; it's an hallucination but sometimes hallucinations are more real and bright than reality.

"Some will picture nothing at all, have no thought or sensation. Don't try to do anything you are not inclined to do. Let yourself go, feel what you want to. No matter how strange your thoughts, do not push them away. Follow them. Don't be afraid of losing reason's thread. Just listen to the sounds; they are sweet sounds to the ear. If you are worried that my words do not seem to penetrate your consciousness, don't worry. Everything will be recorded in your mind, forever. Don't try to focus on your problem or attract my attention to it. Next to you may be patients who are impatient or fidgety. Pay no attention. Please be kind and tolerant.

"I will never be able to tell you the most important thing: how it happens that when you come very, very close to the secret door, it starts to open. Some allow this door to be opened wide, some just leave a little gap so that I can reach in and leave a trace without leaving a trace.

"That is my short instruction. I could have given out a sharp *ustanovka* from the beginning, but I follow the ancient principle: it is not I who command but you who respond. When people move their heads about or wave their hands in the air, they control themselves. If you want to be in a trance, you will be in a trance. It is entirely up to you. This is my *ustanovka*.

"My goal is to influence your body, to reach something that seems to be disobedient. What seems to be solid and immovable is my target; it is in my sights. I am not afraid to hunt it down. I can see that in this instant your mind jumps to where you feel pain. Maybe you have a tumour in your breast and you want to check, 'How do I feel now, did it work, has anything happened?' Maybe you are looking in another direction but I know what I'm doing. Your reactions may be different; I insist on nothing.

"Our seance will be easy, simple. It will end without complications, it will end the moment it ends. One, two, three, four, five. Today we have had a wonderful session. I have put my heart and soul into it. On my right I see sitting among you a spiritual man, a priest. We are working together with you now on both sides. Six, seven. I am so glad he is here with me. Do not open your eyes yet, even if something startles you. I want our session to be very quiet and very soft. You are inside yourself. Don't miss your opportunity: stay there. Eight, nine.

"There are some whose requests I will remember and some I became one with. They can feel that I am with them. You are not mistaken, those of you who feel this. I am waiting for you to respond. I hope it will be a very powerful, miraculous response. That is why we have met here, not just for a chat. Ten, eleven, twelve. People wonder why I count. It is because words are hardly needed now. You anticipate what I say aloud. There are some whose eyelids are stuck together, they are deep inside themselves. Some cannot close their eyes; they try but can't. Some open and shut their eyes. Thirteen, fourteen, fifteen, sixteen, seventeen, eighteen, nineteen, twenty, twenty-one. Forget everything you thought before about my influence; don't make your life difficult. Drop it. Go ahead without this knowledge, without these preconceptions. Never be tired of doing good, let compassion and love fill your hearts. Twenty-two, twenty-three, twenty-four, twenty-five.

"The most important thing today, in our work together, is this secret, this mystery which has its own parameters. It has causes and effects. This mystery will do something: in several days you'll be filled with happiness, unable to believe that the impossible has occurred. There is no place for any negative occurrence. I suggest only joy and positive thoughts. Nothing bad will happen to you. Twenty-six, twenty-seven, twenty-eight, twenty-nine, thirty, thirty-one, thirty-two, thirty-three.

"In a few minutes our seance will be over and we must leave this state. We will leave it carefully. I was very careful in trying to introduce my *ustanovka* to you, in touching, light strokes. My *ustanovka* is well-considered and gentle. Everybody receives his own *ustanovka* and your own organism will decide to which secret places in your body to push this. It will be up to you. You won't believe what's happening but it's already inside you and it works. Many of you now have no pain and are breathing more quietly. You will sleep well, you are calm and quiet and feel no anxiety. So, as I count, you will come out of the trance: thirty-four, thirty-five.

"Now your eyes are opening. You are coming back to life full of energy and strength. You are in control. You know where you are. Your eyes are opened. Those who are present in this theatre can see that everyone is in command of himself. Even that young man who slipped into a trance doesn't move his head anymore. There will be no trances. We are saying goodbye in order to meet again. Goodbye."

6

Crisis of Confidence

I never believed in Mirages,
Nor packed my suitcase for the coming paradise.
A sea of lies devours my teachers
And casts them out beside Magadan.

But we knew how to sense danger
Long before the beginning of the cold,
With the shamelessness of a tart, clarity came
And bolted up our souls.

And though the executions didn't touch us,
We lived, not daring to raise our eyes.
We are also children of Russia's terrible years—
In us the stagnant hard time poured its vodka.

(Song written in 1970 by Vladimir Vysotsky)

*I*n the jauntily ironical tone that he, like all Western correspondents, typically reserved for Kashpirovsky, David Remnick of the *Washington Post* wrote:

> If there is a new cult of personality in the Soviet Union, it is centred not on Mikhail Gorbachev but rather on a Ukrainian psychologist who applies anaesthesia from a distance and has an audience of up to two hundred million people whenever he appears on *Good Evening, Moscow*.

On October 11 Anatoly Kashpirovsky met with reporters at the foreign ministry's press centre. With the redoubtable Soviet spokesman grinning impishly at his side, Kashpirovsky delved into the swampy depths of his own amazingness for a crowd that easily quadrupled the size that ordinarily shows up for a visiting leader from a medium-size country, Spain, say. "People sometimes see me and idolize me," he said. "People love singers and pop stars. It comes and goes. People are very emotional about me, but I remain sober."

His vague answers about his method or statistical analyses of his success rate left most journalists frustrated, but that did not worry the enthusiastic secretaries from the foreign ministry's press centre and the Novosti press agency who packed the seats reserved for the press and clapped repeatedly at his statements.

But with all the adulation, some sharp dissenting voices began to be heard. Such success was unsustainable: it is difficult to imagine the frenzy of excitement Kashpirovsky had created. His six television broadcasts were endlessly repeated through these autumn months of 1989. He raced from one public performance to another, often appearing three or four times a day and filling vast stadia where his adoring public scrambled to get in. He slept only three or four hours each night, trying to do "a hundred times as much work as I did a year ago," and began to feel the strain.

"I never used to tire of my seances," he said, "but I was tired of the fuss that accompanied them and the people around me who dragged me down. I was worn out by slander and scandal-mongering."

On the night of November 9 the citizens of Leningrad were watching Alexander Nevzorov on *600 Seconds*—a very popular nightly news programme featuring crime, corruption and sensation. Suddenly their attention was riveted by a boy in a hospital ward surrounded by doctors and crying relatives. They were stunned by the commentary: "A child has been admitted to the reanimation unit at the Leningrad Regional Children's Hospital. His serious condition, according to the doctors, had been provoked by the seances of Anatoly Kashpirovsky!" The commentary was extremely melodramatic and impressed viewers greatly. Alexander Nevzorov was celebrated for speaking out and naming names. He was going after Kashpirovsky!

When Kashpirovsky learned about Nevzorov's report, he was stunned. He respected Alexander Nevzorov as a serious journalist; Nevzorov had endeared himself to the public, particularly to "democrats", by his lively and fearless investigations. People began to change their minds about him later when his close ties to the KGB, the police and hard-liners opposed to perestroika were eventually revealed. In December 1990 he was shot and wounded at a rendez-vous with a mystery informant. Then the incident was seen as an attack on the liberal media. Afterwards his activities caused him to be branded a Russian chauvinist and reactionary.

Kashpirovsky wanted to do something to counteract the accusation but it was already too late. The following morning brought hundreds of telephone calls to the editorial offices: was it true? Desperate patients felt lost and betrayed. Others gloated, saying: "You see. We told you so. Don't you see now that Kashpirovsky is an evil force?"

The complaints started to pour in, and Kashpirovsky was blamed for just about everything. "I'm another victim of Kashpirovsky's," said P. Lugovskoi, an invalid from Leningrad who called the office of one of the Leningrad newspapers. "During the last twenty years I have called an ambulance only four times. But after the last teleseance the doctors visited me twice. Twelve other people I know of stopped watching the seances because of the insomnia caused by them. We want details; we want to know what happened to the poor child!"

Yevgeny Chazov, the minister of health, promised Kashpirovsky he would try to get to the bottom of this affair and the same evening the chief paediatrician of the Leningrad region appeared on Nevzorov's programme. "The child has been mentally sick from his early childhood," he said. "He inherited his disease from his parents. His father was an alcoholic and his mother was mentally ill." Moreover the boy had been admitted to hospital two weeks previously and had actually been in a coma at the time of the broadcasts. Alexander Nevzorov had to retract his statement.

However, despite Nevzorov's retraction, a chain reaction in the press had begun. On November 13 a favourite Leningrad programme, *Pyatoye Koleso* (*Fifth Wheel*), was on the air. This programme was regularly watched by twenty million people in and around Leningrad,

Moscow, the Baltic republics and northwest Russia. This programme —the Leningrad version of *Vzglyad*—struck viewers by its intelligent treatment of the most burning issues in a society undergoing perestroika. The *Wheel* discussed the problems of returning Afghan veterans, the maltreatment of children in orphanages, war in the Caucasus, privileges of Party apparatchiks, the decrepit Leningrad nuclear power station, details of the killing of the Tsar and his family and other issues considered political dynamite.

Pyatoye Koleso was directed by Bella Kurkova, a brave woman who led an uncompromising struggle with Yury Solovyov, First Secretary of the Leningrad regional committee, and she did a lot to support Yeltsin and Sobchak. Several attempts were made to cut the programme and sack Kurkova. But Leningraders threatened to strike and the regional committee chose not to start a conflict with the people and left Kurkova and her creation alone. *Fifth Wheel* and its director were especially respected by the intelligentsia and in academic circles.

Pavel Boon, the film producer from Kiev, had gone to *Fifth Wheel* and offered his documentary film on Kashpirovsky to its producers who specialized in dealing with paranormal phenomena. They had broadcast several programmes on UFOs, Bigfoot, poltergeists, sorcerers and other peculiar phenomena. David Remnick wrote in *Lenin's Tomb*:

> Russians have always been fascinated by extra-sensory perception and other mystical notions, and now none of the old Soviet restrictions applied any longer. The Gorbachev era was characterized by its profound sense of flux and uncertainty: old women sold copper bracelets in city parks swearing they work as a vaccine against Aids; horoscopes ran in Communist Party newspapers; the official news agency Tass announced that human-like giants and a midget robot, flying in a 'banana-shaped object', had landed in the city of Voronezh.

The *Wheel*'s producers were looking not just for sensational revelations but for the facts to support them. That's why their material was presented in the form of a debate between scientists and proponents of such paranormal phenomena. Kashpirovsky was an unlikely subject for their broadcasts. He always vehemently denied having any supernatural or extrasensory powers. "I'm just an ordinary guy. No one ever hit me over the head with a frying pan and wham! I had this ability. I worked at it. I'm a professional and I'm just good at what I do." Some of the producers believed otherwise: "We were told by some 'sorcerers' that Kashpirovsky during his seances extracts bioenergy from healthy people and gives it to the sick ones. Hence if a healthy person goes to a seance, he will come out sick! We know that teleseances are harmful and must be stopped, but what can you do, when the majority of Leningrad is pro-Kashpirovsky? Even Alexander Nevzorov could not make his criticisms stick."

Anyway, they screened Pavel Boon's film. In it Kashpirovsky looked like the devil, the personification of evil, and Pavel Boon insisted that he was showing the truth. "I was going to make a three-part documentary about Kashpirovsky. But while editing the first part, I came to the conclusion that Kashpirovsky was not what others believed him to be. I could not work with him anymore. I felt I had to tell the truth about him. You must help me open the eyes of the public!"

The film was called *According to Your Faith You Will Receive*, and from the first minute its intention was clear: a howling Kiev stadium, cordons of militia holding back the surging crowds, people driven into a frenzy at the appearance of Kashpirovsky, the piercing sound of Vysotsky's songs. The film was shot from floor level and gave Kashpirovsky a monumental, demonic image. The doctor became a dictator, mowing people down with a wave of his hand while the hypnotized audience smiled idiotically. The producer mixed real scenes with images from a German film of Walpurgisnacht, the Witches' Sabbath. Wagner's *Ride of the Valkyries* gave an expressive accompaniment to the atmosphere. This was dark and melodramatic stuff. Finally, a burning Russian ikon blazed onto the screen to suggest the satanic nature of the seance.

However, the damage done to Kashpirovsky's reputation was nothing to what followed. This was the worst blow of all. In a dramatic television interview, Lesya Yershova, the woman who had smiled and sung through her operation in Tbilisi, claimed that she had really been in agony all along. "If you only knew what that smile cost me, the songs that I started to sing to try to deaden the horrific pain which tormented me from the first minute of the operation to the last," she told the stunned audience.

Suddenly the great Kashpirovsky turned out to be a fraud, an extortioner, Satan himself. Sympathy for the doctor disappeared as if by magic. What if such a scoundrel hypnotized the whole country!

The next day the Leningrad TV centre and newspapers across the country were flooded with telegrams, telephone calls and letters. The wave of fury reached the ministry of health in Moscow and even Gorbachev. Some demanded the teleseances be stopped immediately; others called the broadcast a provocation and called on people to use their common sense: "Are we really as submissive and weak-willed as the people at the Kiev stadium? Are we really not capable of anything ourselves? Is Kashpirovsky really our only hope?" People rang from all over wanting to know the truth. Many demanded that the psychotherapist be put in a mental hospital along with his patients, or in prison.

L. Pyatiletova, a *Pravda* correspondent, interviewed Yevgeny Chazov, the minister of health. "Yevgeny Ivanovich, the readers of *Pravda* are perplexed by your silence regarding the television seances of Dr Kashpirovsky. His supporters want him to set up clinics and to train others in his method. His opponents consider him a public menace. Why is the ministry silent? Is it because you calculate that while Kashpirovsky is at work the ministry does not have to spend foreign currency on drugs and equipment? After all, it is so much cheaper to let the people believe they can heal themselves in front of their television sets."

Chazov replied: "I had a meeting with Dr Kashpirovsky. We proposed creating one or two laboratories to study him. But so far he has not agreed. Do his performances do any good? I believe they can help people who have been subjected to psycho-emotional stress, whose ailments are psychosomatic, but not that he can heal cancer. Do they do any harm? Well, Kashpirovsky is, after all, a doctor, a psychotherapist, and very careful during his performances."

Meanwhile, believing there is never smoke without fire, people began to panic. Soviet people, as always, believed everything shown on TV, the voice of indisputable authority, and many reported that their pains had come back. Those who had given up smoking or drinking as a result of the teleseances resumed their previous indulgences and blamed Kashpirovsky.

Major newspapers responded at once. As if having forgotten that they themselves had helped to create the idol, they joined in painting him black. *Literaturnaya Gazeta* devoted almost half a page to the confessions of Lesya Yershova: "The whole operation and everything connected with it was just a pack of lies. I admit I took the most active part in those lies. I was suffocating with pain but I smiled and sang. My hands were shaking, I was held down, I scratched everyone standing near the operating table. But I endured it because I really did want to help Kashpirovsky conduct an operation without drugs. I am ashamed that I have kept silent for so long; I kept on hoping that Kashpirovsky would keep his promises and take care of me. But he asked me not to pester him with my complaints and requests. I don't know what to do. Everyone trusts him. When I just mentioned that he had deceived me on *Gart* (a Ukrainian TV programme), I got a stream of threatening telephone calls."

The article was called *The Price of Sensation*. Its author, Sergey Kiselev, *Literaturnaya Gazeta*'s own correspondent for the Ukraine, added in conclusion: "Perhaps this letter will make believers in non-traditional forms of treatment sober up, and make those responsible for medical research and the health service investigate the activities of people who claim to have special powers and who perform with the approval of the authorities."

Kiselev's article was followed by another of a similar tone in *Izvestia* by Professor Leskov, in which he wrote of the Kashpirovsky phenomenon as "a sign of the collapse of ideological values, at a time when people are tired and disenchanted with existing realities. Who would argue that faith in rapid social improvements and in the humanity of science is being severely buffeted? These psychotherapists are so popular because they do, to a certain extent, fill the vacuum. The longing for old times, when one could live without taking responsibilities, is still strong." *Izvestia* argued that his therapy was negative because it induced passivity at a time when perestroika was trying to mobilize people. It created "hypnosis addiction" in his audiences and increased their all-round suggestibility.

Daily more new evidence was revealed of the damaging influence of the teleseances. "In Kiev people are queueing up to receive psychiatric help after watching Kashpirovsky on television," said a doctor in one of Kiev's psychiatric hospitals "They have been diagnosed with the so-called Kashpirovsky syndrome."

"Do you want to know what the Kashpirovsky syndrome really is?" asked Yury Kazin, a member of Parliament. "It is when people do not want to do anything. They sit in front of their TV sets and just wait for changes for the better."

Meanwhile, Kashpirovsky's seances were still in full swing and attracted even more people, many of whom were just curious to take a look at him. Kashpirovsky himself was in turmoil, though in his performances he gave no clue. "Nobody knew what I went through in those days," Kashpirovsky told me, recalling the events of 1989. "With millions of fans I still felt so lonely. There was no one to lean on. My relationship with Valentina had reached a dead end. At the age of fifty I learned that the saying 'prosperity makes friends and adversity tries them' is wrong. Prosperity tries everybody, even those closest to you. After so many years of poverty and hardship, I found out that wealth and prosperity turned her head. We stopped understanding each other.

"My mother was no longer healthy and did not want to bother me with her problems. She had an operation. And I was so busy that I overlooked the moment when I could have helped her. My life turned into a nightmare with telephone calls from grateful patients, offended patients, racketeers, extortioners, blackmailers. Some mafiosi types threatened Seryozha, my son, trying to extort money. So I, on the quiet, had to send him with a trusted friend to the Crimea for a year to live and study in Yalta and then to Poland. He would not go to bed without a gun under his pillow. I had to hire bodyguards for myself too.

"I could work twenty-four hours a day and I would never get tired. But I got tired of people and so-called friends, like Sherbachev and Belozerov, who not only turned away from me but began to act against me." (Sherbachev had taken an active part in the episode with Lesya Yershova, and Belozerov had put Chumak on the screen.) "And others—even those whom I had helped. Look at Lesya, whose life I saved. It's not easy to come to terms with treachery." Kashpirovsky felt alone and betrayed. He thought there was no one in the whole world to whom he could turn for help, no one whom he could trust.

He was mistaken. Thousands of people were ready to die for him if needed. Many of his fans sincerely believed he could cope, as he never complained or asked for pity or consolation. Kashpirovsky himself hoped that Mikhail Gorbachev would intervene and stop the attacks by journalists. He had helped Gorbachev's mother with her back problem. She was a great fan.

Olga Ignatova, the other patient from Tbilisi, appeared on Moscow TV on November 19 and pitched in: "You must leave him alone! I'm surprised that none of the journalists ever asked *me* if I had felt any pain during the operation. I can't understand why they never bothered to check with me or to ask themselves what Lesya's motives really were. I can confirm without any equivocation that I did not have any pains at all during the operation."

Help also came from an unexpected source. Six months before the fateful *Wheel* ran over Kashpirovsky, Leningrad TV had set up a new editorial board, dealing with programmes on literature and the arts, called *Lyra*. The *Lyra* producers had also seen Pavel Boon's film about Kashpirovsky, but their opinion was that the film was a deception, a piece of vulgar, unprofessional work. They did not trust Boon, who said: "I had no intention of destroying Kashpirovsky, but I was carried away by the material. Afterwards I was threatened and hunted by Kashpirovsky's people who demanded that the film be sold to them. Kashpirovsky beat me up—can you imagine that?" It all looked like a bad whodunnit. The producers Tatiana Bogdanova and Valentin Soshnikov decided to determine the truth to clear the air.

They couldn't be sure of Kashpirovsky's cooperation. "I don't think he will talk to Leningrad television. He's had enough of you," said Alexander Ivannitsky, the chief editor of the sports programmes on Ostankino TV, over the telephone. "Oh, we understand how he feels and we would like to help him. We have nothing to do with *Fifth Wheel*. We are a different programme," said Tatiana Bogdanova. They spent hours dialling his Moscow contact number, and finally Kashpirovsky came to the telephone. "I have nothing to talk about with Leningrad television!" he said tersely and hung up.

Lyra decided to try again. This time he agreed to talk. They wanted him to come to Leningrad to appear live and present his side of the story. The date was set for November 25. In the morning of November 21 they met at his hotel. But what they saw shocked them. Kashpirovsky looked completely different from the commanding presence they had seen so many times on their screens. He looked terrible, with great bags under his eyes. He smiled but the smile could not mask the feelings of hurt and confusion. "Hello!" he said. "I'm glad you could make it." Only his voice reminded them of the Kashpirovsky they knew.

"Anatoly Mikhailovich, let us help you," they said. "We'll give you three hours on the air so you can talk about anything you want without any limitations. Will that be enough?" Kashpirovsky was astounded. It appeared that Leningrad was not alone in the search for the truth about Kashpirovsky. Moscow finally responded to public opinion. Moscow philosophers, psychotherapists and journalists decided to hold a conference devoted to the phenomenon of Dr Kashpirovsky.

Psychotherapy—Limits of Reality was the title of the discussion this time. It was "the first splash in the ocean of scientific responsibility," as one of the participants called it. Anatoly Kashpirovsky did not stay for the entire discussion but gave a passionate speech in which he deplored the image that had been created of him as some sort of descendant of Hitler. Soon after his speech he excused himself and left for a seance at the Ostankino TV centre.

"We live in a country of wonders," said D. Doubrovsky, doctor of philosophy, opening the discussion. "We can be proud of ourselves: no other country offers its citizens such a variety of television services. Millions of viewers are experiencing the hypnotic boom. More than two hundred hypnotists perform in different cities today. Alan Chumak charges health-giving water in millions of flats at one go via the TV and *Vechernaya Moskva* publishes his picture, which he says has a charge that lasts ten days. V. Avdeyev performs on Moscow television and assures viewers that he is capable of training psychics and teaching them how to perform astral projection to other planets, giving them not only health but life everlasting. What's happening to us? Have we lost all sense of reality?"

In fact, Kashpirovsky received a great deal of support at this meeting while earnest professors discussed his powers. There was a lengthy debate on whether the number of deaths in Moscow had risen above the average while he broadcast his seances, whether the "psycho-ecology" of the nation was being upset. However, while the academics argued to and fro, a group of Kashpirovsky's opponents demanded that he should no longer be allowed access to the nation's television.

"I didn't find the conference useful," said Kashpirovsky. "To my mind it was simply a waste of time. I was given an opportunity to make a statement, but it was like casting pearls before swine. And they were the cream of Soviet psychotherapy." He arrived in Leningrad hoping that this time his appeal would fall on fertile ground. *Lyra* had kept its word. The programme *Bessonnitsa* (*Insomnia*) was broadcast at midnight. While Kashpirovsky was preparing to keep himself and the people of Leningrad awake, the Moscow newspaper *Sovetskaya Rossia* was publishing reports from the conference, which had ended the day before.

In Leningrad the attitude to Kashpirovsky was complex. Many people believed what had been shown on *Fifth Wheel* and thought Kashpirovsky had only himself to blame, that he was a typical star and that he did not care about his patients. "He is too rude. His fame is the only thing that matters to him." Kashpirovsky despaired of this. "I want to say that to live and work in an environment full of distrust is impossible. Why do people, even intelligent people, believe all sorts of nonsense: that I am the devil, that I cause terrible problems? How can I overcome this? Even if I give no seances and I shut myself in a room and stay there, some will say that all misfortunes are my doing. This is a true witch-hunt. What am I to do? Forgive them for they know not what they do."

Before *Insomnia*, the *Lyra* programme, was broadcast, Kashpirovsky had to meet Academician Natalia Bekhtereva, head of the Institute of Experimental Medicine. She agreed to take part in *Insomnia* on condition that Kashpirovsky came to see her before they went on the air. She used to support him but, after all the allegations, she wanted to know the truth. Kashpirovsky appreciated her support and valued her judgement more than that of any other colleagues.

At the institute a crowd of more than three hundred people

wanted to talk to Kashpirovsky, instead of the fifty who were expected. After a general discussion, Kashpirovsky and Bekhtereva spent an hour talking privately, discussing possible cooperation in the future.

On the day of the broadcast, scientists, doctors, psychologists and lawyers came to the studio. Apart from Bekhtereva and Kashpirovsky, there were the sociologist M. Mezhevich (doctor of philosophical sciences), the famous Leningrad lawyer Y. Gilinsky (doctor of jurisprudence), P. Bul and B. Karvasarsky (both doctors of medical sciences), the surgeon Academician G. Ioseliani from Tbilisi and Olga Ignatova, on whom he had operated. The second patient, Lesya Yershova, who had "betrayed" him, did not come.

Valentin Soshnikov presented the programme. Then the camera focussed on Kashpirovsky. The city of Leningrad and about half of the Soviet Union saw a man worn out by troubles. He looked shrivelled under the lights and at first his speech came haltingly. He was obviously nervous. But then he pulled himself together.

The programme began with video material taken by the journalist Mark Rivkin during the operation in Tbilisi. The producers invited some surgeons from Leningrad clinics, and to their surprise the surgeons got really excited about what they were seeing. Ioseliani, the surgeon who performed the operation, and Kashpirovsky were showered with questions: What kind of preparation was there before the operation? How had the patients been chosen? How did the post-operative period go? They asked Olga Ignatova if she had felt any pain during the operation. She repeated that she had not.

At this point someone stood up in the middle of the audience and said: "Comrades, be on your guard! Kashpirovsky is hypnotizing us and the viewers!" "I'm not here to hypnotize anybody, but to tell the truth about myself," interjected Kashpirovsky. "I want to emphasize that my work is not limited to hypnosis alone; I use the technique of *ustanovka* as a means of affecting the functional systems of the human body. I was blamed for asking people to read out testimonials. The reading of telegrams and success stories at the beginning of a session has nothing to do with self-advertisement. The aim here is to create an atmosphere that will be conducive to the realization of my *ustanovka*."

Professor Pavel Bul, author of the book *The Technique of Hypnosis and Suggestion*, spoke at length: "I thought of using hypnosis via television back in the 1960s. I was invited to the Leningrad studio to demonstrate some of my hypnotic abilities. My colleague and I suggested that viewers should clench their fists and then release them at our command. Everything seemed fine. But then hundreds of telephone calls came to the Leningrad TV station. It turned out that many people had exceptionally high suggestibility. They were not able to unclench their fingers on their own. All night long we had to go round the town to free the victims. This innocent experiment demonstrated how television healing could turn out." He also spoke about the necessity of feedback. "Television seances lack a personal contact that is an essential condition for a psychotherapist to communicate with a patient. Doctors should never forget the main law of medicine: not to harm the patient. The doctor must be aware of the effect of his treatment at all times."

Professor Bul also said that he himself had tried out everything that today had become known as Kashpirovsky's miracles both in surgery and in the treatment of medical conditions. "I could give a long list of diseases and operations with successful results and any number of examples on how hypnosis can be carried out at a distance by a variety of means: telephone, radio, tape-recorder, or just by an ordinary photograph or letter."

Then Natalia Bekhtereva spoke. "Kashpirovsky has a special gift which needs to be studied. What is necessary are experiments that will evaluate the changes in the bodies of his patients and, perhaps, in Kashpirovsky's body as well. He is a talented doctor and in our institute I witnessed how he helped patients with serious brain disorders. We did blood analyses before and after his treatment and found changes in blood chemistry and electrical brain activity. I'm sure this deserves thorough research. I believe we could work together." Her support surprised many. Kashpirovsky felt at ease—she had a considerable reputation and not only in medical circles.

Although *Insomnia* was on the air for more than three hours, the city of Leningrad watched it right to the end. Though Leningrad academic circles did not display much enthusiasm for it, the staff of *Lyra* had achieved what they had been after—the support of the public.

Again a torrent of letters arrived at the television studio the day after the programme. These were almost all expressions of gratitude and support. The viewers who did not believe Lesya Yershova's story were united in an urge to defend Kashpirovsky. Many were affected by the way he had answered the question: "Don't you feel lonely in spite of all your talents?" For a moment everything became still. One could hear the crackling of projector lights. Kashpirovsky paused and took a deep breath. Then he said: "Yes, I am lonely. At times I have the feeling that I live on a razor's edge." People were touched and demanded that Kashpirovsky should be left alone and given an opportunity to continue his work.

"Now I know that in Leningrad I have lots of friends," said Kashpirovsky to the producers of *Lyra*. "I'll give you a ring from Kiev to let you know how things are going. OK?" "Come to Leningrad soon!" they asked him. "Yes, I'll be back in January. We are planning to begin our work with Natalia Bekhtereva." The *Lyra* producers were sure they had finally won the argument. They were wrong.

Despite the success of the programme, reports of people traumatized by Kashpirovsky continued to appear in the newspapers, sufferers from the "Kashpirovsky syndrome". It was claimed that people had fallen into spontaneous trance at the sound of his voice and would stay in this state for hours, sometimes for days. Kashpirovsky's opponents warned of a "psychic epidemic". A special appearance on national television was broadcast so that he could clear these unhappy somnambulists of their condition. But eventually the ministry of health banned his teleseances pending further elucidation of his results. To make things even worse *Argumenty i Facty*, the newspaper known as the voice of perestroika, published extracts from some of Kashpirovsky's many interviews with an extremely pointed bias, for example: "The whole country can be made to roar with laughter ... Everything can be made to collapse" or "I have learned about crowds like no one else has. I have no rivals in manipulating crowds, in achieving what I want." And even more: "Naturally, these are distractions from the acute problems of everyday life. But perhaps that is not so bad after all? From that point of view my performances are political acts" and so on. Kashpirovsky had never learnt to be diplomatic, often put his foot in it and with his impatience and lack of unction put many people's backs up.

Lyra prepared to launch itself into battle once again. The producers asked Kashpirovsky to come to Leningrad and told him they were ready to help. They organized a conference, to be televised, which attracted journalists from all over the country. On February 5, 1990, Kashpirovsky flew into Leningrad. He telephoned Tatiana Bogdanova: "I have just arrived from Narodichi, a small town near Chernobyl. The level of radiation is crazy. They eat food grown in radioactive soil and drink contaminated water. Horses are being born with eight legs. Horrible! And it seems that nobody cares. There are still children there. I was intending to conduct several seances for the sick but because of poor organization, they were not publicized. But still, I had some creditable results. And the flowers! I've never seen so many flowers. They brought me so many that they filled the hotel corridor with them. I could hardly walk through." He was so moved by the plight of the children there that later, at his own expense, he transferred fifty children from Chernobyl to Poland for treatment.

More importantly for *Lyra* he had brought with him his trump card—Lesya Yershova. She was prepared to make a public recantation. "She had once more appealed to me for help. She needed to have a tooth removed, and I could not refuse her—after all I am her doctor," said Kashpirovsky.

This was one of the oddest programmes ever shown on television. Kashpirovsky sat at a table flanked by the *Lyra* producers. The studio was crammed with journalists. Lesya was in the front row facing him, and when questioned, retracted everything she had said and claimed she had been misunderstood and bullied. She had never really meant to say she was in pain. She claimed to have been upset that Kashpirovsky had had no time for her after the operation, that she felt rejected and hurt. "If I had been asked what was the happiest moment of my life, I would have said when I was cut open and felt no pain." After the operation she had "consulted people who turned out to be enemies of Anatoly Mikhailovich. I turned to Valentin Sherbachev, who I thought was his friend. But he didn't even hear me out. He just turned the camera on me and I was told to say what I had to say and to say it quickly. I said too much."

Listening to this "repentant Magdalene", journalists could hardly control their indignation. They could not believe that someone could be capable of such treachery. Lesya nodded her head and mumbled apologies.

She was a troubled woman, clearly so suggestible that she could have been influenced by anyone at any time. Her voice and manner were those of a confused little girl and when questioned she contradicted herself at every turn. Kashpirovsky's own judgement at having allowed her to become his patient for such an important operation must be questioned. She was certainly madly in love with him, and during the interview it was difficult to say who looked more hurt and wounded, she or Kashpirovsky.

At the end of the programme, Kashpirovsky looked weary. "I'm tired of all the lies," he said, "I'm ready to give up." But he and the *Lyra* team, the journalists and the many thousands of viewers felt he had been vindicated. Dr Ioseliani, who had performed the operation, had always stated categorically that it would have been quite impossible for Lesya Yershova to have undergone such extensive surgery—it took two and a half hours—if she had felt any pain. He would have known immediately.

The programme provoked another huge response, a great wave of support for Kashpirovsky and his television seances. But a couple of days later Kashpirovsky was in deep trouble again. This time he was being accused of rape, and a court case had already been instigated. The newspapers were full of it.

Kommersant wrote:

> On January 28 Mrs V. came to Kashpirovsky's last seance. According to her, she managed to talk to him and thanked him for a successful treatment. She claims that Kashpirovsky offered her an individual seance in his hotel room. At about nine o'clock she was standing outside his door among a crowd of his devotees who evidently didn't leave even at night. Then two people in white coats appeared from nowhere and took her into his room. A minute later the only clothes still on her were her boots. Mrs V. considers the most likely reason to have been hypnosis. She recovered from the trance in about an hour, outside the door, where she remembered that she had been sexually abused. As a result the statement of Mrs V., aged forty-eight and mother of three children, was lying on the prosecutor's desk. Her husband at that time was at sea. On the same day at noon Kashpirovsky left the town.

In *Komsomolskaya Pravda* the correspondent V. Kosyak expressed his opinion about these events:

> It is hard to believe that such a famous personality would risk his reputation so thoughtlessly. We will let you know as soon as the truth is established.

Kosyak had obtained his information from the prosecutor's office at Mariupol, where proceedings had been started against Kashpirovsky.

The country was divided. Some said that this proved how evil he really was, others that the woman was just another hysterical fan desperate for attention. Kashpirovsky flew back to Mariupol to talk to the chief prosecutor. According to some accounts he was completely unable to cope with the situation calmly and diplomatically, became incredibly rude and told the prosecutor to shove his accusations up his arse. He swore that the woman was mad and denied the charges in the strongest possible terms. He said he was not even in his hotel at the time, a claim later confirmed by his secretary, that there were no men in white coats and that he had never even met this woman.

There were hints of some sort of financial scandal involving Kashpirovsky and the sponsors of his performances in Mariupol. Enormous profits were rumoured to have been made—five hundred thousand roubles by the city cooperative alone, an enormous sum at that time—and the president of the city council was reprimanded. Many considered the rape story to have been part of a plot by local racketeers to extort money from Kashpirovsky. Others suggested that some kind of deal between him and his alleged victim had gone wrong and that they had fallen out as a result. A story circulated that two of the woman's sons, both with dubious connections, had offered to persuade their mother to drop charges in exchange for a nice new motorcar.

Though irritated by Kashpirovsky's manner, the prosecutor did drop the case shortly afterwards. But yet again his reputation had been badly damaged. While all these accusations and passions raged, with a typically perverse sense of timing, he left for America.

The trip to the United States was his first journey beyond Soviet borders. He performed in front of emigrés in New York, San

Francisco and Chicago. He enjoyed great success but was constantly pursued by the rape story and anxieties over his financial affairs. He became persuaded that he was being exploited, that he was losing out somewhere. Having worked his way through a succession of managers, his tours were now organized by Michael Zimmerman, who arranged for him to meet Mohammed Ali, the highlight of his trip. Kashpirovsky's visit abroad was ignored in the Soviet press. Even information sent by the Tass correspondent in America about his visit to the United Nations was not mentioned. He had given a press conference there to the NGOs (non-governmental organizations) on his plan to set up a clinic for sick children from Chernobyl. "I was told that during the seventy days of my absence, nothing was mentioned about my tour. In America I received proposals from American doctors to discuss the possibility of doing research on the dissolution of scar tissue. I declined this type of cooperation only because I really want to do this work in my own country."

Then in April he was off to Israel, where there was already a long history of interest in hypnosis and hypnotherapy. The Israelis took him seriously, and he felt wanted and needed again. "When I was in Israel, I liked it very much. I often think warmly about my visit to the Promised Land, about the benevolence and hospitality of the emigrés. I had such a wonderful rest there and I loved the people so much I did not want to leave them. Maybe because of that some idiot writing an article in *Ogonyok* called me a Zionist. As to the anti-semitic mood that exists now in Russia and the Ukraine, that will go on and even perestroika will not destroy it. There has always been a fifth column stirring people up against the Jews. I don't like it."

On leaving Israel he flew to Poland. "If there is one piece of news that has depressed Russians even more than the austerities forecast in President Gorbachev's economic reform plan, it is confirmation that the psychotherapist Anatoly Kashpirovsky and his family have emigrated to Poland," wrote *The Times* of London on November 1, 1990. "Kashpirovsky is idolized by millions of Russians for his calming late-night television performances. With his penetrating gaze, he adjures careworn Russians to relax, cast off their troubles and be kind to their neighbours. Strangely, perhaps, Kashpirovsky's choice of Poland for his new home has distressed people as much, if not more, than the rumour of his emigration. There is a ready understanding of why someone successful might want to emigrate to the West—but to Poland?"

"These journalists are completely out of their minds," responded Kashpirovsky. "One day they blame me for the deaths of people in Moscow, then they criticize me for emigrating."

Vesta, an insurance company in Lodz, invited Kashpirovsky to Poland. Seances were arranged not only in Lodz but also in Vrotslav, Gdansk, Poznan and at major venues in Warsaw. He met Lech Walensa on various occasions. "So many journalists crowded into his office that, to tell the truth, I felt uncomfortable," Kashpirovsky remembered. "On the whole the reception I was given struck me by its informality and lack of red tape. Walensa thanked me for helping him to get rid of his back pains. He showed genuine interest in psychotherapy and suggested that appropriate conditions should be created in Poland to conduct essential scientific research. I received a completely serious invitation from him of permanent residence in Poland. 'Solidarity,' Walensa said to me, 'will always keep solidarity with you in times of triumph and in black days of failure. It's spring in Poland now and I'm happy that the shoots of friendship between Poles and the Soviet people, of whom you are the embodiment, have been sown in genuinely favourable soil.'"

Poland received Kashpirovsky as one of her own, remembering that he was Polish on his mother's side. There was a real pilgrimage to his seances: they came to be healed, they came from all over, from Germany, Czechoslovakia and Bulgaria. Discussion programmes began to appear on television, with scientists, specialists and doctors taking part. As ticket prices were high, at Walensa's request Kashpirovsky gave some charity seances for working families who were not well off. The meetings were held, in the main, in Catholic churches where, for the first time, as one of the priests remarked, the Russian language was heard. In contrast to his experiences in Russia, Kashpirovsky's relationship with the priesthood in Poland was good. The seances began with prayers and ceremonial singing, and they ended in the same way. As everywhere else, *talantlivy*—"talented patients", as Kashpirovsky called them, those who had overcome disease—came to the microphone to talk about their cures.

He was awarded the Viktor prize—the award given to the most popular people on Polish television. Among holders of the award were Pope John-Paul II and Lech Walensa.

During one of the seances in Sopot, before an audience of five thousand, a woman brought flowers to Kashpirovsky. She had just thrown away the walking-stick with which she had walked for many years and was coming to thank him. But he asked her to place the flowers on the grave of the unknown Russian soldier instead of giving them to him. Silence fell in the hall, for this was the period when the Soviet embassy in Warsaw was being stoned and the monuments and graves of Soviet troops were being destroyed. Kashpirovsky thought he also would be stoned, but instead of this, applause broke out. He realized that he had gauged the mood of his Catholic audience correctly—they considered the desecration of graves to be immoral. There were articles about this incident in the Polish press, but not a word appeared in the Soviet press.

He flew off to Czechoslovakia and then to Bulgaria, where he was met as a VIP. He was warmly received by the prime minister, Dimitr Petrov. He also met with his colleagues, Bulgarian psychotherapists. He knew that in Bulgaria there had always been much interest in hypnosis and suggestology.

Despite some philosophical differences, discussion was cordial. They shared the opinion that suggestion is a method of reaching and making use of the unknown reserves, powers and abilities of the human mind. One of the great pioneers in the field was the Bulgarian doctor Georgi Lozanov, who had been working with patients since the 1960s. He was director of the Institute of Suggestology and Parapsychology in Sofia. Kashpirovsky was shown the film of the first operation using Lozanov's methods, which had taken place in Bykovo in August 1965. He was told Lozanov also had had problems after the operation. His work too had aroused much criticism. A commission was set up. About a thousand doctors attended to see films of the operation, to debate and to discuss the procedure. After these discussions Lozanov brought out the patient, who told them how satisfied he was. Three years after the operation he was still in splendid condition. And so Lozanov was left alone.

Whenever Kashpirovsky returned home from his travels he always looked carefully at what had been written about him in the press. It was said that he had gone to the West to make a fast buck, and it was hinted that he might stay permanently in some well-fed foreign country. But for some reason or other no mention was made of the fact that his appearances abroad had attracted thousands of people, nor that there were no complaints about his influence being harmful. The press kept quiet also about his appearances in Chernobyl and Nagorno-Karabakh and other flashpoints in his country.

Kashpirovsky went to Kafan, a small settlement not far from Nagorno-Karabakh on February 7. "There was so much snow that the roads were dangerous. Early in the morning we left from Yerevan and arrived in Kafan very late at night. The mountains were so high that at times our road passed above the clouds. When we arrived we were met by armed people. We did not know then that in a few days our guards would be shot. Only Ashot and Arthur, who accompanied us everywhere and did not stay in Kafan, have survived. On the next day our host, the chief militiaman, who had under his command men who barely knew how to hold a weapon, took us for a ride to see the border between Armenia and Azerbaijan. He was a Ukrainian in the middle of this ethnic conflict. His name was Yury.

I went to Kafan because some time earlier they had asked me to perform for the survivors of the Leninakan earthquake. Kafan was the epicentre of the war between the Armenians and the Azeris—a very troubled place. So I understood that I could not refuse. I did not want people to think I was afraid. I said to my friends: 'I cannot make you go. Only those who really want to come should do so.' So there were few people with me.

"Before we left Kafan for Yerevan, the local head of the administration invited us to dinner. 'Now you must go to Azerbaijan,' he whispered into my ear. I liked the people there, the way they try to sort things out. I did not give them any kind of advice. I did not want to interfere with their problems. But I did say that the war was caused by the leadership of the country.

"When we returned to Yerevan I had to perform in a hall for nine thousand people, but it was packed to overflowing. I performed in my usual black poloneck, in spite of the extreme cold. The temperature inside was minus five degrees. And I did not want to put on anything extra to show I was feeling the cold. I thought of my audience, who had to live under such terrible circumstances. After three hours I froze to death. The next day they put two heating stoves under my table. I was so involved with my performance and warmed by a nice warmth from under the table that I did not realize that something was going wrong. Suddenly I noticed smoke. My trousers were on fire.

"People were sitting there covered with blankets. Then the electricity went off. For two hours they sat there with no electricity, but no one left. That performance lasted about six hours.

"After that we went to Leninakan. Families were living in small huts and tents. It was extremely cold. They used candles because there was no electricity. Mikhail Sergeyevich Gorbachev had made many promises but nothing had been done. I gave my performance in the theatre, the only building that had survived the earthquake. Everything else had been destroyed."

7

In His Own Words

The conscious mind may be compared to a fountain playing in the sun and falling back into the great subterranean pool of the subconscious from which it arose.

(Sigmund Freud)

*I*n January 1991 a conference in Kiev investigated Kashpirovsky's work. Participants tried to get to the bottom of his medico-psychotherapeutic activity, as their colleagues in Moscow and Leningrad had tried before them. But this time a real attempt was made to achieve some understanding of the facts, in so far as they could be agreed upon, and to establish a basis for further research.

The conference was attended by two hundred and twenty-five participants from various parts of the Soviet Union, Australia, Austria, Poland and Sweden. Among them were representatives from the scientific community, the government, the clergy and the media.

Kashpirovsky had set up a department to codify statistical evidence of his cures at the International Psychotherapeutic Centre, which he sponsored, in Kiev. "I had to organize the centre, because I was receiving an enormous amount of mail. At times there were a hundred and fifty to two hundred thousand letters per month. I consider it valid medical evidence when people themselves state that after watching my teleseances, they were rid of some disease. I know the scientific community says this is merely anecdotal, but even so this huge weight of evidence cannot just be brushed aside. People write from all over the Soviet Union and abroad."

By the beginning of 1991, when 1,126,000 letters had been received, Kashpirovsky joked that he was a candidate for the *Guinness Book of Records*. Such a huge amount of mail was enormously encouraging, but it also created problems. Kashpirovsky hoped the medical authorities in Moscow or Kiev would be interested in reading these letters or at least in providing him with help to analyse them. But no one seemed interested.

S. Krivushenko, from Kashpirovsky's centre, presented a summary of the results:

> We [a team of fifteen people] analysed 451,118 letters received from those who watched the teleseances. Among them 183,128 contained definite information about the effects of healing; 178,349 or 97.6 percent reported favourable results; 395 or 0.5 percent negative results and 3,960 or 2.17 percent no effect.
>
> After five seances on Ukrainian television we received 36,200 letters. Because the seances concentrated on the healing of enuresis, we received 6,500 letters concerning this ailment. Of them 4,066 or 62.5 percent reported total healing, and 2,399 or 36.9 percent reported no improvement in the condition, 35 letters or 0.5 percent contained information about side-effects. Seven thousand other letters reported healings of various diseases.
>
> Analysis of the results at a live performance conducted in Moscow and Kiev is based on the return of questionnaires given out. In total we received 4,017 questionnaires; among them 95 percent reported positive results and 3.9 percent no results. Negative results were reported by 1.1 percent. After six seances conducted over national television we received 382,000 letters. Positive results were reported by 147,852 or 38.6 percent, negative results were reported by 337 or 0.09 percent. More than 230,000 letters were requests for the continuation of the television seances.

L. Yunda, director of the International Psychotherapeutic Centre in Kiev, said:

> I started to work at the centre established by A. Kashpirovsky

three years ago. During this period the centre treated 15,911 patients. The most numerous group had neurotic disorders; the second, allergic and skin diseases; the third, joint problems; and the fourth, cardiovascular problems.

Treatment was conducted using three methods of patient selection. In the first group, the control group, selected patients were chosen nosologically [classified by disease]. They were treated by conventional psychotherapeutic methods. The second group was a mixed group and the treatment was by Kashpirovsky, using his method of influencing the subcortical centre. The third group used Kashpirovsky's method and augmented it with auto-rehabilitation programmes, which consisted of healing sessions and exercises at home. We analysed the results. In the control group 67.7 percent had a positive effect, 31.6 percent no effect and 0.8 percent had negative results. In the second group 83.2 percent had positive results, 16.6 percent no effect and 0.3 percent negative effects. In the third group 91 percent had positive effects, 8.8 percent no effect and 0.2 percent negative results.

We paid special attention to the negative results. The patients who had the highest percentage of negative or no effect belonged to the group with neurotic disorders. Among other groups negative results were an order of magnitude lower. The conclusion is that psychotherapy should be limited in the presence of psychological pathology.

Kashpirovsky then continued: "I have learned from my bitter experience in dealing with the national press and medical circles in the capital, and so I have prepared myself in advance for this report. I will try to take into account all the main bones of contention." He analysed speeches by scientists in Moscow and Leningrad and also criticism by journalists. In 1990 alone more than forty articles criticized him. He realized that the high percentage of success in his work did not convince the specialists, and that without the support of the medical authorities and without a sympathetic attitude by the administrative authorities, he would lose everything he had created, despite his tremendous popularity. The ministry of health, having banned his teleseances, was now threatening to close down his public performances, much to the disgust of the wider public, who read all kinds of nefarious political double-dealing into the move. Kashpirovsky felt that Gorbachev himself might have been behind the ban on television seances. In a speech Gorbachev had said he was not like Kashpirovsky—he couldn't cure the nation with a click of his fingers. There were suggestions that the leader felt the seances distracted people from concentrating on the political realities of their situation.

Kashpirovsky understood that the evidence of his own eyes and the testimony of his patients was insufficient for the Moscow and Leningrad professors. He felt he had to try to convince them, to communicate what he knew to be the truth. He wanted the statistics, so painstakingly collected at the Kiev centre, to be put into the equation so that an unbiased evaluation could take place. Of course these statistics were open to as much doubt as any other subjective evidence, but they did at least suggest that many thousands of people genuinely believed they had benefited from his influence. Kashpirovsky's own belief in himself, in the reality of his method and the veracity of the evidence of these cures, was absolute.

He found it particularly hard that he had received such adverse notices in the Russian press, which seemed to discount all his achievements but was only too eager to jump on any hint of a problem. "Not a single visitor to my seances in the USA, Poland, Israel or elsewhere abroad has ever accused me of attempting to ruin his or her health nor the health of the nation. Polish television received 850,000 letters, and 65 percent reported positive results. Strange as it may seem, people did not blame me if healing had not taken place." But in Russia the press was not ready to give him its support; it would not publish any articles he wrote.

He needed to provide himself with some kind of platform from which he could address his detractors and present his case. In his speech to the conference he not only tried to answer his critics, but summed up his own ideas about his psychotherapeutic methodology, till now scattered in various utterances.

"This is my first opportunity to speak to the scientific community, to the people who really understand what telepsychotherapy is all about," he began. "For a long time it has been considered that psychotherapy has its own well-defined parameters. In my opinion this is wrong. The certainty that present psychotherapeutic methods and approaches are not subject to any kind of change or doubt has for a long time kept psychotherapy within very tight and restricted boundaries and deprived it of any prospect for development. In our country this kind of system can be seen in personality-oriented, reconstructive psychotherapy with its individual, family or group approaches and its corresponding methods of verbal and non-verbal suggestion.

"Thanks to television psychotherapeutic seances, psychotherapy in the Soviet Union has been raised, over the last three years, to a previously unknown height. Hundreds of millions of citizens of our own country and the countries of Europe have participated in these programmes. This boom in psychotherapy has spread across the oceans to the USA, Australia and other countries.

"I worked in the same place for twenty-five years, at a psychiatric hospital and for more than twenty years I appeared with the Znanie society, demonstrating so-called psychological experiments. People were not satisfied with just listening to lectures about the work of I. M. Sechenov, V. M. Bekhterev and I. P. Pavlov and hearing about complicated neurological phenomena. They wanted to see for themselves what could be done. At first these lectures were called Hypnosis and Suggestion, later they became known as The Secrets of the Human Psyche, and I moved further and further away from the common, narrow understanding of psychotherapy. I am not afraid of exaggerating when I say that psychotherapy in our country is sick with hypnosis. For many people the word psychotherapy means hypnosis. Looking back at the past, I am glad that I stopped using hypnotic suggestion, just as, in his day, Sigmund Freud had rejected it.

"I have abandoned the dogmas which overload our psychotherapeutic science. There are various schools, various directions and approaches, but the essence is the same. All psychotherapeutic schools, including our Soviet schools, are basically concerned with curing neuroses. One needs only to open any book on psychotherapy to be convinced of this. There you will read that only diseases like hysteria, neurasthenia, neurotic fears, harmful habits and insomnia can be cured by means of psychotherapy. A few books will mention that psychotherapy can cure hypertension, stomach ulcers, some forms of bronchial asthma and skin diseases, and nothing else! If you want to know what can cure hernia and how, you'll be directed to look in textbooks on surgery. As for gynaecological diseases, ovarian cysts, blocked fallopian tubes, fibroids, erosion or prolapse of the uterus, you will find treatment described only in the appropriate gynaecological, oncological or surgical textbooks.

"If you touch on vascular disease then, again, you will not find the slightest reference to them in any psychotherapy textbook because psychotherapy has been concerned with only one thing, the treatment of functional diseases. No wonder, since the method of suggestion always had the same approach: to influence one's consciousness. For example, a person experiences fear. They say to him: 'You no longer feel fear, you can do this, that or the other.' But this is an appeal to the conscious mind.

"We talk about the huge possibilities of the human psyche, but often we use examples which are just conjurers' tricks. When people talk about the possibilities of the human psyche, they refer to people who can walk barefoot on glass or burning coals, or who can multiply six-figure numbers in their heads. We talk about and we argue about telepathic capabilities and many other things. But we don't often talk about the unlimited possibilities of a person's influence over his own body.

"So, can a person influence his own body? Let's suppose that someone has developed a tumour in the stomach. Will not the patient turn to all the saints and to everything on earth in order to be cured? Does he not entreat, beseech, threaten this tumour, does he not get down on his knees in front of it? And the result? It's always the same, as a rule, the tumour wins.

"The conscious mind is not always successful in influencing the body, not in the way we would want it to. At the same time we constantly talk about the psyche and the nervous system of a person governing everything in that person, and this is wholly true. But, nevertheless, how does the nervous system carry out this control?

"I consider the work of Sigmund Freud as the basis for this knowledge, for he wrote a great deal about the unconscious and the subconscious. There is, of course, conscious influence and control and there is the whole sphere of unconsciousness. According to Pavlov all animal behaviour is based on conditioned and unconditioned reflexes, on unconscious reactions. Thus, for example, a bee builds its honeycomb, and an ant its anthill and so on. I would like to look at some simple examples to show the great role of the subconscious, and then apply this to the human sphere.

"It has been noted how spontaneously the inhibition of reproduction takes place in a cage, in captivity. Animals do not reproduce because they see steel bars, although they don't think about this. Their life experience, stored in the genetic memory, in the subconscious sphere, gives them the information that they must not reproduce. And this powerful, reliable information about bars, cages and other confined spaces, which their ancestors also had experienced, inhibits their subconscious reproductive function. Such is the strength of subconscious suggestion. With this in mind, I developed my own direction for psychotherapy, which has as its base the powerful influence of the subconscious on the body.

"My work implies the influence of the subconscious through the conscious. The conscious is the anteroom leading to that mysterious room where the subconscious is concealed. It must not be bypassed, since that is where the *ustanovka* is formed. Many scientists, including Freud, understood this intuitively. Even hypnosis was an attempt to distract the conscious mind in order to reach the subconscious.

"Suggestion reaches us, according to V. M. Bekhterev, not through the front door, but through the back entrance, once the watchful caretaker, the critical mind, has been removed. Is this not the origin of the hypnotic trend in psychotherapy in our country? But the error lay precisely in the fact that 'criticism' had to be removed through hypnosis. Therefore, psychotherapy became more and more closely linked to hypnotherapy, because consciousness does not disappear in a hypnotized subject but simply takes on a new form, possibly a narrower one. If the conscious is influenced, then it is not because the person has fallen asleep, but because a powerful *ustanovka* has been induced to activate some sort of program in our biocomputer, our nervous system. When Freud assessed the unconscious, he did not sense its full depth, because he directed his powerful mind to find a treatment for mental illness and created the theory and practice of psychoanalysis. Is it possible to apply psychoanalysis to the treatment of hernia, tumours, commissural disease? No, it is not. Psychoanalysis is used to treat neuroses. Moreover, this must be done *tête-à-tête*, since the patient unburdens himself to the doctor and involuntarily reveals his problems. Freud partially opened the door to the subconscious but he did not give many patients an opportunity to get rid of somatic diseases by psychotherapeutic means.

"I consider that the most important part of my work lies in influencing the subconscious and the body, via the conscious. We have a large number of cases where hernias disappeared after psychotherapy sessions, and not just simple umbilical hernias but more complicated ones, such as inguinal, diaphragmatic, oesophageal. There has been a mass phenomenon of dissolution of scars and scar tissue. But what sort of mechanism is present in these cases? We know that the pharmacological preparation lidase, which is of animal origin, can affect cellular tissue, dissolving or reducing it. But it will work only on newly formed scars. Old cellular scar formations remain unchanged. Therefore the search for causative effects on scars, irrespective of the time of their formation, is important. The possibility of affecting cellular tissue by psychotherapy is very important.

"Everyone remembers the day when that famous surgeon Christian Barnard carried out his first heart transplant. Mankind breathed a sigh of relief. At last a way had been found to get a new heart. But where could such a number of hearts be found? And how complicated was the care of the patient with the transplanted heart! No one could possibly have imagined, years ago, that such a thing was possible. Such a lengthy and difficult procedure! But when we began to receive letters from patients who described recovery from heart attacks after attending seances, who had evidence that their internal scars had begun to disappear, doctors just would not believe it.

"I consider that psychotherapeutic work with the mechanisms of connective and other types of tissue has great prospects. For example, elements of connective, muscular and endothelial tissue are present in blood vessels and also in their walls. We have thousands of examples of the varicose dilation of veins disappearing in many patients, and the curing of chronic thrombophlebitis. How can one help but not devote some thought to this? Finally, chest pains cease. All this has important scientific significance. I consider that the processes of reparation and physiological regeneration of endothelial, muscular and connective tissues should be thoroughly researched. As we have already isolated lidase from animal tendons to facilitate the dissolution of new scars, then, evidently, it is worth searching for biochemical substances that a human can produce, which can affect old cellular scars. Indeed, we have all known for a long time that a group of biologically active substances, with their own distinct medicinal forms, are produced within the human body.

"Four groups of these substances have been isolated within the organism. The first are antibodies. Hormones were discovered next. The third group comprises the prostaglandins; interferon is a prostaglandin. Note that all these groups are derived from the organism. The fourth group of substances are those which can be derived under dynamic conditions—as a result of psychological influence. The best examples are drugs which can increase physiological strength, ability to work and endurance. These substances can stimulate other functions of the body and psychic and even morphological changes.

"The number of diseases susceptible to psychotherapeutic treatment is huge. I never imagined that the first seances in the Ukraine, which were intended for children suffering from enuresis, would produce such a large number of cures from other somatic diseases. A large amount of documentary evidence exists and from it selected facts must be isolated. Many diseases have been cured which competent psychologists, doctors and specialists in their fields considered incurable.

"Quite a long time ago, I gave public lectures and seances and I drew people's attention to the huge number of people who came to me asking for cures of somatic diseases. Why would they come to me, old ladies requesting cures for blindness or some other organic disease, vascular, osteo, hernial diseases, tumours and so on? I believe that it was not only wishful thinking, but that in their subconscious lay the unique information that such a cure was possible. Time and again I saw myself that fracture marks would disappear without trace, or that osseous growths would dissolve.

"I will give you an example. I was in Uzbekistan. A young man in the audience got up and said: 'I am Rafat Reskiev, former world boxing champion, classified as an invalid.' X-rays had shown that he had sustained multiple fractures to his hands. He said: 'After your psychotherapy teleseances I was taken out of the invalid category, as X-rays showed no traces of the former fractures.' There are many such examples. Our very tissues and our bones, which are considered to be far less developed than the brain and which belong to an earlier stage of our evolution as human beings, are the best reagents. The *ustanovka* bypasses the conscious mind and reacts directly with the cells of the body, activating their genetic knowledge."

It is worth noting here that now Kashpirovsky no longer uses the word *ustanovka* to describe this process, considering that it has too many connotations. He prefers, simply, to use the word "information". He gives his audience, his patients, "information", which allows them to access the "information" in their own bodies. In fact he seems, intuitively and in non-scientific language, to be moving towards a fundamentally scientific understanding of the nature of life. DNA molecules, the building blocks of life, are nothing but coded information. He seems to be suggesting that he works by somehow activating processes at this level.

"Soviet psychotherapy considers the brain as the best reagent. However, I am convinced that it is not. Moreover, its reactions are temporary. Therefore any progress achieved with the help of psychotherapy does not last long. It will be temporary. For example, today a patient is irritable; tomorrow, as a result of treatment his irritability goes away; but the day after tomorrow it comes back again! But if a scar has disappeared, why should it appear again? When a cataract has dissolved, why should it come back? It appeared in the first place as a result of a trauma or inflammation. Therefore, in this case, our achievements are permanent, since they are connected with the soma and not with functional disorders of the nervous system.

"People believe that lipomas, fatty tumours, new but benign formations, are incurable and that surgery is the only form of treatment. In fact there is one route to be followed: a person must be approached from within, he must be relieved of disease by natural means, by stimulating his own remarkable sources. Deliverance from diseases—incurable ones, somatic in many cases—by natural means is my greatest achievement. This achievement does not belong to me only, but to an evolutionary process in modern psychotherapy and psychology. This is the direction in which we should all be moving.

"We do know a lot about ourselves, but there is a lot we do not know. We know what is accessible to our conscious mind, our analysis, our eyes, our hands. Suppose there is a stomach tumour. It is still as small as a poppy seed. Do we know this? We do and we don't. We do not know because as yet it has not begun to cause us problems. We will find out about the tumour only later, when the X-ray is taken, when there is a disturbance in the function of an organ and we experience pain. But when there are no obvious disturbances in physical function, how are we to guess at its existence? All the same we do have knowledge of a sort. Our body knows and has already started to take certain steps. Here there is no connection between this knowledge that the body has and the conscious mind.

"But suppose the following experiment is performed. We irritate the little tumour with a probe introduced into the stomach. Will it be painful? It will. This means there is a link between this tumour and the corresponding representation in the brain. There is a channel of communication, and since it exists, then there must be information that the tumour exists. But for the time being our consciousness is 'asleep'.

"What is my treatment based on? Not on curing a disease, but on the treatment of the sick person, in the same way that the great therapist S. P. Botkin treated people in his day. I would say that it is based not so much on treating a person, as on returning memories of the norm of perfection of his organism to him. I suggest that such a memory matrix of the norm exists. A disturbance or an informational failure in the matrix causes the development of a variety of diseases.

"I think that during a seance there is a distraction of the conscious mind and a corresponding activation in our biocomputer, according to the *ustanovka*, for healing. Control is distracted or switched off and our genetic knowledge is allowed to function. In our biocomputer's memory we have stored all the knowledge of the norm and its variants, and this knowledge is stored in the form of distributive matrices. Via the subconscious the body finds for itself the form of reaction, a result of stimulation by psychological factors, in order to return the body once again to the state of perfection. From then on, everything proceeds automatically.

"If we cut our hand, we just don't think about how it is going to heal, about primary or secondary accretion. This happens automatically. So, in the organism there is a program which contains the 'memory of the norm'. Clearly such a memory exists. If the organism had no such memory, it would have no idea how to proceed. So the psychotherapy that I am talking about is based on a scientific approach to the treatment of somatic diseases. Science just does not realize it yet. Unfortunately, the presence of psychology in medicine is minimal, because few doctors would use such psychological elements in their treatment.

"All words have problems, and the word 'healing', with its quasi-religious connotations, gives perhaps the wrong idea for this process of returning to the norm of health. Perhaps it is a sort of rehabilitation rather than healing? Rehabilitation on the basis of the body's own memory, with consequent tissue regeneration?

"I was particularly appalled by the health minister's ban on such an approach because there is so little access to official medicine here in this country. There aren't enough drugs, equipment, good hospitals. But we do have this opportunity to go down the route I have suggested: to explore through psychotherapy the control of this subconscious memory, to refine the method of the presentation of information, by which I mean the *ustanovka*, by which this memory is activated. The ministry of health wants to stop all healing sessions until further research is done on the results; but if anything does need to be researched under laboratory conditions, it is this mechanism of influence, this *ustanovka*.

"There is a story about someone who came to visit a naturalist, but found that he was out. He sat in an armchair and started to read a newspaper. Suddenly he looked under the bed and saw a big snake. He immediately remembered tales of reptiles hypnotizing their victims with their gaze and he thought: 'What if it hypnotizes me?' Hardly had this thought occurred to him than his hand began to twitch. He was already on all fours, his eyes popping out of their sockets, staring at the snake, reaching towards the snake, crawling right towards its jaws, although he didn't make it that far. His naturalist friend returned to an awful scene. His visitor was dead. Under the bed was a stuffed snake, with shoe buttons for eyes. What happened? Let's try to analyse it.

"Information about such a tragic outcome, which came through the conscious sphere, was so terrible that death occurred from anticipation of such a death. Fear, which was caused by an unusual irritant, was so powerful that it caused death more surely than any actual snakebite. Too much scotophobine, the fear hormone, was released by the subconscious biocomputer and this led to the tragedy. We have the means of life and death within ourselves. If we are ready to believe that we can kill ourselves in such a dramatic way, psychologically, why not allow that we can heal ourselves too?

"During seances, I often read extracts from the works of Wolfgang Goethe, Mikhail Sholokhov, Alexander Pushkin and others, and various sayings of Eastern sages and gradually prepare the distraction of the conscious at an intellectual level. It seems to me that a literary work can be a psychotherapeutic factor—bibliotherapy! Such literary works can summon our imagination into play, and this can result in a variety of consequences. However, my method of treatment is not medical at all, but medical results are achieved. This has persuaded me that the less medical the approach in psychology, the more psychology there is in medicine. It sounds paradoxical, but let us remember that the 'return to the norm' is an approach which abandons normal medical practice with its often crude interventions. I am a doctor who stopped being a doctor in order to treat people better. In fact, I believe absolutely in the old saying that the body is its own best doctor. I treat people by helping them to stir up their own internal resources.

"Well, now I'd like to talk about something a little different but important. People wonder why I encourage people to talk positively about their experiences of cure or read out telegrams at the beginning of my seances. This has been ridiculed. But obviously the preliminary directive and the preliminary information patients receive is enormously significant. Information which is positive encourages and facilitates healing and recovery. In just the same way information which is negative, false or unnecessary to a person can destroy his defence mechanism and block the rehabilitation process of the organism, his organs and tissues. This has to be taken into account by anyone trying to get to the bottom of these complex phenomena.

"People come to the seances with a mindset formed by information received from newspapers, magazines, the television, conversations with friends and so on. The phenomenon of suggestion is not rare or peculiar; it is part of all human intercourse. I try to establish the possibility of cure in peoples' consciousness, not to hypnotize them into a trance, which is far too narrow and limited.

"Why did I settle on the idea of teletherapy? Because I could see the enormous number of people in need of treatment. Let us take just one example: enuresis. This is a disease which tablets, injections and physical methods cannot cure. It is cured by the creation of a new directive, new information, for psychotherapy is a science about biological information technology. This is what true psychotherapy is all about! It is a combination of biological IT and biological directive.

"The medical psychotherapist is the bio-informant for the human organism. What does he do? He immerses the patient, let us say, into a state of hypnosis. What does he do next? He gives the appropriate commands. And how does he hypnotize? With information! 'Your hands and feet feel heavy ...' What is this? It's information. 'Your head is spinning.' Information. 'You won't stammer anymore ...' Information. And if he has a confident face? A confident, strong-willed face? Is this not information about future success? And if his gestures are decisive? This is also information that he does not doubt your disease will be conquered. Most of all the information must be convincing and reliable.

"Now, if I shout 'Fire! Everything's burning!' you would not be frightened because the information is not convincing. The task of the psychotherapist is to make the information convincing, then to ensure it enters firmly into the subconscious where it will begin to work. I would say that psychotherapy's success depends on the way in which the information is given. Unfortunately our psychotherapy is tuned to one channel of communication, the verbal channel. But information can be conveyed by gesture too, or by silence. There can be sounds, colours, smells that might influence huge numbers of chronically sick people in a positive way.

"I thought of television therapy and its potential for reaching masses of people. Teletherapy which would help a person to return to the norm via positive information, as opposed to what we have to swallow every day: sad, terrible, irreparable news. I provided people with a positive example, and the more positive examples there are in the audience, the more influential the seance is, the higher the percentage of responses. At this point, before I say anything else about teletherapy, I want to clear up why I performed anaesthesias on television.

"My achievement does not lie in the application of psychotherapy to surgery. Many doctors, on many occasions before me, have conducted operations using psychological suggestion. In the nineteenth century James Braid did about three hundred of them. But who did it first doesn't matter. What does matter is that I succeeded in proving, on television, that it is possible to carry out anaesthesia from a distance without applying hypnosis, which is understood by many as occurring during a sleeping state.

"I want to give an example to illustrate the difference between anaesthesia carried out in the immediate presence of the patient, and that carried out via television. Let's suppose that any one of you were to get up now and stand on the edge of the stage, with your back towards the audience. There is a risk of falling, but the fall is not so terrible. Now stand above a ravine. Could you stand with your back to the abyss? You couldn't, although the probability of falling is the same, but the circumstances are different!

"So, conducting a televised operation is the same as standing with your back to an abyss. Put yourself in the patient's position. He's in the operating theatre and he hears the clanking of the instruments, he'll be cut open any moment now, but there's no syringe with a drug for him. Try to feel what he is feeling and you will understand how complicated the psychotherapist's role is here as he attempts to overcome the patient's barrier of fear. And what kind of trust can there be in a doctor who is not convinced of the power of his skill? I don't think these operations were given the appreciation they deserved. Why did I need to do them? Simply to show in a very direct and convincing way that it is possible to influence profoundly a person's subconscious via television. I have proved that via television it is possible to transmit psychotherapeutic information and this information can be utterly reliable. It was only after the television operations that programmes on Ukrainian television demonstrating the world's first television psychotherapy seances were possible. They were a dramatic demonstration to a world that needed convincing.

"When I first started conducting teleseances for children suffering from enuresis, we quite unexpectedly received evidence that a whole range of other diseases and symptoms had disappeared in both the children and in others watching the seances. I was able to draw two conclusions from this unforeseen reaction:

"First, the rule that it is the patient, not the illness, that needs psychotherapeutic treatment was shown to be correct. On the other hand, one previously incontestable rule was proven to be out of date—the one which states that a therapist must know the history of the disease, the specifics of the disease. One has to treat a person as a whole to stimulate his defensive mechanisms. Thus the organism by itself will manage to find the diseases that are partially hidden from doctor and patient. By trying to cure a patient of a specific disease, we distract his attention from the more serious underlying problem, the cause of that disease.

"Second, it became clear that the most important thing about telepsychotherapy was its effect on the psyche. Evidently, when people saw a person on television able to produce anaesthesia during a surgical operation, their faith in him became boundless. They accepted that whatever he said or did was designed to put their health right. As a consequence, they responded by getting better. They received one single comprehensive piece of information, namely: he wants to help us, to cure us. The surgical operations shown on the telebridge played a huge role in creating this effect. They became a sort of catalyst which launched the whole phenomenon. This is the phenomenon of Man himself! And I never forgot that I was dealing with real Ivanovs and Petrenkos and other people sitting in the audience or by their television screens. I listened to each one.

"There have been great healers throughout history but I might add that there have also been great patients, who have recovered because of a glance or the touch of a hand. At a seance you might have a group of twenty diabetics, but not all of them will be cured. Those who do recover might be called 'great patients'. Evidently, they can access those essential elements which the organism is able to produce in some brilliant way to make its own internal medicine. Therefore it is correct to talk about remarkable doctors and patients.

One might even say that the great healers always had great patients, but great patients don't always have great healers.

"Telepsychotherapy is reproached for its lack of feedback from patients. But it's not quite like that. My opponents doubt my thirty years' experience as a psychotherapist. My experience always helps me to anticipate what can happen in the audience, what sort of reactions could arise. What have I to fear? All I do is give information about recovery, in a direct and indirect way. My work could be simply called the instilling of information about positive outcomes. Why criticize me when there are so many negative influences at work in the world? Like in the news or at rock concerts, where so often there are hidden calls for violence? And videofilms with their blood baths? That's why reproaches made in my direction are so unjust and ignorant. I can say straight out that negative reactions to psychotherapeutic treatment don't happen. I can affirm this as a tried and tested truth.

"Recently I read in a newspaper that the Ukraine has more than two million mental patients. These are the patients who are officially listed in hospitals, at dispensaries or as out-patients. And how many more are there who are not registered? In Vinnitsa, over a period of twenty-five years, I observed many patients. There was no teletherapy for them. They had so many problems with the awful side-effects of the drugs they were given. There was no criticism from the ministry of health about the ill-effects of their treatment!

"And when the ministry tells me that my data is insufficient, that they are not facts and that my records should contain the case histories of individual illnesses, I can reply only that they are records as far as I am concerned, whether they have the ministry's stamp of approval or not. When Chazov was the minister of health, he supported teletherapy, and at first the new minister, I. Denisov, also supported us. Now I sense that he too has fallen under the hypnotic powers of the press! I consider that letters with testimonials are a valid record. They should be examined, but we should not simply agree with all of them. We are trying to evaluate them, but there are over a million letters—some of them even with the stamp of the ministry of health. What, after all, was preventing our health services, individual doctors or hospitals, from selecting groups of patients and recording their case histories before and after the television seances?

"And why are the Moscow and Leningrad institutes not carrying out appropriate research? Who is preventing them from making videotapes of my seances on national television and conducting treatment on groups of patients in medical institutions? I agree that research is needed: we've got to find out exactly what happens and why it happens, and then come to a conclusion. I think this neglect can be explained by a total disinterest in the health of the nation and perhaps also by an absence of the necessary technical means. It is far simpler to blame me for everything.

"So, we have all gathered here to think about what has happened and what to do next. I beg you to understand," said Kashpirovsky as he concluded his lecture, "that it is not I who should be considered as the phenomenon. I am simply its epicentre. The real phenomenon is Man and his latent reserves, the enormous potential that all possess."

After Kashpirovsky finished his speech, other participants started presenting their papers. Dr V. Menzul, for example, chief of the Paediatric Burn Centre in Moscow, said:

> I want to underline that of the children in the burn centre, all of whom watched all six seances, not a single one had an adverse reaction. We noted positive reactions in all children. I'd like to cite one example. A boy, twelve years old, had burns over fifty percent of his body. I operated on him three times. His immune system started to reject skin grafts. Then he began to watch Kashpirovsky's seances. His condition started to improve immediately and within two weeks his wounds were healed with no further problems. I support the idea of telepsychotherapy and the foundation of psychotherapeutic centres in our country.

Then Dr V. Krepkaya, a gynaecologist from Kiev, stated:

> I attended Kashpirovsky's seances in June 1988 out of curiosity, and for a time I did not think suggestion could be used to treat gynaecological problems. But women who attended seances in 1988–1989 noted improvement in their health. I decided to do some research. We divided patients into three groups:
> (1) Patients of Dr Kashpirovsky who attended 4-6 seances either in person or by television. In this group we had women who

were emotionally unstable, but who had a deep trust in Kashpirovsky as a doctor. As a result of his treatment 76.2 percent showed improvements in all sorts of disorders from fibroma of the uterus to breast cancer.

(2) A group of women was treated with conventional medical methods and reinforced by one to three seances of Dr Kashpirovsky. Within this group 81.8 percent showed improvement.

(3) This group was treated conventionally and showed improvement in only 31.2 percent. We also observed negative reactions in 1.9 percent. These patients were observed to have insomnia, fatigue, irritability. I consider it necessary to do further studies.

Dr N. Lipgart, chief psychotherapist of the Ukraine, from Kiev, had this to say:

I'm disappointed that at this conference there are no practising psychotherapists, nor are there any specialists from psychotherapeutic clinics, nor any representatives from the Ukrainian academic world. Whether you like it or not, there are people who have reproduced your method and in particular psychotherapist Danilov, who successfully uses your method in Psychosomatic Polyclinic Number 6 in Kharkov. I believe that you used direct and indirect suggestion in a wakeful state and also in a hypnotic state. It is a pity that you do not agree with this. We psychotherapists consider you to be a hypnologist, a very talented hypnologist. What we see during your teleseances is a hypnotic state in the audience, and it is in your favour, because in a hypnotic state suggestion is more effective.

Anatoly Mikhailovich, I understand you want to widen the scope of psychotherapy and bring it to every home. But there is the possibility of totally unpredictable results. Because of the interaction between the patient, the television and your suggestion, it is not known how your suggestion will act. You are trying to direct it. You are giving an appropriate mindset, but the human psyche is often unpredictable. You should not sweep negative results under the carpet. According to you, the positive results are the results of your healing, but the negative results you attribute to pure coincidence. Both come from the same source.

Dr P. Tsai, from Kharkov, told the conference:

There are 175 psychotherapists in the Ukraine. We often meet to discuss our work. We noted that some patients, after viewing your teleseances, had a worsening of their condition. To overcome this problem, I used to say to a patient: 'Tomorrow you'll be watching a teleseance and after that you will feel better. And my patients did not show any side-effects. I believe that teleseances must be resumed, and tele-healing should be reinforced by other psychotherapists' *ustanovka*.

At the conference about sixty reports were presented. Most of the doctors spoke in support and in defence of Kashpirovsky's methods. In conclusion a range of hopeful resolutions were passed. The Kiev conference, however, received no serious scientific or public response. Its results were not mentioned in the mass media. The opinions of its participants, in so far as they were heard at all, were dismissed out of hand in academic circles. What had most disturbed the critics, the teleseances, were no longer an irritant because they had been banned and the conference did nothing to alter this. Though his healing sessions continued around the country, so did the criticisms.

Whatever one may think of Kashpirovsky, he certainly managed to bring all the lunatics out of the cupboard. One of his fiercest opponents was a man called Dichev, who wrote in the newspaper *Vechernaya Moskva* warning that Kashpirovsky could kill people by his use of a "combination of music with killer-phrases, amplified by the television twenty-five thousand times." But Kashpirovsky remained defiant: "In spite of the attacks of my enemies and their ridiculous accusations that I am making zombies out of Gorbachev and Yeltsin, that I am participating in Zionist plots or other nonsense, my seances still attract tens of thousands of people."

More seriously, journalists continued to direct their fire at him. He was accused of belonging to the "business-hypno-narco-mafia" and given short shrift in national newspapers like *Izvestia*:

> I can see the social damage brought by the seances with the help of national television. The intellectual wretchedness and emotional mumbo-jumbo which accompanied the performances of Kashpirovsky undermined the personality and created a pathogenic mentality. It was especially harmful to children's psyches. To my mind his intellectual equipment is very poor. Besides, he is under the

influence of an *idée fixe*, to cure the whole of humanity in one sweep.

Undoubtedly his position in the minds and hearts of the people was steadily eroded by this continual rubbishing. "Whether television healing produced results or not," said Kashpirovsky, "for a large number of suffering people it was the last available chance, the last hope thrown to those tossed overboard and left to fend for themselves in a desperate economic situation. But who ever cared about the people in our State?"

His grand schemes for mass television healing sessions had been destroyed and besides there were now dozens of mystics, psychics and faith-healers jamming the airwaves and diminishing, by association, his impact. People just didn't, or couldn't, discriminate anymore. The new national passion were the Mexican soap operas shown daily on television. They seemed far more real and comprehensible than the world outside. For the whole country was, at this time, in complete turmoil and a greater drama was unfolding all around.

In 1991 Gorbachev warned that "if there is no control, the future will bring anarchy, chaos and, worse yet, civil war." The Soviet Union was disintegrating. Already Lithuania, Latvia, Estonia, Armenia, Georgia and Moldavia had fundamentally redefined their ties with Moscow. On August 19, tanks rolled through the streets of Moscow and surrounded the City Hall in an attempted coup by the right wing. Boris Yeltsin, a key figure on the barricades, was later elected president of Russia.

Kashpirovsky had always thought of himself as a Soviet man. He wept to see what was happening. "You know, many people in the Soviet Union still believe they live in the strongest country in the world. And when they see that their country is being torn apart and with such pain and bloodshed, they feel hurt. In the Ukraine the situation is such that the republic wants to be independent, but this drive for independence should not become a confrontation with other republics or people of other nationalities. There should not be a militant nationalism. Independence should become a true freedom and should unite people everywhere."

His attitude towards Yeltsin was ambivalent. "I'd respect leaders who carried out their promises. I don't like it when people flip-flop and kowtow, like Yeltsin did before Gorbachev. But still I sympathize with Yeltsin, although he is not the kind of leader that Russia needs to lead her out of chaos. I wish I could have more spare time: then I'd try to do what they could not accomplish."

Despite such protestations, others were not slow to realize Kashpirovsky's political potential. His huge popularity, especially with the grassroots, his charismatic public image, made him an obvious target for any political party that cared, or dared, to take him on board. So overtures were made and he began his association with a political leader whose views, behaviour and personality were even more controversial, unpredictable and explosive than his own.

8

Politics and the Man

The while with liberty we burn,
The while our hearts are quick for honour,
My friend, to our land we dedicate
The soul's exquisite raptures!
Comrade, believe: it will arise,
The star of captivating bliss,
Russia will rouse herself from sleep,
And on the ruins of despotism
Our names will be inscribed!

(To Chadayev, Alexander Pushkin 1818)

*I*n December 1993 Kashpirovsky called me on the phone: "Let me introduce myself," he said. "You are speaking to a member of the Russian state Duma." He said it laughingly but his voice was full of pride and self-satisfaction. "I was elected on Zhirinovsky's ticket."

The rise of Vladimir Zhirinovsky and his so-called Liberal Democratic Party of Russia had surprised Western commentators and many Russians, but his nationalist, right-wing, anti-semitic, imperialist views had also struck a deep chord in a time of confusion. When he ran for the presidency in June 1991, against Yeltsin and others, Zhirinovsky won six million votes, almost eight percent of the electorate. This was passed off as some kind of aberration, a protest vote. Many laughed as they saw him hurling flowerpots at Jewish protesters or heard him ranting on about bringing the breakaway republics to their knees by burying nuclear waste along their borders and blowing radioactive particles at them with giant fans. This soon changed to alarm when he and his party, in the December 1993 parliamentary elections, took nearly twenty-five percent of the vote.

Kashpirovsky's route to the state Duma seems to have bypassed any normal political evolution. He had never met Zhirinovsky, never attended any of his political meetings nor gone through any process of political selection himself. He was invited to be one of that party's candidates at the end of 1993, accepted, and found himself a deputy. This was made possible by a change in the electoral system instituted by Boris Yeltsin. The first post-perestroika system of electing individual deputies as representatives of constituencies had been replaced by a system of giving parties a block number of seats in the Duma proportionate to the number of votes they had received. The party was then able to allocate the seats to anyone they wished, as long as they had been registered on the party list.

Though Kashpirovsky may not have been actively involved in party politics at this time, he certainly had political ambitions and had been heard to say on a number of occasions that he himself might run for president! He had received thousands of letters from his fans encouraging him to do so. He seems to have believed that Zhirinovsky might help him in this, or at least make him vice-president. Zhirinovsky had declared himself an admirer and supported his plans for mass television healing sessions. He also obviously understood Kashpirovsky's enormous pulling power and was often seen on TV with a poster of Kashpirovsky, eyes blazing, at his back. This led many of his opponents to believe he had used Kashpirovsky's hypnotic powers to enthral the nation. Konstantin Borovoi, the businessman who opened Russia's post-Communist stock exchange, the chairman of the Party for Economic Freedom, wanted the elections declared null and void because of this.

From 1991 until the 1993 elections, Kashpirovsky had actually spent much of his time abroad, mainly in America. He was one of the many ex-Soviet citizens who found life more comfortable outside the borders of the old Union and was, of course, accused of desertion. He took an apartment on Long Island, put his somewhat wayward son

Seryozha into college and was quite obviously doing well. However, he did want to return. He was not at ease in the United States, and his private life was a mess. He divorced his wife Valentina after twenty-five years of often tempestuous marriage. "I did not want to divorce my wife," he said. "After all, we've been through so much together. But I saw no other way out of it." He really did seem to be suffering badly.

Then, a year later in 1992, he visited the Czech republic. The same crowds of devotees came up to him after the seance to touch their idol and to thank him for their healings. It was the usual scene; but that day his eyes met the eyes of a young woman. "How many eyes have I seen during my performances? But this pair made me stop and look. At that moment I understood I could not live without them. It was love at first sight." Irina was Czech, the mother of two girls and in the process of divorcing her husband. They were married soon after, and she accompanied him on all his travels, from city to city, from country to country. "She gives me that which I lacked before. With her I gained a sense of family, of being at home. Each day I love her more and more." Kashpirovsky's happiness and contentment were plain to see. He did not want anybody to interfere or intrude on it. Their marriage was kept secret—even from Valentina.

Then the story broke. "Famous psychotherapist marries foreigner in secret ceremony" read the headline in a Moscow newspaper. A former faithful admirer, Vasilkova, feeling jilted, had decided to get even with him for marrying Irina and leaked the news. Kashpirovsky was devastated by this betrayal. Valentina, his ex-wife, was enraged. "Why couldn't you have told me you were going to get married? People won't leave me alone. They call me, they come to the door, they follow me on the street. The whole of Kiev wants to give me 'the happy news,'" she screamed down the telephone to Kashpirovsky in America. "She did not understand that I kept the marriage secret for her own sake. I did not want to hurt her. But she would not listen." A slight misjudgement, perhaps.

Realizing that another tie had been cut, that he was drifting further away from home, he made various attempts to re-enter the world he had left behind. He did not want to return just to live the life of an ordinary citizen, but to do something important, to achieve something. This need of his goes a long way toward explaining his opportunistic involvement with the LDP. However, at first he tried to stick more closely to his original vocation and went back to St Petersburg, or Leningrad as he still persisted in calling it, in the spring of 1992 to try to establish a charitable foundation for needy children in Russia. He came full of enthusiasm. "I had meetings with Anatoly Sobchak (the liberal mayor of St Petersburg), who supported my idea of a fund and promised cooperation. I visited his home and we discussed the continuation of my healing sessions. His wife, Ludmila, was very supportive. She said: 'People lack clothing, food and medicine. We appreciate your concern and willingness to help.' I like Anatoly Sobchak. He is very clever, educated, and not just out for money. I also liked being in Leningrad. I feel at ease there. I thought I might settle down there. I can't stay in the Ukraine with Kravchuk's policy of nationalism. It is stupid. There has never been antagonism between Ukrainians and Russians. Not that I remember!"

His enthusiasm for the creation of his international fund died down when he tried to register the foundation in the USA. He learned that the process of registration alone would take two years at best, that the laws were very restrictive and would allow no commercial activity under its name.

The only way to support the fund was to finance it out of his own resources or to find other sponsors in Russia and elsewhere. "I addressed several of the new businessmen in Russia. I went to Konstantin Borovoi asking him to participate in the fund. But he refused to give any money and, actually, I did not like the way he looked. A serious businessman would never wear jeans and sneakers. We did not find much in common." Borovoi's version is rather different. He claims that Kashpirovsky came to him offering his political support in return for financial support of the fund. Borovoi says he wanted nothing to do with him.

Neither did the city council of St Petersburg want him. They resisted his attempt to get residency in the city, having joined in the calls for a ban on his mass performances there. "We decided to take such measures because of the innumerable complaints of the people of St Petersburg," they told journalists, and indicated that they had the support of Professor L. Rubina, the chief psychiatrist of the city:

"The activities of Kashpirovsky should be limited, and the use of television for his seances should be categorically prohibited. It is not a limitation on the freedom of speech, but a ban on illegal medical practice."

Kashpirovsky also fell foul of the Russian Orthodox church, desperately fighting a forlorn battle against foreign evangelists, loony sects and myriad healers and astrologers. In its pamphlet *The Orthodox Church on Healers, UFOs, Television, Faith-Healers and the Occult*, the church says "Our ancestors realized what a danger such people were," and compares their activities to the most terrible crimes. Audiences are "obsessed by forces we call demonic."

"I call upon you not to step over the threshold of Kashpirovsky's show!" stormed the local bishop in Krasnodar. "Stay at home! Do you realize the horror of finding yourself in Satan's den?" Kashpirovsky was indignant. "Why don't they stop the charlatans who heal with their sexual organs?" (This was a reference to healers like Zolotov who became notorious for their "orgasmic" healing sessions.) "Why should they ban me, a medical doctor? What else can you expect in this uncivilized country. But the people discern who is real and who is not."

It was not only in Russia itself that he had difficulties. Shortly before the Pope visited Lithuania and Latvia in 1993, Kashpirovsky was denied an entry visa. With his wife, Irina, he arrived at a hotel in the Latvian town of Daugavpils late at night. Suddenly a detachment of armed soldiers stepped into the hall. "Are you Mr Kashpirovsky?" they asked him. "You must leave Latvia at once. The train for Moscow leaves in half an hour." "Why? What's the matter?" Kashpirovsky couldn't believe it. "Your papers are not in order." "But I received the visa in the Latvian consulate in Moscow." "We have our orders. Please, proceed now. We don't want to use force." But Kashpirovsky did not want to give up. "Look," he said. "The train is leaving shortly, so we won't have enough time to catch it. And I don't have tickets. Nothing can happen if we stay overnight." His persuasion worked. "But be prepared to leave first thing in the morning," they said before leaving.

Next morning Kashpirovsky was not in a hurry to wake up. "I was told they were already there, waiting for us to leave. I decided to get even with them by slowly eating my breakfast and doing everything possible to stretch out the time. I knew they wanted me out of the country because of the visit by the Pope. They were afraid he would protest about my presence in Latvia with him. They are idiots! I knew that my visa was OK and I could have insisted on staying there. But I lost interest in staying in such a silly country .

"I always respected the church," said Kashpirovsky. "And I am on friendly terms with many priests and clergymen. But some of them decided to gain political capital by denouncing me. Unfortunately people follow their orders not to attend my seances. They don't want to be accused of having connections with the devil!"

So Kashpirovsky was feeling embattled and wanted to fight back. Then he met Aleksei Mitrofanov, a producer for national television, who wanted to make a film about him. In the course of their discussions, Mitrofanov came up with an amazing plan. They would send Kashpirovsky into space! There, while gaily orbiting the earth, he would anaesthetize a patient. The first telebridge operation from outer space! The proposal was apparently considered seriously by the Centre for Space Flights. Kashpirovsky, never lacking in self-confidence, was disappointed to receive a letter from Ryumin, the deputy-general of the centre, that all scheduled flights for the next three years were already booked up. "They told me I would need at least two months of training, but I told them I had no time to waste and that I was ready to go tomorrow."

Though all this talk of outer space came to nothing, the contact with Mitrofanov seems to have propelled him further into Zhirinovsky's orbit, for Mitrofanov was Zhirinovsky's shadow minister of culture. Although it has been difficult to establish each step precisely, by November 1993 Kashpirovsky was listed in the newspaper *Rossiskaya Gazeta* as a deputy for the LDP and was expressing admiration for the views of its leader.

"Zhirinovsky will be a good president," said Kashpirovsky. "He is a fine politician and is really concerned about Russia's future. They say he is a fascist but he, unlike Yeltsin, has not killed anybody yet. Why does nobody call Yeltsin a fascist? What else can you call a president who shoots at his own people? How could he use tanks to fire at the Parliament?" (The storming of the White House in October 1993, when Yeltsin sent in troops to evict his political opponents, who had occupied the building.) "It was Gorbachev's policy which brought the Soviet Union to its knees. Yeltsin is continuing the same policy and now Russia is in such a state that no one is afraid of us anymore. Before, they feared us and thus respected us. People say that America and the West planned and engineered the collapse of the Soviet Union. Gorbachev and Yeltsin just fulfilled their plans. They are responsible for the worst crime of all by destroying the Soviet Union. It's because of them that people are getting killed everywhere. If Gorbachev would have conducted his policies correctly, there would never have been such conflicts as in Nagorno-Karabakh, Dushanbe and other places.

"Zhirinovsky wants the Union back together. And here he finds my support. I also believe that we must do everything to bring all the republics back to the Union. Those mongrel governments of the so-called sovereign republics that are trying to break away from Russia are asking for a kick up the arse. What you read about Zhirinovsky is just a bunch of lies. It's all journalists' dirty work. They humiliated me and lied about me. Now they are doing the same to destroy Zhirinovsky's image. They portray him as a fool, a fascist, a warmonger.

"I have nothing against Zhirinovsky. I know that he feels the same about me. So I like everybody who likes me. I've never met him and I'm not sure I will ever meet him. But I'm grateful to him for his support. I'd support him in the future. I would give my support to implement those ideas which I consider normal and humane. Journalists concocted a story, linking us together, two odious personalities. I still do not understand why they continue to attack me. They never leave me alone.

"If I were president, I would put the people first. These democrats are busy discussing economic problems, glasnost and the rest. In villages, however, people are not interested in this. They need tractors, land, freedom to act and justice! If they had been given this, everything would have been different. A good president should be concerned about making people happy! Give them what they need and they would work like crazy. The president does not have to be a financial genius. All he needs is common sense. He should go among people, listen to their problems, give them solutions and build a state for the people. Our politicians just make life more difficult. After my first visit to America I brought back a hundred thousand disposable syringes. It took me a year to make some hospitals accept them for free. I spoke with different people, those who say that they are concerned with the people's problems. It was only with extreme difficulty and the help of the leader of Rukh (the nationalist Ukrainian organization) that I eventually managed to deliver them to a hospital.

"All I see is falsehood. What I hate most is that these leaders have changed colour so easily, with no problem or feeling of regret. I would never do that! Years ago in Vinnitsa, when my application for membership of the Communist Party was turned down, I felt belittled. In those years to be a Party member meant to be officially recognized. They said I was politically unreliable. I suffered because I was not recognized. I wish I could look in the eyes of the hospital Party leader and people like him now—those who have thrown away their Party cards so quickly. I would have never thrown mine away. I would have stayed with my party to the bitter end. Those who have changed their colours once may change them again. I do not trust such people. My position is clear. Once you've lost, commit *hara-kiri*, like the Japanese did. But our leaders are ready to do anything, even kiss the hands of the priests they once denounced just to keep their positions and their power!

"Eduard Shevardnadze, for example. When he was elected chairman of the Georgian parliament, he immediately announced that he was no longer an atheist. He was even baptized. He has an ikon in his office now, though at one time he had Stalin's portrait on the wall. And Yeltsin is no better with his policies of flirting with the church.

"What we need now is authoritarian rule, law and order. We need good laws on private property and land ownership. We need a group of professionals who would oversee the implementation of these laws. I would reorganize the police, so they would look like American policemen; buy them uniforms and equipment so they would command respect. I would introduce summary executions of those criminals who are destroying our quality of life. My son-in-law was recently mugged in Kiev but the police did nothing. Others would quickly learn how to behave properly. Zhirinovsky got six million votes in the last election though his campaign was not well organized.

With me running on his ticket, I'm sure he could get many more."

And, of course, he did.

However, the fact that Kashpirovsky was standing for election in the new parliament while out of the country caused some annoyance. He was accused of turning the election into a farce and "mocking the attempts of the Russian people to create a proper parliament." Kashpirovsky excused himself by saying he had to leave for America on an extended working trip and that he hardly had to canvass for votes because there was no one in Russia who did not know him. "I made a statement before I left. I told them that I could be of use because I understand people's needs so very well. And besides, I was already accused by the press of using my so-called powers to make people vote for me. I didn't want them to have any excuse to declare my election invalid."

As it turned out, the coming elections failed to excite many. People were so sure of the victory of Yeltsin's party, Russia's Choice, that they did not go to vote. Vast numbers felt completely alienated from the political process. A Russian businessman explained: "We don't expect politicians to do anything for us. They may pass good laws, but they do not realize how bureaucrats are blocking things. You cannot imagine how difficult it is to start your own business now. The local laws contradict the laws of the central government. Everybody tries to tax you. And all they want is their bribes, as it used to be in the past. In that way Russia has not changed. Politicians in this country were never businessmen themselves, so they don't really understand what business needs."

So Zhirinovsky, the "Last Hope of a Cheated and Humiliated People," as his campaign slogan read, gained a massive foothold in the Duma not only by the force of his ragbag of nationalist ideology, but also by considerable default. After his victory he said: "I know you're sick of politicians. Many of you did not bother to vote. Why would you? You are tired of the promises and the lies. But I'll give you results immediately, so you needn't wait for them. If you support me, I'll diminish taxes to help you to develop businesses. We must stop foreigners with their chewing gums, stockings and McDonalds."

Explanations for the popularity of Zhirinovsky's party were varied. Many thought that people were simply tired of Yeltsin's "shock therapy" reforms, that they wanted to see a change in their daily lives. Mikhail Gorbachev said, "I do not believe even now that the Russian people and our army were really serious in voting for such a chauvinistic programme. Our people voted for him only to show the government their rejection of its policy." There was considerable reluctance to allow that Zhirinovsky's views represented anything very significant in the national psyche. Konstantin Borovoi, as mentioned earlier, was convinced that it was all Kashpirovsky's fault. He said on Russian television: "The people who voted for Zhirinovsky in the Duma elections were under Kashpirovsky's hypnotic influence. Therefore they voted for Zhirinovsky unconsciously in a state of trance."

Borovoi even gathered psychologists, psychiatrists and hypnotists to investigate precisely how Kashpirovsky had manipulated the Russian electorate. "Mysticism and medical technology have been used for political aims on a giant scale—maybe for the first time in human history," he said. "This is banned by international agreement and special articles in the criminal code." But the meeting could not agree. None of the experts could prove that Kashpirovsky had given Zhirinovsky lessons in mass hypnosis, as some suggested, nor that his powers were an infringement of human rights.

This was the first time the Russian people had witnessed the power of television in a "democratic" election. Many voted for the most entertaining TV personality during the campaign. Every day for a month Zhirinovsky appeared on the screen laughing and joking, generally making a fool of himself. He was the first Russian politician to manipulate the media in this way. He appealed directly to the people. At times he was serious, and unlike in 1991 he didn't promise "I'll give you bread, money, vodka." He said instead: "I'll give you jobs and you will work very hard, but you will earn good money. I'll see that every single mother will get a husband. I am one of you. I was called by fate to save Russia, which has been unlucky with its leaders."

When Richard Nixon went to Russia, he met Zhirinovsky and assessed him thus:

> Mr Zhirinovsky is a ruthless, shrewd demagogue. But after examining him at length on issues ranging from his views on foreign

policy to his attitude toward the USA and anti-semitism, I share the view of President Leonid Kravchuk of the Ukraine: he will not be elected president of Russia. He lacks the presence and conviction to lead a great nation. For Hitler, anti-semitism was a faith; for Mr Zhirinovsky, it is a tactic, a cynical attempt to exploit popular biases.

One of Zhirinovsky's top associates said later that he had intentionally adopted the extravagant posture of a holy fool. For centuries these *yurodiviye* were opposition figures, given considerable licence to speak out against authority. "Although Russians have always had a soft spot for holy fools, they have never chosen them as their leaders—as Mr Zhirinovsky will soon discover when he enters the presidential sweepstakes."

The opening of Russia's state Duma was farcical. "The first day's tragicomic events included bodyguards being battered with cameras, arguments among the Liberal Democratic camp and a carnival-like parliamentary session," wrote the St Petersburg press. And, of course, the leader of the LDP was the centre of attention. The people of Russia watched the performance with laughter, as if forgetting that the Duma was supposed to solve their problems. Zhirinovsky used the occasion to scold Bill Clinton for having refused to meet him, the leader of the "most powerful political faction in Russia."

Kashpirovsky did not manage to attend the opening of the Duma but very soon he was having to defend his affiliation. "I feel awkward that I'm under the roof of such a bloc, but I believe that my actions will justify my decision and that people will be grateful for it later. I am a doctor who has entered politics with the best of intentions. People listen to me because I understand their problems and hardships." However, not everyone did understand nor were they prepared to listen to him any longer. His audiences in America, many of them Jewish Russian emigrés, were particularly incensed, shouted at him during his healing sessions and began to stay away in droves. So, just three months after his election, he decided to dump Zhirinovsky and wrote a letter to I. P. Rybkin, the chairman of the state Duma:

> I, Anatoly Kashpirovsky, doctor by profession, in 1993 actively entered political life in Russia and became a member of the Russian parliament. This move was not by chance, although it was surprising

to many who believed a doctor should do nothing else but work as a doctor.

There were two reasons for this decision. First of all, the nonstop disintegration and agony of my motherland caused by politicians lacking vision. Disintegration was not necessary. If the leadership had been more careful and flexible, it could have turned our once strong state onto the road to democracy without destroying the Union, without bloodshed and without those consequences which made millions of people suffer so much. Becoming a member of Parliament, I hoped to fight for humanitarian ideals, for Russia, Peace and Humanity.

The other reason for my participation in political life was to defend my discovery, one of the most important discoveries in the history of mankind. But this was ridiculed—and my name was ruined by cynical ignorant people, though the discovery was appreciated by many scientists.

Entering the election campaign, I was convinced that any political faction I belonged to would have to give priority to my ideas for the health and happiness of the people. And that is why I accepted the invitation by the Liberal Democratic Party to campaign with them for election to the Russian Parliament. I couldn't disagree with the statements set out in their political programme such as keeping the state's territory intact, keeping private property sacred and untouchable, keeping the decision on national questions within the constitution and the law, freedom of religion, equality of civil rights without discrimination, non-intervention in internal affairs, free education and health care. I am sure that these slogans attracted many of the votes for V. Zhirinovsky.

However, as soon as he was elected to the Parliament, V. Zhirinovsky began waving the flag of racism and threatening the world with war. I consider the position taken by the Liberal Democratic Party's leader to be presumptuous, reckless and dangerous. V. Zhirinovsky has wiped out every good thing in his political programme and as a result those who voted for him were deceived.

Therefore, I do not want my name to be associated with the leader of the Liberal Democratic Party, V. Zhirinovsky. I cannot remain in the same faction with a politician of such persuasion and I officially hereby announce my resignation from this faction.

Anatoly Kashpirovsky
New York, 3 March 1994

A correspondent of *Novoye Russkoye Slovo*, V. Kozlovsky, asked Kashpirovsky how he came to such a decision:

"I had no contacts with Zhirinovsky because I was in the USA. I just read what he had said and did not know whether to believe it or not. It was hard to believe that he could make such shocking, ludicrous statements. I wanted to gather more information. And now that I'm convinced that he is, in fact, saying these things, I have decided to have nothing to do with him. I shall take a different route in politics."

—What is it that you do not accept in Zhirinovsky?

"His aggression, his aggressive statements, his intentions to start a war."

—Are you sure that he wants to start a war?

"Yes, I heard him saying that. Personally I have nothing against him. But I don't like what he says."

—Are you going to participate in the work of the Duma?

"Yes, I hope that for some time I'll remain a deputy of the Duma, but I'm afraid that I'll be all by myself there."

—In what sense?

"Well, what faction do I belong to? Who am I?"

—Is it necessary to belong to a faction in order to participate in the parliament?

"One must be more prepared than I am and know one's way around better. I thought that if I left Zhirinovsky, I had stopped being a deputy. Just a few days ago I learned that this is not the case."

—Even though you have been elected on his ticket?

"Yes. If I had known this earlier, I would have made my mind up sooner. I was hesitating. I don't want to betray anybody. I don't like to betray. But in this case Vladimir had put himself and his followers in such a position that there is only one way out of it: to leave him."

—How can you participate in the work of the Duma while living in the USA?

"I don't live in the USA. I'm leaving it soon. I had certain scientific and personal plans here. Now I'm going to return home. I think I'll leave in April. I have a one-room apartment, just a tiny apartment in Galushkina, in the suburbs of Moscow."

—Are you planning to attend the sessions of the Duma?

"I wish I could come and see them. But I wonder if they will tolerate my absence till April. They may ask, 'Where is our deputy? Where has he been hanging around?'"

—Do you think they will exclude you for your absence?

"Probably. I consider that the state Duma is a very serious institution, and one should participate in its work seriously. Very seriously. Perhaps there will be some question of my resignation from the Duma. I respect this institution. I did not have any assignment within the LDP, any particular role or portfolio. I think they totally forgot about me and never gave me any assignments."

—Did you have any contacts with them?

"I called Vengerovsky, the deputy leader, twice. He called me once. He said: 'Our party is moving fast, because none of the parties has gained so many votes during such a short period of time, and it is the only strong party in Russia. So if it collapses, everything will collapse. At this moment we are in a state of formation, so to speak.' I wanted to influence Zhirinovsky, to help him to become better. Unfortunately, he does not want to listen to the voice of reason. I cannot stay in the same party with him."

"He's a traitor!" said Zhirinovsky when he learned about Kashpirovsky's withdrawal. "A deputy who leaves our party should resign his seat. He should submit his resignation so that we can consider other candidates. We have a hundred people on our waiting list.

"Personally, I have nothing against Kashpirovsky. But if he doesn't want to be with us, he should withdraw. He should have thought what kind of party we were before the elections. Now after having won the elections, we have became more relaxed and democratic. To make a statement saying we are different from what he expected is rubbish! We were more rigid and aggressive before the elections. Now, enjoying our victory, we have become mild and calm. That is why his claims are groundless! He knew where he was going, what kind of party we are. Our party stands for patriotism. If he has been under pressure from Zionist circles and nationalistic Ukrainian circles, then he should have said: 'You know, guys, I live in America, it is tough here, I'm under pressure, I'm threatened, let me go.' Then just resign quietly and go. But to play a game like this by saying, 'I'm no longer in the faction of LDP!' Why did he enter the party then? Didn't he know what kind of party it is? I can't approve of such an attitude."

Others in the LDP were equally upset. Aleksandr Shemyakin,

Zhirinovsky's chief of staff, told the newspaper *Sevodnya* that Kashpirovsky had "never attended a single meeting of the Duma. Kashpirovsky has shown himself to be a dilettante, to say the least. My aide, after reading that statement, called it childish prattle. When one is sitting on the other side of the world and has no idea of the situation in Russia, it's frivolous to draw such conclusions. It is not clear whether the LDP faction will take any action to strip Mr Kashpirovsky of his Deputy's credentials. However, he doesn't show any noticeable desire to participate in the work of the Russian parliament, either."

Kashpirovsky's declaration created no great sensation among the general public. In America, Israel and Poland, Kashpirovsky's fans were relieved. "At least now I can go to Israel and Poland," he said. He was by no means the only deputy to abandon the LDP. The head of the St Petersburg faction of the LDP followed his example along with other members. Besides, the Liberal Democratic Party's rating in the local elections was lower than anticipated—which came as a surprise after Zhirinovsky's resounding victory on the parliamentary level.

In a survey of 1,500 people by the Russian Centre for Public Opinion and Market Research at the end of March, 63 percent said they did not trust Zhirinovsky at all. "It was some kind of splash," said Gennady Burbulis, referring to the December results. "Three months were enough to realize that it is not going to bring any benefits to the country."

"He knows his only route to power is by making these aggressive statements so that he can remain on top of this wave of popularity," said Andrei N. Zavidiya, a businessman who ran on Zhirinovsky's ticket in the 1991 presidential election and who broke with him in the winter of 1994. He also said that Zhirinovsky's financial support had been drying up lately, as he and other Russian businessmen took their money elsewhere.

> On April 4 Vladimir Zhirinovsky put on a show which gave some idea of what he might do if he ever came to power. The fifth congress of his Liberal Democratic Party of Russia, held in a meeting hall on Moscow's outskirts, began with a line-up on stage of "Zhirinovsky's Falcons", 18 young men in blue uniforms and black

boots, some wearing dark glasses, all with sidearms strapped to their waists. But the crowning moment came when the 343 delegates, with not a single dissenting voice, not even a whimper of debate, raised their pink party cards in unison and voted to make Zhirinovsky their dictator, with full powers to control all party affairs, from finances to appointments, until April 2, 2004. With the same vote the delegates also agreed not to bother meeting again until 1997—one year after Zhirinovsky, by his most conservative estimate, will have become president of Russia, heading a "one-party government."

(Celestine Bohlen, *New York Times*, April 5, 1994)

Two months later Kashpirovsky returned to Russia and took up his place in the Duma. *Komsomolskaya Pravda* reported the "Return of the Prodigal Son":

In today's television reporting on the Duma's session we thought we noticed the very familiar face of the least disciplined member of the Russian parliament. Our suspicions turned to certainty when, after his appearance, all the members of parliament were seen to have fallen asleep. Yes, we were right. Anatoly Kashpirovsky is back to his duties.

Soon after, he was seen regularly hob-nobbing with his erstwhile leader and other members of the party he had renounced. An article appeared in *Time* magazine on the occasion of Zhirinovsky's 48th birthday:

Say what you will about Vladimir Zhirinovsky, but the man knows how to throw a party. For his 48th birthday, "probably the last before I return this nation to its historic greatness," as he put it that night, Russia's most compelling—and notorious—politician invited everybody, from President Boris Yeltsin to a czarist honour guard in full battle dress, to celebrate with him at Moscow's grandly decaying Budapest Restaurant. President Yeltsin declined to attend. But the czarists were out in force, and so were a pride of sleek blondes who called themselves the Zhirinovsky Girls.

Russia's most famous hypnotist and faith-healer, Anatoly Kashpirovsky—whose television appearances still weaken the knees of tens of thousands of elderly women—turned up to say that someday the anniversary of Zhirinovsky's birth would be celebrated with the same joy as Lenin's once was.

"He is the brightest, cleanest, most courageous man we have," said the wiry Kashpirovsky, himself a member of parliament who only months before had bitterly split from Zhirinovsky's party and denounced its leader. "He is the only man who can lead this country out of the darkness and into the light."

What can one possibly say? Except, perhaps, that Kashpirovsky has always been his own worst enemy. It seems that Zhirinovsky had offered him the post of minister of health that April and had invited him along on a trip to "talk to the people." He used Kashpirovsky to warm up his audiences, both of them impressed by the other's skill in handling crowds. Kashpirovsky expressed his admiration: "I love Vladimir. He is never afraid of speaking his mind. He and everything he says is distorted by the press who criticize him for being rude, but he is straightforward. He has real global vision. Whenever I introduced him to the audience, I told them not to prejudge him, to listen carefully because he knows how to achieve the goals we all want." There was, indeed, great fellow feeling between the two men and obvious similarities in their personalities: strength, fearlessness, outspokenness, disdain of criticism, immense self-belief, an almost sexual energy which attracted and repelled, the ability to inspire deep devotion and adulation and absolute hatred. The great psychologist —not just by force of training but on a profound, intuitive level—and the great demagogue. Almost a dream ticket?

In the Duma, Kashpirovsky now sat at the leader's right hand. His admiration grew. "We are like people at the bottom of a well; we see all sorts of obstacles on our way up. But Zhirinovsky sees a clear way out. He knows how to save the nation." But he was disappointed by the Duma itself: "Although there are many well-meaning and well-educated people, there is no unity among the members. We are like the swan, crawfish and pike from Krilov's famous fable: each pulls in his own way and in his own direction. And the worst of all is that the Duma has no power. We are like puppets, controlled by Yeltsin. That is why everything we do comes to nothing. I have never thought much of Yeltsin. He is neither capable nor suitable as president. Now he looks like a walking corpse, even worse than Brezhnev at the end of his life. A few weeks ago he told us that he was very pleased that Russia was becoming more civilized, that there was more order in the country and that in the Duma the deputies were less confused and calmer. It is complete nonsense. I think he has just lost track of what is really happening in the country. His popularity has vanished forever; no one now is more hated than Yeltsin."

In fact, Kashpirovsky became so frustrated by the lack of progress that he began to stay away from many sessions of the Duma and concentrate more upon his own affairs. He had always said quite clearly, whenever interviewed about his political career, if it may be called such, that he was in politics primarily to try to push through his plan of healing the nation by telepsychotherapy, as he called it. He always considered himself a doctor first. Despite many other inconsistencies, in this he was always firm. "My mission is much more important than any political faction or system." So he continued to give healing seances, though less intensively than before. He was also working on a great new scheme, which he modestly anticipated would explode like "an atom bomb" on medical science. This was an extension of his theory that by distracting the conscious mind it was possible to activate the subconscious into setting off the natural regenerative powers of the body. He insisted that everything he did and said during a seance was aimed at establishing and promoting this process of distraction. He always emphasized that the words he used were not, in themselves, important, and that sound, gesture and visual imagery could also work. Now he was trying to develop this further and wanted to find a way of working with very young children, something that would attract them and not bore them. He was working on a series of images, visual symbols, which could be shown on television. He was terribly excited by this project, which he had started to think about while in America, though it was still some way off completion.

Then, in December 1994, Russia embarked upon its disastrous Chechen war. Dzhokhar Dudayev, a former Soviet airforce general and maverick president of Chechnya, had been waving the flag of independence since 1991 and tension had been steadily growing. There was much resentment on both sides. Russians were fed up with

Chechen mafia gangs, closely linked to their government, with their activism in the Caucasus (they had been implicated in the conflict between Georgia and Abkhazia) and with Dudayev's unwillingness to come to heel. The Chechens grew increasingly annoyed at Moscow's attempts at control, saw their chance to reclaim their own destiny and took it. Local skirmishes spiralled and Yeltsin, or rather Pavel Grachev, his right-hand man in the military, sent in the army. Grachev declared that "a single parachute regiment would solve the Chechen problem in two hours." Never has a man spat in the face of history quite so inaccurately. The Chechen wars of the previous century were Russia's fiercest colonial wars; though Georgia was incorporated into the Russian empire in 1801, and all the southern lands were quickly taken, it took the Russian army a further 60 years, at terrible cost, to subdue the Chechens. Their great leader, Shamil, was made of the stuff of legends and when he was finally, in old age, led off into exile in Russia, even the Russians honoured him wherever he went.

So when Yeltsin appeared on television insisting that Chechnya was part of Russia, he was guilty, at best, of wishful thinking. One major factor in the conflict was oil. The crucial pipeline from Baku passes through Grozny, the Chechen capital, on its way into Russia and the potential energy resources of the area are staggering. The Caspian region has been described as the greatest source of energy for the twenty-first century. Estimates of reserves make it bigger and more important even than the Persian Gulf has been. Activity among the oil companies in the area is now intense but bedevilled by political problems, and Chechnya and its pipeline are central to Russian calculations. The Russian government has been desperately trying to persuade Western governments and companies to route their oil through the existing pipeline through Chechnya and not through a proposed new line that bypasses Russia and cuts down through Georgia and on into Turkey. To lose control of the area at such a time was seen as a disaster.

And so the war went on and, as the months passed, grew more and more unpopular. The death toll mounted, the army felt embittered, the command structure seems to have been a fiasco. The suffering was pitiful. Chechens and Russians alike were driven from their homes, and television showed frightful pictures of carnage.

Russian mothers were seen wandering about trying to locate sons the army was too terrified to tell them had died.

To Zhirinovsky the war was a mistake only in so far as it had been badly prosecuted. Kashpirovsky was torn. Although he thought the war was a disaster, he could not bring himself to let go of the idea that Chechnya was an integral part of Russia and was driven to support Zhirinovsky by the incompetence and the dithering of the government. So they worked together in the Duma, both fiercely critical of government policy. When Yerin, the minister of the interior, gave a speech to the deputies, Zhirinovsky, typically, burst out: "You are a son of a bitch. You are a coward. Because of you innocent people are being killed. But you are standing here in front of the Duma, trying to tell us that everything is under control. You should be hanged immediately!" The minister was unable to continue his speech, burst into tears and had to leave the chamber.

The next day deputies complained that they could not work under such conditions, that it was intolerable to be interrupted in this manner and that Zhirinovsky should be restrained. Kashpirovsky stepped forward to the microphone and said: "These people cannot finish their presentations so I shall do it for them. It seems the essence of what they are trying to say is that they want their powers to be broadened. They are right. Our president has deprived the Duma of all its rights. However, I expect a minister to stand up for himself better and not behave like a noble maid and leave the room when the going gets tough." He then left, only to be overtaken a minute later by a colleague who told him he was being attacked for what he had said by deputy Yakunin, an ex-priest. Kashpirovsky returned to hear the deputy saying that he was the devil, the embodiment of evil and that they should all say their prayers together in the Duma to counteract his influence. As he started on the Lord's Prayer, Kashpirovsky grabbed the microphone and assured the deputies that he was not hypnotizing anyone. Had he been giving out his *ustanovka*, he would have ensured that deputy Yakunin would have arrived wearing just his underpants!

At first Kashpirovsky had considered his duties as deputy very seriously, but very soon he realized that the Duma existed only to satisfy the appearance of democracy in Russia. In reality, the Duma was impotent and had little impact on Yeltsin's government. When they realized this, the deputies entertained themselves during the sessions, talking and laughing and paying little attention to the proceedings. However, they did manage to pass a series of laws which secured their own pensions after retirement. Even those not re-elected would still receive three-quarters of their salary for the rest of their lives. They also granted themselves a host of other privileges including Moscow apartments. They were quietly expecting re-election, when parliament dissolved in panic at the news of war in Chechnya.

Then, on June 14, 1995, Chechen commandos under the leadership of Shamil Basayev crossed into southern Russia and stormed the town of Budyonnovsk. They herded together two thousand hostages (or three or four thousand, depending on the source) and shut them up in the hospital, along with themselves. Basayev threatened to kill the lot unless the Russians cleared out of Chechnya and finished the war. He delivered an ultimatum consisting of ten points, none of which were acceptable to the Russians. Yeltsin had just flown off to Canada, and Pavel Grachev, his loyal supporter, veteran of the Afghan war, sent in a team of crack troops to storm the building. A bloodbath ensued with a hundred and fifty (again estimates vary) innocent civilians mown down in the crossfire and some deliberately killed by the Chechens before the Russians were forced to disengage. Basayev personally executed five Russian airforce officers. He himself had suffered terribly during the fighting in Chechnya: his wife, his six children and his brothers had all been wiped out by a Russian bomb.

Amazingly, Grachev was on the point of ordering a second attempt when Victor Chernomirdin, the prime minister and man in charge while Yeltsin was away, managed to restrain him. Kashpirovsky, with the blessing of the chairman, Rybkin, decided that he should and could do something to help. So he jumped onto the first available military aircraft and flew down to Stavropol, from where he phoned through to the hospital. He alone was able to arrange a meeting with Basayev. He was not the only deputy there. Zhirinovsky and others placed themselves between the troops and the hospital as a living shield. But Kashpirovsky was intrepid as always. Just as he had gone to Nagorno-Karabakh during the fighting there, or to Chernobyl after the nuclear disaster, he leaped in without hesitation.

When he arrived at the hospital, he was horrified by what he saw. To this day he cannot forget that night: desperate hostages waving white towels and sheets from the windows, begging the Russian troops not to shoot; tense Alpha Group commandos surrounding the hospital from all sides, arms at the ready; whistling bullets from the sporadic shooting which continued throughout the night despite the ceasefire. There was a very real danger of another Russian attack at any moment. Kashpirovsky declared himself willing to stay there and die with the rest of the hostages. "Along the walls of the corridors, in two or three rows, a great crowd were standing or lying, perhaps three thousand people. This picture cannot be described. In the service area were naked dead bodies swimming in pools of blood. There were many corpses in the wards as well; children without clothing were hiding under the beds; many were wounded. A terrible sight."

He was ushered into a room by Islambek, Basayev's aide-de-camp. Several women huddled in one corner. Two Chechens were seated on chairs. One was Shamil Basayev. The Chechen leader was very calm and showed no emotion. Kashpirovsky struck up an immediate rapport and spent more than seven hours with him. He persuaded him to let some of the hostages go. First five pregnant women were released, then thirty-two more hostages. He also persuaded Basayev to scale down his original ten conditions to two. Eventually they received news that Chernomirdin had agreed to negotiate on this basis and that talks on ending the war could begin. The hostages could be freed.

So Kashpirovsky, believing his job finished, flew back to Moscow. However, such is the controversy that everything he does arouses, that instead of being welcomed as a hero, the press took him to task. First they accused him of simply trying to hog the limelight, then of having left the hospital too soon, next of failing to hypnotize Basayev while he had the opportunity, and finally of vastly overestimating his own importance in the whole procedure. Deeply wounded by all of this, he wrote to I. P. Rybkin, the chairman of the state Duma:

> Esteemed Ivan Petrovich,
>
> I am addressing you in order to restore my good name and my reputation as a deputy. I could never have imagined that my good intentions in going to negotiate with the Chechens could have been so perversely represented.

When I asked the state Duma to send me to Budyonnovsk I fully understood the situation. It was imperative to start negotiations before a second attempt at storming the hospital was made and hundreds more lives were lost. When I arrived at the hospital, despite all my years of working as a doctor and seeing death and suffering every day, I was unprepared for what I saw. I had never imagined such desperation, hopelessness and anger as I saw in the eyes of the hostages, fired upon by their own Russian troops.

I did my best to help prepare the way for successful negotiations and indeed worked out positions which later became the basis for negotiation between V. Chernomirdin and S. Basayev. Shamil Basayev approved of what I was trying to do and freed a number of hostages as a result.

I left the hospital only after repeated assurances from Chernomirdin that the hospital would not be stormed again and that a truce would now ensue. The Russian army commander, Stepashin, advised me to go as there was nothing left for me to do. All my actions were coordinated by him and by the deputy head of administration in the Stavropol region, A. V. Korobeynikov. Unlike others there who were itching to storm the hospital again, these two were dead against it, and Stepashin displayed the highest degree of professionalism and made all the right decisions in a very difficult situation. When I was in the hospital I coordinated all my actions with him over the telephone and had his complete understanding.

Korobeynikov too gave precise orders, did not panic and proved himself master of the situation.

When I was in the hospital, Basayev was prepared to negotiate directly with me, provided that I was given the authority to guarantee the conditions we had negotiated. Unfortunately, the next day, Sunday, this authority was given to C. A. Kovalyev (well known dissident and human-rights activist). His arrival caused considerable irritation and aroused the suspicions of Shamil, eventually delaying his departure and increasing the number of hostages he took with him. The Cossacks too were against his inclusion in the discussions. Afterwards, in the process of self-glorification, he has continually tried to distort and diminish my role in these events.

I ask you to instigate an enquiry into these events so that the efforts of the deputies of the Duma, including your own personal input, may be revealed in their true light.

A. Kashpirovsky
June 23, 1995

Chairman Rybkin replied the same day to the state Duma, diplomatically but supportively, and received a round of applause:

"Esteemed colleagues, some of our deputies participated in operation Live Shield, where more than twelve hundred hostages who had been kept by force in the hospital in Budyonnovsk were liberated. In the first stage Anatoly Mikhailovich [Kashpirovsky] spent eight hours in the hospital in conversation with the leader of the terrorists. Two of the conditions which laid out the basis for negotiations between the prime minister and Basayev were worked out by him. I witnessed this because I spent every day and night with the deputies involved. I would like to thank them all from the bottom of my heart."

Kashpirovsky was profoundly affected by the crisis. He, like many others, felt that the whole policy of confrontation in Chechnya had been an appalling mistake, that negotiations at the highest level should have taken place months before and that lives had been carelessly thrown away at Budyonnovsk. He even felt some admiration and sympathy for Basayev, the young Chechen commander, even though he had ordered the killing of the Russian soldiers and civilians he was holding hostage. He also felt that he himself should have been the one to finish the final stages of negotiation and not Kovalyev. Whether this was just a clash of personalities or Kashpirovsky's egoism or a quarrel of real substance is difficult to ascertain. Though Kovalyev had done his work well, the local Cossacks also objected to him because, they claimed, they had previously sent him information, as a representative of the president, objecting to the killing and humiliation of the Chechen people, to which he had not, for whatever reason, responded. Kashpirovsky was bitterly conscious of his own government's humiliation, that "the prime minister of a great country was on his knees, begging terrorists to free the hostages, that he was practically a tool in their hands."

The whole affair caused him to rethink his political stance. He was warm in his praise for Zhirinovsky's quick response to the crisis and his attempts to talk to Basayev. However, the Chechens had refused to negotiate with him because of his aggressive and imperialist policies. He had dismissed their aspirations for an independent Chechen state and proposed a North Caucasian Republic, an idea that had a brief airing back in the early 1920s before the Bolshevik takeover, with Chechens, Russians, Cossacks and others all sharing in a combined republic, as a gubernial division of Russia. But Kashpirovsky could no longer agree with Zhirinovsky. He went to party headquarters to give his account of his activities in Budyonnovsk:

"I finished my report. There was no comment from Zhirinovsky. He did not look at me. I got up and moved towards the door and opened it, waiting for him to say something. But he continued to talk to someone else. I knew that if I left the room now it would be forever, I would never come back. But still there was no reaction. I stepped outside and then, with all my strength, slammed the huge door shut behind me."

So, once again, he left the man he had once thought would be his "best friend". He had expected Zhirinovsky to stand up and defend him, but this never happened. He felt betrayed and humiliated. So he thanked Zhirinovsky for having made him a deputy and wrote another letter to the Duma announcing his withdrawal from the LDP and his intention of joining Rybkin's faction.

"Rybkin is a very clever, nice, calm person. He has a good nature and he leads the Duma well. He always smiles, never raises his voice and remembers the names of all the deputies. He likes me and I am sure he will make a very good president. With my help he stands a good chance of winning. I can guarantee a large number of votes. After I withdrew from the LDP, many deputies congratulated me. Even Yakunin (the ex-priest who had inveighed against his evil influence) came up and kissed me."

Kashpirovsky has always cast himself in a heroic mould. He craves the large stage, the grand gesture, the noble deed. He sees himself as a man of the people, a Soviet man, yet always his own man. Ever obsessed by his psychotherapeutic evangelism, convinced of the huge importance of his mission and the purity of his dream, he now treads the muddy waters of Russian politics, still surprised that any mud should stick to him. The complexity of his character, the contradictions of his nature, the turmoil of his life, echo those of his country. He can be seen almost as a paradigm of his times. Everything he does divides opinion; every step he takes is open to question and doubt, his future impossible to foretell. Is he a great man with an important message, a plausible charlatan or a self-deluding egoist? Is he Saint or Satan, both or neither?

Rumours circulate round him like thick clouds. He has recently been heard again to say that he will run for president himself in the 1996 elections. Anatoly Mikhailovich Kashpirovsky as president of Russia? Unbelievable! But with this man, at this time, and in that country, anything is possible.

TO BE CONTINUED ...

Bibliography

NEWSPAPER AND MAGAZINE REPORTS

Alexandrova, Lyudmila
- Lukava: no split in Liberal-Democratic faction, ITAR-Tass, April 5, 1994.
- Zhirinovsky, like Yeltsin, plans a trip down the Volga, ITAR-Tass, August 2, 1994.

(Anonymous)
- Zhirinovskogo k vlasti, Kashpirovskogo v kosmos (Zhirinovsky to power, Kashpirovsky into space), *Novoye Russkoye Slovo*, New York, August 7, 1992.

Archangelsky, A.
- Rasputinshina na poroghe? (Rasputinshina is coming?) *Literaturnaya Gazeta* 1989, no.50.

Ardashnikov, V.
- Nashestvie shamanov (Plague of the shamans), *Novoye Russkoye Slovo*, New York, July 31, 1992.

Arseniev, Vladimir
- Kashpirovsky zdyes bolshe ne vrachuet (Kashpirovsky does not work here anymore), *Izvestia*, Moscow 1991, no.85.

Barashev, N., and N. Gogol
- Choudo v tom, chto chuda nyet (There is no miracle in the miracle), *Pravda*, September 1989.

Belitsky, V.
- Chudesa po utram (Miracles in the mornings), *Trud*, Moscow 1988.

Blokhin, N.
- Obmanytuye nadezhdy (Deceived by hope), *Literaturnaya Gazeta*, Moscow, December 13, 1989.

Boudreaux, Richard
- Russian loses round, gets in fight, *Los Angeles Times*, April 9, 1994.
- New faith and furore in Russia, *Los Angeles Times*, March 17, 1994.

Butler, Juliet
- Magical mystery cures, *The Times*, London, April 9, 1994.

Carpenter, Dave
- Mystic healer has ties to some high places: the Kremlin and the cosmos, *Los Angeles Times*, May 21, 1995.
- Cults: Russian pagans, *The Observer*, May 14, 1995.

Chernyshov, Vadim
- Match veka minzdrav protiv Kashpirovskogo (Match of the century, public-health ministry versus Kashpirovsky), *Sovetskaya Rossiya* 1991, no17.

Chukseyev, Vitaly
- Russian faith-healer blasts Zhirinovsky, quits his faction, Tass, March 5, 1994.

Clark, Victoria
- If you want a witch, *Life*, New York, May 14, 1995.

Dejevsky, Mary
- Perestroika idols are toppled, *The Times*, London, November 1990.

de Waal, Thomas
- Roll up for the Duma show, *Moscow Times*, July 22, 1994

Dichev, Todor
- Bioroboty uzhe ne phantastika (Biorobots are no longer fantasy), *7 Dnei*, Minsk, May 1991.

Faradzheva, Y.
- Ya stremlus k nevozmozhnomy (I am striving for the impossible), *Volzhskaya Pravda*, Volgograd 1991, no. 89.

Filipov, David
- Zhirinovsky win illegal, *Moscow Times*, April 14, 1994.

Fromer, Issak
- Anatoly Kashpirovsky vukhodit iz LDPR (Anatoly Kashpirovsky leaves the LDPR), *Rakurs* 1995, no.9.

Gerasimov, Y.
- Kontsert dlya psihoterapevta s orkestrom (Concert for the psychotherapist with orchestra), *Anomalia*, St Petersburg 1992, no.6.

Goldberg, Carey
- Russia's new parliament off to a wild start, *Los Angeles Times*, January 12, 1994.

Gorbunova, Yelena
- Professia—psichiatr (Profession—psychiatrist), *Trud*, Moscow, February 16, 1988.

Gordievich, A.
- Zdravstvui, dyadya Kashpirovsky! (Hello, uncle Kashpirovsky!), *Domovoi*, Kiev, December 1989.

Gordon, Dmitri
- Kashpirovsky, *Ukrvuzpoligraf*, Kiev 1992.
- Nachinalis seansi ... molitvoi (The seances started with prayer), *Vechernii*, Kiev 1990.

Gould, Jennifer
- 'Bad Vlad' cruises for support: vodka and vitriol on the Volga are part of Zhirinovsky's riverboat campaign, *Toronto Star*, September 11, 1994.

Gradov, Georgii
- Doktor Kashpirovsky: "Mne udalos naiti potainuyu dver v cheloveke i otkrut yeyo" (Dr Kashpirovsky: I found a secret door in a person and opened it), *Tainy Zdorovia*, Tass-Leningrad 1991, no.9.

Grant, Alexander
- Anatoly Kashpirovsky: "Otkrytie eshcho nuzhno otkryt" (Discovery needs to be discovered), *Novoye Russkoye Slovo*, New York, November 9–10, 1991.
- Malchik v trusikah protiv dyadi s borodoi (Boy in short trousers versus old man with beard), *Novoye Russkoye Slovo*, New York, May 11–12, 1991.

Guskov, Vyacheslav
- Zhirinovsky, Kashpirovsky visit Kostroma, ITAR-Tass, August 12, 1994.

Ipatova, Natalia
- Kashpirovskogo nye zapretili (Kashpirovsky's sessions are not banned), *Smena*, St Petersburg 1992, no.17.

Karachayev, Ivan
- Smert pod gipnozom (Death under hypnosis), *Novoye Russkoye Slovo*, New York 1993, February 17.

Kashpirovsky, Anatoly
- Dayu ustanovku (I give ustanovka), *Rakurs*, New York, no.10.
- Ya ispytal ot zhurnalistov ne toldo dobro (I experienced not only good from journalists), *Komsomolskaya Pravda*, Moscow, 1991, no.6.

Kissin, M.
- Yeshcho o Kashpirovskom (More about Kashpirovsky), *Golos Rodiny*, USA 1989.

Knox, Kathleen
- Simple cures: just meditate, *The Prague Post*, June 15–21, 1994.

Kolesniko, Andrei
- The other Boris Yeltsin, *Moscow News*, April 22, 1994.

Kondakov, V., and A. Shahunyants
- Navazhdeniye (Evil suggestion), *Sovetskaya Rossiya*, Moscow 1990.

Korshunov, A.
- Lichnost, o kotoroi seichas govoriat (Someone who is so much talked about—interview with Anatoly Kashpirovsky), *Sovetsky Sport*, September 24, 1989.

Koshvanets, V.
- Vo vsem vinovat Kashpirovsky (Kashpirovsky is to blame for everything), *St Peterburgskie Vedomosti*, St Petersburg, December 22, 1993.

Kozlovky, Vladimir
- Kashpirovsky otmezhevyvayetsa ot Zhirinovskogo, no vozrazhaet protiv yego ubiistva (Kashpirovsky distances himself from Zhirinovsky, but is against his murder), *Novoye Russkoye Slovo*, New York, March 1994.
- Television healer leaves LDPR—Anatoly Kashpirovsky discovers aggressiveness in Zhirinovsky, *Sevodnya*, Moscow, March 10, 1994.
- Zhirinovsky poprosil Kashpirovskogo napisat zayavleniye ob ukhode (Zhirinovsky asked Kashpirovsky to resign), *Novoye Russkoye Slovo*, New York, March 14, 1994.

Ladny, V.
- Syn ot Kashpirovskogo (The son from Kashpirovsky), *Komsomolskaya Pravda*, New York 1995, no.40.

Lebedev, V.
- Besovstvo (Possession), *Trud*, Moscow 1991, no.13.

Leskov, S.
- Minzdrav dayet ustanovku (Public-health ministry sets policy line—more about A. Kashpirovsky's sessions), *Izvestia*, Moscow, January 4, 1990.

Limonov, Eduard
- Limonov protiv Zhirinovskogo (Limonov versus Zhirinovsky), Konts Veka, Moscow 1994.

Lishak, Arnold
- Kto vy, Doctor Kashpirovsky? (Who are you, Dr Kashpirovsky?), *Mir*, Philadelphia 1991, no.348.

MacKenzie, Jean
- Yeltsin, not premier, is aim of Duma's ire, *Moscow Times*, June 22, 1995, no.737

Manucharova, Y.
- Phenomen Kashpirovskogo (The Kashpirovsky phenomenon), *Izvestia*, Moscow, August 29, 1989

Matlin, Vladimir
- Vladimir Zhirinovsky's doubtful followers, *Washington Post*, March 21, 1994

McCabe, Michael
- Noted Soviet faith-healer appears in San Francisco, *San Francisco Chronicle*, February 24, 1990

Megarill, Y.
- Kyda vedet nas ofitsialnaya medicina? (Where is established medicine leading us?), *Novoye Russkoye Slovo*, New York 1992

Miller, Kay
- Profiles of the key players in the new parliament, *Star Tribune*, January 11, 1994

Milov, N.
- Zhirinovsky calls for early presidential elections, ITAR-Tass, August 15, 1994

Nazaretyan, Akop
- When a nation's self-image begins to change, *Moscow Times*, June 14, 1995, no.731

Nove, Alec
- Just call me czar, *The Herald*, Glasgow, January 18, 1994

Novikov, Ivan
- Terrorists' actions in Budennovsk are "punitive operation", ITAR-Tass, June 21, 1995

Rakhanskaya, Valentina
- Nayedine so vsemi (I am alone with everyone), Kiev 1990

Remnick, David
- Soviets under a spell, *Washington Post*, October 12, 1989

Reznik, Simyon
- Paving the way for the red-brown Russian nightmare, *Washington Times*, January 11, 1994

Salniko, D.
- Kto zhe samui-samui? (Who is number one?), *Molodaya Gvardiya*, Kursk, January 1, 1990

Shcherbachev, Valentin
- Vnysheniye vmesto narkoza (Suggestion instead of narcosis), *Trud*, Moscow, April 1988

Shenkman, Stiv
- Phenomen borbi s Kashpirovskim (The struggle with Kashpirovsky phenomenon), *Phizkultura i Sport*, Moscow 1990, no.5

Shepotyev, F.
- Yavleniye unikalnoye (Unique phenomena), *Vecherny Donetsk*, September 10, 1990

Shlaen, Semen
- Ne tolko penitsillin i ne tolko spid (Not only penicillin and not only aids), *Novoye Russkoye Slovo*, New York, 1992.

Shturman, Dora
- Etogo nye mozhet byt, potomu chto nye mozhet byt nikogda (It cannot be, because it can never happen), *Novoye Russkoye Slovo*, New York, November 6, 1992

Shyshov, A., and A. Gasparnyan
- Phenomen Kashpirovskogo, *Sovetskaya Kultura*, November 11, 1989

Sieff, Martin
- Reputed Rasputin advises Yeltsin: ex-KGB officer dabbles in occult, *Washington Times*, May 24, 1995

Solovyov, V.
- Sharlatany (Charlatans), *Novoye Russkoye Slovo*, New York, December 13, 1989

Specter, Michael
- Russian lawmakers chastise government, *New York Times*, June 19, 1994
- The great Russia will live again, *New York Times*, June 19, 1994
- Zhirinovsky, *New York Times*, June 19, 1994

Steele, Jonathan
- Russian superstar hypnotist holds viewers spellbound, *The Guardian*, London, October 16, 1989

Syrchenko, Tatiana
- Kashpirovsky skazal: Prikhoditye! (Kashpirovsky said: Come!), *Komsomolets Kirgizhii*, Frunze, September 26, 1990
- Sudite ne toropyas (Don't rush to judgement), *Leningradskaya Pravda*, Leningrad, April 19, 1990

Thoenes, Sander
- Two deputies abandon Zhirinovsky, *Moscow Times*, April 1994

Umnov, V.
- A. Kashpirovsky: ya znayu, kak upravlyat tolpoi (I know how to control the crowd), *Komsomolskaya Pravda*, Moscow, November 22, 1990

Urbanowicz, Juliusz
- Vladimir Zhirinovsky: the unwanted friend, *The Warsaw Voice*, March 20, 1994

Vasilkova, Yelena
- Meli, Yemelya (Keep talking, Yemelya), *Rabochaya Tribuna*, Moscow 1990.
- Nam ne dano predugadat (We cannot predict), *Rabochaya Tribuna*, Moscow 1991.

Velichko, O., and E. Kessariisky
- Zhirinovsky travels along the Volga, ITAR-Tass, August 11, 1994

Womack, Helen
- Hypnotist seeks power, *The Independent*, London, December 11, 1993

Yarmolinets, Vadim
- Allan Chumak: "Lubov vutaskivayet s togo sveta" (Love brings people from the other side), *Novoye Russkoye Slovo*, New York, May 19, 1995
- Professor Raikov: "Gipnoz spaset mir!" (Hypnosis will save the world!), *Novoye Russkoye Slovo*, New York, May 19, 1995

Yemelyanenko, Vladimir
- The state meets its match, *Moscow News*, December 2, 1994

Young, Cathy
- Zhirinovsky up close, *The American Spectator*, February 1994

Zeidman, I.
- Muzhchina goda? (Man of the year?); Muzhchina i Zhenschina, kto oni?, *Sovetskaya Molodezh* (results of opinion polls), Moscow, December 12, 1989

Zhakharchenko, Viktor
- Tak kto zhe vy, Doktor Kashpirovsky? (After all, Dr Kashpirovsky, who are you?), *Chydesa i Priklyuchenia*, Moscow 1992, no.3

Zuichenko, Al
- Konstantin Borovoi claims that Zhirinovsky won with the help of a sex symbol, *Sevodnya*, December 16, 1994

BOOKS AND ACADEMIC JOURNALS

Amada, Gerald
A Guide to Psychotherapy, Ballantine Books, USA 1995.

Bekhterev, Vladimir
Vnushenie i Chudesnie Istseleniya (Suggestion and Miraculous Recoveries), Vestnik Znania, Leningrad, 1925 no.5.

Bogdanova, T. S., and V. D. Soshnikov
Bessonnitsa ili tri mesyatsa s Kashpirovskim (Insomnia or three months with Kashpirovsky), IMA-Press, Leningrad, 1990.

Bul, Pavel
Technika ghipnoza i vnyshenia (On Hypnosis and Suggestion), LIO Redactor, St Petersburg, 1992.

Calloway, Paul
Russian/Soviet and Western Psychiatry, Wiley, New York 1993.

Ellenverger, Henri
The Discovery of the Unconscious, Basic Books, USA 1970.

Estabrooks, G. H.
Using Hypnotism, Coles Publishing, Canada 1980.

Gerke, R.
O Gipnoze i Vnushenii (Hypnosis and Suggestion), Riga 1966.

Gris, Henry, and William Dick
The New Soviet Psychic Discoveries, Souvenir Press, England 1979.

Guiley, Rosemary Ellen
Encyclopedia of Mystical Paranormal Experience, Harper, San Francisco 1991.

Ioffe, Anatoly
   Zapiski Vracha-Gipnotizera (Notes of a Hypnotherapist), Kemerovo Publishing, Kemerova, USSR 1966.
Kakabadze, V. L.
   Sbornik Statyei (A collection of articles on the 100th anniversary of the founder of the Georgian Psychological School), Metsinereba, Tbilisi, Georgia 1986.
Karle, Hellmut W. A.
   Thorsons Introductory Guide to Hypnotherapy, Thorsons, London 1992.
Karvasarsky, Boris D.
   Psyhoterapia (Psychotherapy), Medicina, Moscow 1985.
Kashpirovsky, Anatoly
   Gruppovaya Nespetsificheskaya Psikhoterapia (Nonspecific Group Therapy), TEK, Moscow 1993.
   Lekarstvo? ... Vnutri Nas! (Medicine? ... is Inside Us!), Moscow 1990.
   Materiali 1-i Ukrainskoi Nauchno-Prakticheskoi Konferentsii (Material from the Ukrainian Scientific-Practical Conference), Kiev, January 28-30, 1991.
   Mysli na Pyti k Vam (Thoughts on the way to You), EKOS, St Petersburg 1993.
   Psihoterapevticheskii Phenomen Kashpirovskogo (The Psychotherapeutic Phenomenon of Kashpirovsky), Moscow 1992.
Lahusen, Thomas
   Late Soviet Culture from Perestroika to Novostroika, Duke University Press, London 1993.
Massie, Suzanne
   Land of the Firebird: The Beauty of Old Russia, Simon and Schuster, New York 1980.
Morgovsky, A.
   Seansy A. Kashpirovskogo, Zagadki, Legendy, Realnost (The Sessions of A. Kashpirovsky, Puzzles, Legends, Reality), Prometey Publishing, Moscow 1990.
Mosin, I.
   Tainy XX veka (Mysteries of the 20th Century), Moskovsky Rabochii, Moscow 1990.
Ostrander, Sheila, and Lynn Schroeder
   Psychic Discoveries Behind the Iron Curtain, Bantam Books, USA 1971.
Parker, Tony
   Russian Voices, Henry Holt and Company, New York 1992.
Raigorodetsky, Y.
   Iskustvo Vnusheniya (The Art of Suggestion), Dneprkniga, Dnepropetrovsk 1990.
Reber, Arthur S.
   The Penguin Dictionary of Psychology, Penguin, London 1985.
Remnick, David
   Lenin's Tomb, Random House, New York 1993.
Rozhnov, Vladimir E.
   Rukovodstvo po Psikhoterapii, Medicina, Moscow 1974.
Rozhnova, M., and V. Rozhnov
   Istoria Gipnoza (History of Hypnosis), Moscow 1989.
Sheehy, Gail
   The Man who Changed the World: The Lives of Mikhail S. Gorbachev, Harper Perennial, USA 1990.

Shenkman, Stiv
Phenomen Kashpirovskogo, Yakhtsman, Moscow 1992.
Siegel, Bernie S.
Love, Medicine and Miracles, Harper and Row, New York 1986.
Smith, Hedrick
The New Russians, Avon Books, New York 1991.
The Russians, Ballantine Books, New York 1973.
Stites, Richard
Russian Popular Culture: Entertainment and Society since 1900, Cambridge University Press, Cambridge 1992.
Temple, Robert
Open to Suggestion: The Uses and Abuses of Hypnosis, Thorsons, England 1989.
Turovsky, Valerii
Bezh Geroya (Without a Hero), Stolitsa, Moscow 1992.
Wilson, Andrew, and Nina Bachkatov
Russia and the Commonwealth A to Z, Harper Perennial, USA 1992.
Yeltsin, Boris
The Struggle for Russia, Times Books, USA 1995.
Zickel, Raymond
Soviet Union: A Country Study, US Government Printing Office 1991.

Index

A

Abkhazia	193
abominable snowman	86
acupressure	56
acupuncture	25
Afghan war	101, 195
Aids	86, 134
Alekseyev, Vasya	76
Alexandrov, Anatoly	82
Alexandrovsk	45
Ali, Mohammed	148
All-Union Institute of Neurophysiology	123
Alma Ata	82-83, 92
Amada, Gerald	36
America, United States of	*xiii*, 12, 42-43, 67, 73, 85, 117, 148, 156-157, 176-178, 181-183, 185, 187-189, 192
anaesthesia	
—see Hypnotism, anaesthesia under	
Andropov	72
Aniva Bay	44
Argumenty i Facty (TV programme)	144
Armenia	173
Armstrong, Neil	42
Arons, Harry	33
astrology	25, 179
atheism	10
"Athletic and Psychological Training for the Harmony of Body and Mind"	80
aura	25, 84
Australia	153
Austria	153
autogenous training	61, 75-76
Avdeyev	140
Azerbaijan	151

B

Bachkatov, Nina	80
Baikal, Lake	62-63
Baku	193
Baltic republics	62, 134
Barnard, Christian	160
Basayev, Shamil	195-196, 198
Before and After Midnight (TV programme)	87
Bekhterev, V. M.	*xviii*, 22, 37, 157, 159
Bekhtereva, Natalia	141-144
Belorussia	7-9
Belozerov, Vadim	*xiii*, 85-86, 88, 93, 120-121, 138
Bessonnitsa (TV programme)	141
bibliotherapy	165
Bigfoot	134
bioenergy	120, 123-124, 135
Bob, Vasili Ivanovich	15
bodybuilding	50, 74
Bogdanova, Tatiana	139, 145
Bogdanovich, L.	19
Bohlen, Celestine	190
Bondar, Nikolai	85, 88
Bondar, Valentina	108
Boon, Pavel	102-103, 134-135, 139
Borovoi, Konstantin	176

Botkin, S. P. 163
Braid, James 28, 38, 167
Brezhnev, Leonid
   xiv, xvi, 51, 59, 67-68, 70-72, 192
Brezhnev, Galina 71
Brighton Beach *xv*
Bubnova, Inessa 121
Budyonnovsk 195, 197
Bul, Pavel 61, 142-143
Bulgaria 149-150
Burbulis, Gennady 189
Bykovo 150

C

Calloway, Paul 19
Canada 53, 195
Caspian region 193
Caucasus 62, 134, 193, 198-199
Centre of the Cyclone (Boon) 103
Chazov, Yevgeny 67, 133, 136, 169
Chechnya 192-199
  hostage crisis in 195-199
  mafia gangs in 193
  oil pipeline in 193
  war in 192-193
Chekhov, Anton 41, 43
Chekhov Drama Theatre 44
Chelyabinsk 42, 92
Chernenko 72
Chernobyl 99, 145, 148, 151, 195
Chernomirdin, Victor 195
chess 68
Chicago 148
Chita 42
Chumak, Alan 63, 120-122, 138, 140
Clinton, Bill 185
Communist Party 3, 59, 72, 134, 182
Congress of People's Deputies 119
Congress of Soviets 114
Cossacks 197-198
Coué 28
Czech Republic 66, 120, 149-150, 177

D

Dagi 46
Danilov 171
Davitashvili, Dzhuna 71, 84
Denisov, I. 169
Dichev 172
Dnepropetrovsk 63
Doctor Zhivago (Pasternak) 23
Donaghue, Phil 85
Donetsk 34, 36
Doubrovsky 22-24
du Maurier, George 38
Dudayev, Dzhokhar 192
Duma
   175-176, 183-185, 187-192, 194-199
Dzhigiti 5

E

Eastabrooks, G. H. 33
elections 114-115, 176, 182-189, 195, 200
Elliotson, John 38
Emerson *xviii-xix*
emigrés, Soviet *xv*, 148, 185
Esdaile, John 39
Estonia 173
extrasensory perception (ESP)
   xvii, 25, 71, 84, 121, 134-135

F

faith-healers 25, 173, 190
Feodosia 74, 77
Fifth Wheel (TV) 133-134, 139, 141
Filatov 34
Finland 3
folk healers 11, 86
Freud, Sigmund 22-23, 153, 157-160
Frolov, Konstantin 81-83, 97

G

Gagarin, Yury 14
Gart (TV programme) 137
Gdansk 149
General Techniques of Hypnotism
  (Weizenhoffer) 33

Georgia   109, 115, 117-119, 173, 193
Georgian television   107, 119
Germany   3-5, 8, 102, 149
Gervets, Isaac   9
Gilinsky, Y.   142
Gilyaks--*see* Nivkhi
glasnost   23, 26, 72-73, 85, 121, 181
Glaza v Glaza (TV programme)   105
Goethe, Wolfgang   165
Good Evening, Moscow (TV)   131
Gorbachev, Mikhail   xiii, 23, 36, 72-73, 85, 97, 101, 114, 118-120, 131, 134, 136, 139, 148, 152, 156, 172-174, 181, 184
Gorkom   96
Gorky   43
Goryachi Krest (Vlasov)   77
Grabovskaya, Lyubov   84, 87-88, 90, 93
Grachev, Pavel   193, 195
Greene, Graham   99
group counselling   19
group therapy   70
Grozny   193
Guide to Psychotherapy, A (Amada)   36
Gulyaev, Pavel   84

H

healing   xviii, 37, 38, 49, 71, 82-83, 90-93, 96, 97, 99-130, 143, 154, 156, 163-165, 171-173, 177, 192
  adverse reactions to   133, 138, 144
  evidence for cures   107, 153-156, 160-161, 168
  seances   xvii, 37, 71, 78, 82, 91-93, 103, 105-107, 120-129, 132-133, 135-138, 140-141, 144-146, 149-150, 153-156, 160-165, 167-173, 177-180, 185, 192
  TV ban on   11, 27-28, 37, 144, 155-156, 164, 172, 178-179, 184
Hitler, Adolf   3, 5, 11, 140, 185
hooligans   17, 26
120 Minutes (TV programme)   120
Hungary   120

hypnosis   xiii, xvii, 22, 24-28, 30, 33, 36-39, 43, 48, 50-54, 57, 60-63, 68, 70-71, 81, 87, 89, 93, 102, 122-124, 135-136, 140-143, 146, 148, 150, 159, 164-167, 184, 190, 196
  anaesthesia under   38-39, 52-54, 57, 84-85, 87-90, 93, 104, 107-108, 112-114, 117, 131, 167-168, 180
  and asthma   90-92, 107, 157
  and breast cancer   171
  and cancer   xvii, 52, 88, 103, 126, 136
  and depression   19, 24, 108
  and eczema   xvi
  and enuresis   70, 82-83, 85, 87, 92, 96, 105-106, 154, 161, 166, 168
  and haemophilia   39
  and irritability   171
  and Karpov–Korchnoi chess match   68
  and obesity   70, 90, 92, 95-96
  and phobias   24, 36
  and psychotherapy   22, 159
  and scars   5, 35, 66, 125-126, 148, 160-162
  and sleep   37, 60, 76, 94, 133, 141, 143, 157, 171
  and skin grafts   170
  and smoking   38, 70, 94, 137
  and stuttering   23-24, 60, 70, 91-92
  and suggestion   27-29, 68, 157
  and television   30, 87-90, 108-114
  and ulcers   35, 90, 157
  at a distance   143
  dangers of   27
  evidence for effectiveness   38-39
  Party control over   68
  rapid   23, 33
"hypnosis addiction"   137
Hypnosis Without Miracles (Rozhnov)   89
hypnotarium   70, 91, 96
hypnotherapy   36, 38, 83, 124, 148, 159
Hypnotism Act   28

I

Ignatova, Olga 108, 110, 122, 139, 142
Institute of Experimental Medicine 141
Institute of Suggestology and Parapsychology, Sofia 150
International Psychotherapeutic Centre 153-154
Ioseliani, G. 109, 112-113, 117, 142, 146
Iosifovna, Tamara *xviii*
Irkutsk 62
Islambek 196
Israel 148
Ivan the Terrible 1
Ivannitsky, Alexander 121, 139
Izvestia 123, 137, 172

J

Japan 44, 47-48, 93, 182

K

Karpov–Korchnoi chess match 68
Karvasarsky, B. 142
Kashpirovsky, Anatoly—
  and antisemitism 145
  and Chechen hostages 195-198
  and the church 1-2, 100, 149, 179-180
  and the Communist Party
    3, 59, 72, 134, 182
  and healing—*see* Healing
  and hypnosis —*see* Hypnosis
  and marriage 25, 177
  and neurosis
    19, 24-25, 36, 60, 90, 92, 155, 157, 160
  and obesity clinic 70, 95-96
  and the press 156
  and rape under hypnosis 147
  and resignation from LDP 185
  and television *xiii-xiv*, 30, 81-83, 85-86,
    90-91, 93-94, 96, 101, 104-108, 114,
    116-118, 120-125, 132, 135-136,
    138-141, 144-145, 149-150, 154, 156,
    166-173, 179-180, 184, 190, 192
  and use of hypnosis in anaesthesia
    —*see* Anaesthesia

(Kashpirovsky, Anatoly—*continued*)
  and Viktor prize 150
  and weightlifting 18, 67, 73-79, 85
  as deputy in Duma 175
  as the devil 2, 21, 51, 110, 118, 135,
    141, 180, 194
  as middleweight champion of the
    Ukraine 15
  as physical-training therapist 18
  as president 200
  as psychologist to the national team 74
  as psychotherapist *xiii*, *xvii*, 60-61,
    74-75, 80, 87, 90, 123-124, 136-137,
    140, 148, 150, 166-167, 169, 172
  as stage hypnotist 32-36, 41-43, 49,
    61-63
  as student *xvii*, 14, 16, 18, 23, 88
  asceticism of 14, 32, 49
  children of 18, 26, 62, 69
    (*see also* Kashpirovsky, Serzhoya)
  expulsion from Latvia 179
  financial affairs 102-103, 148, 178
  financial scandal 147
  popularity of *xiii*, 2, 57, 69, 106,
    117, 122-123, 132, 155, 174
  poverty of 19-20, 138
  in space 14, 180
  sporting achievement of
    10-11, 15, 18, 67, 74, 77, 119
  "supernatural" powers of
    xvii, 48, 51, 78, 84, 135
  on videotape 125-129
"Kashpirovsky phenomenon" 123
"Kashpirovsky syndrome" 138, 144
Kashpirovsky, Irina 177
Kashpirovsky, Seryozha *xvii*, 26, 74, 77,
  80, 116, 118-119, 138, 177
Kashpirovsky, Valentina
  25, 51-52, 95, 138, 177
Kazakhstan 4-5, 11, 43, 82
Kazin, Yury 138
KGB *xiv*, 36, 42, 44, 59, 66,
  71-72, 119, 133
Kharkov 21-22, 24, 27, 60, 171
Kharkov University 22
Khmelnitsky 2

Khodyrev	115	Leningrad Regional Children's Hospital	
Kholmsk	44		132
Khrapaty, Anatoly	74	*Lenin's Tomb* (Remnick)	43, 134
Khrushchev, Nikita	11-12, 16, 23	Leskov, Professor	137
agricultural reforms	24	Liberal Democratic Party	
"Thaw"	22-23, 25, 84		175, 180, 186, 189, 199
Kichigin, Gena	50	Lipgart, N.	171
Kiev	xiii, 10, 78, 85-90, 95, 99-103,	literacy	31
	105-107, 109, 114-116, 121, 134-138,	*Literaturnaya Gazeta*	137
	144, 153-154, 156, 170-172, 177, 182	Lithuania	173, 179
Kiev Institute of Neurosurgery	87	Lodz	149
Kiselev	137	London, Jack	6, 9, 46
Klepach, Valentina	53	Los Angeles	xv
kolkhozes	6, 12, 16, 106	*Love, Medicine and Miracles* (Segal)	75
Kommersant	146	Lozanov, Georgi	150
Komsomol	11-12, 115	Luzhniki	74, 80
Komsomolskaya Pravda	147, 190	Luzhniki sports stadium	85
Korchnoi	68	Lvov	3, 101, 103
Koreans	47, 55-56		
Korobeynikov, A. V.	197	**M**	
Korol, Piotr	15	Marchuk, Gury	82
Korolyov, Vladimir	88	Markovtsy	5
Korosten	33	martial arts	80-81
Kosyak, V.	147	Marxism-Leninism	21
Kotangli	46	materialism	22
Kovalyev, C. A.	197-198	Medvedev, Aleksei	79
Krasnoyarsk	42	Medzhibozh	2, 8
Kravchuk	178	*Meeting with Dr Kashpirovsky, A*	
Krepkaya, V.	170	(TV programme)	121
Krilov	191	Megrelishvili, Zurab	110
Krivushenko, S.	154	Menzul, V.	170
Krut	12	Mesmer	28, 38, 48
Kulagina	25	Messing, Wolf	25, 33
Kuprin	29	Mezhevich, M.	142
Kurkova, Bella	134	Mgachi	45
Kuznetsov, Pavel	78	Mikhalkov, Sergey	96-97
		military academy	69
L		miners	34-36
Latvia	173, 179	ministry of foreign affairs	94
Lee, Bruce	80	ministry of health	59, 69, 71, 100, 106,
Lenin	14, 44, 67, 71, 191		113, 122-123, 136, 144, 155, 164, 169
Leninakan	151	Minsk	7
Leningrad	22, 61, 73, 84, 115, 125,	Mitrofanov, Aleksei	180
	132-136, 139-145, 153-156, 169, 178	Moldavia	173
(*see also* St Petersburg)		Molochnye Kotiki	46

Moonlit Night (Kuprin) 29
Moscow 22, 27-28, 44, 59, 61, 65-69, 71, 73, 80-83, 87, 96, 103, 115, 119-121, 134, 136, 139-141, 149, 173, 190, 193, 196
MVD 59, 100
mysticism 120, 134, 173, 184

N

Nagorno-Karabakh 151
Nakhodka 50
narcopsychotherapy 60
Nazis 4
Nevelskoy, Gennady 41, 44, 55
Nevzorov, Alexander 132-133, 135
New Jersey *xiv*
New York *xiii, xv, xvii*, 148, 186
New York Times 190
Nivkhi 46-47
Nixon, Richard 184
Notes of a Psychiatrist (Bogdanovich) 19
Novosti press agency 132
Nysh 46

O

Obkom 8, 44, 96
Odessa 15, 27, 71
Ogonyok 148
Okha 46-47
Olympics 15, 24, 65-67, 74, 76-77, 79, 85
Open to Suggestion: the uses and abuses of hypnosis (Temple) 38
Orthodox Church on Healers, UFOs, Television, Faith-Healers and the Occult 179
Ostankino 121-122, 139-140

P

Paediatric Burn Centre 170
Palace of Sports 73, 80
paranormal, the 25, 134
parapsychology 71, 86, 120, 123
Party for Economic Freedom 176
Pasternak 23
Pavlov, I. P. *xviii*, 19, 22, 29, 32, 36-37, 157-158

Pavlov Psychiatric Hospital, Kiev 100
perestroika *xiii*, 44, 72-73, 85, 120-121, 133-134, 137, 144, 148, 176
Petrov, Dimitr 150
philharmonic societies, lectures in 25
Pirogov 14
Pisarenko, Anatoly 74, 85, 101
Platonov, Konstantin *xviii*, 22-23, 32, 36
Pochenkov mine 34
Podolsk 77, 80, 82-83, 85
Poland 3, 138, 145-149, 153, 156, 189
Politburo 66, 71-72
poltergeists 134
Pope John-Paul II 150, 179
Potyemkin 65
Poznan 149
Pozner, Vladimir 85
propiska 20
Proskurov 2
psychic 25, 37, 118, 140, 144, 161, 173
psychoanalysis 22, 104, 159
psycho-emotional stress relief 34
psychokinesis 25
psychology 19, 22, 37, 125, 163-165
psychology and dialectical materialism 22
psychosomatic 39, 136, 171
psychotherapy *xvii*, 21-22, 25, 27, 32, 34-37, 50, 60-61, 69, 81-84, 96, 100, 117, 149, 155-167, 170-172, 192
and athletics 75
and the military 83
and neuroses 157-174
and physical diseases 157-174
Psychotherapy—Limits of Reality (TV) 140
Pugachova, Alla 94
Pushkin, Alexander 1, 21, 87, 165, 175
putevka 42
Pyatiletova, L. 136
Pyatoye Koleso—see *Fifth Wheel*

Q

Quiet Flows the Don (Sholokhov) 112

R

Raikov, Vladimir 61, 122
Rasputin 39, 94, 124
Remnick, David 43, 131, 134
Reskiev, Rafat 161
Rigert, David 74-75, 79
Rivkin, Mark 107-108, 111, 117, 120, 142
Rodionov, General 119
Rosenbaum, Aleksander 94
Rossiskaya Gazeta 180
Rozhnov, Vladimir
    27-28, 30, 34-35, 61, 89
Rubina, L. 178
Rukh 182
Russia and the Commonwealth A–Z
  (Wilson and Bachkatov) 80
Russian and Western Psychiatry (Calloway) 19
Russia's Choice 183
Rybak, Igor 24
Rybkin, Ivan Petrovich 185, 195-199
Ryumin 180
Ryzhkov 72

S

St Petersburg 1, 178, 185, 189
Sakhalin 41-45, 47-49, 54-56, 68
Sakharov, Andrei 119
San Francisco *xv*, 148
Sarkisyan, Yurik 76
Satan 2, 118, 135-136, 179
Schultz, J. H. 61
Sechenov, I. M. 28, 32, 157
Segal, Bernie 75
Serdyuk 100
Sevodnya 189
Shamil 193
Shcherbitsky, Volodymyr 99, 105
Shebunino 44
Shemyakin, Aleksandr 188
Shenkman, Steve 121
Sherbachev, Valentin
    85-86, 90, 101-105, 138, 145
Shevardnadze, Eduard 116, 182
Shlaen, Semyon 53-54, 57
Sholokhov, Mikhail 112, 165
Siberia 12, 42-43, 49, 62, 92
Sidorenko, Vladimir 116-118
Simonov, P. 123-125
600 Seconds (TV programme) 132
Smena 91
Smertin, Gennady 27, 71
Sobchak, Anatoly 134, 178
socialist propaganda 65
Sokol 69
Solovyov, Yury 115, 134
Solzhenitsyn, Alexander 23, 96
Sopot 150
sorcerers 10, 134-135
Soshnikov, Valentin 139, 142
Sovetskaya Rossia (newspaper) 141
Sovetskaya Rossia (whaling ship) 51
Soviet Academy of Sciences 81, 107
Soviet medicine 19
Soviet psychiatry 19
Soviet psychotherapy 22, 37, 141, 157, 162
Soviet Union *xiii*, 2, 6, 8, 10, 12, 19, 22,
    34, 36, 44, 47, 52, 59, 62, 68, 74, 76, 77,
    100, 104, 118, 122, 131, 142, 153-157
  alcoholism in 31-32, 47
  disintegration of 173, 181
  health system in *xiii*, 19, 59
  military 3, 36, 41-42, 66, 69, 193
  poverty in 31
  psychiatric hospitals in 59, 138
  sport in 10, 11, 18, 65-67, 74, 78
sovkhozes 12
Spinoza 99
Stabrov, Vitaly 76
Stalin 2, 8, 11, 23, 33, 66-67, 182
  "Family of Peoples" 3
  murder camps 48
Stavnitsa 2, 4, 6
Stepashin 197
Strait of Laperuz 44
St Petersburg (*see also* Leningrad) 178
suggestion 28, 38, 56, 60-61, 78, 89, 114,
    123-124, 150, 157-159, 166-167, 170-171
  (*see also* Hypnosis and suggestion)
Suleimanov, Khafiz 76-77
Supreme Soviet *xii*, 114

Svengali	38	USA—*see* America	
Sweden	153	*Using Hypnotism* (Eastabrooks)	33
Sypko, Zhenya	76-77	Ussuriysk	61

ustanovka   37-38, 56, 61, 128-129, 142, 159, 162-164, 172, 194

T

Tabachnikov	34	Uzbekistan	161
talantlivy	149, 168	Uznadze, Dmitri	37, 61
Tass	134, 148		
Tatar Gulf	44		

V

Tbilisi   71, 105, 107-109, 114-121, 135, 139, 142

		Vasiliyev	84
		Vechernaya Moskva (TV)	140, 172
Tbilisi Institute of Clinical and Experimental Surgery	109	Velvovsky	22
		Vengerovsky	188
Technique of Hypnosis and Suggestion (Bul)	143	Vesta (insurance company)	149
		videotape	125-129

Techniques of Speed Hypnosis (Arons)   33

Vinnitsa   10, 12-20, 24, 26-31, 52, 57, 68-71, 74, 81, 83-88, 90-96, 169, 182

telepathy	25, 84, 123, 158	Vinnitsa hospital	93
telepathic hypnosis	84	conditions in	19
telepsychotherapy	168-169	Virgin Lands	11
Teleshevskaya, Maria	60	Vladivostok	49
television		Vlasov, Yury	77-78
—*see* Kashpirovsky and television		Voronezh	4, 134
Temple, Robert	38	*Vremya* (TV programme)	73
Thatcher, Margaret	73	Vrotslav	149
Times, The	148	Vrublevskaya, Valeriya	105, 109
Tolstoy, Alexei	43, 65	Vysotsky, Vladimir	102, 131, 135

trance   xiv-xv, 24, 33, 51, 61, 63, 68, 70, 76, 78, 92-93, 102, 104, 110-111, 124, 126-129, 144, 146, 166, 184

Vzglyad (TV)   xiii, 85-87, 94, 96, 134

W

Tretyakov	44		
Trilby (du Maurier)	38	Walensa, Lech	149-150
Tsai, P.	171	Warsaw	149
Tsarevich Alexis	39	*Washington Post*	131
Tsarevich Dmitri	1	Weizenhoffer	33
Turkey	193	Wilson, Andrew	80
Tyutchev, Fyodor	41	witchcraft	25

Word as Physiological and Therapeutic Factor, The (Platonov)   22

U

Y

UFOs	86, 134	Yakovlev	85
		Yakunin	194, 199

Ukraine   2-10, 13, 22, 24, 43, 95, 99-100, 106, 109, 114, 117, 169, 171, 173, 178

		Yampol	28, 58
antisemitism in	148		

Yeltsin, Boris   71, 115, 120, 134, 172-176, 180-183, 190-193, 195

TV seances in	105-107, 154, 161, 168	
nationalist movement	58, 182, 188	
Ukrainian civilians, murder of	3	
United Nations	148	

Yerevan	151
Yerin	194
Yershova, Lesya	108-109, 111-114, 117, 122, 135, 137-138, 142, 144-146
Yevtushenko, Yevgeny	94
yoga	50, 61
Yunda, L.	154
Yushchenko psychiatric hospital	91
Yuzhno-Sakhalin	42, 44, 47

Z

Zakharevich, Yury	74, 79-80
Zarya Vostoka	105
Zavidiya, Andrei N.	189
Zhirinovsky, Vladimir	175-176, 180-191, 194-195, 198-199
anti-semitism of	184
racism of	186
Zhirinovsky's Falcons	189
Zhirovitsy	7
Zhmerenka	18
Zhvanetsky, Mikhail	72
Zimmerman, Mikhail	*xiv-xv*, 148
Znanie Society	27-28, 41-42, 44, 54, 157
Zolotov	179
Zuchar	68